The Bible's Prophets

The Bible's
Prophets

An Introduction for Christians and Jews

David J. Zucker

WIPF & STOCK · Eugene, Oregon

THE BIBLE'S PROPHETS
An Introduction for Christians and Jews

Copyright © 2013 David J. Zucker. All rights reserved. Except for brief quotations in critical publications or reviews, no part of this book may be reproduced in any manner without prior written permission from the publisher. Write: Permissions, Wipf and Stock Publishers, 199 W. 8th Ave., Suite 3, Eugene, OR 97401.

Wipf & Stock
An Imprint of Wipf and Stock Publishers
199 W. 8th Ave., Suite 3
Eugene, OR 97401

www.wipfandstock.com

ISBN 13: 978-1-62032-737-1

Manufactured in the U.S.A.

New Revised Standard Version Bible, copyright 1989, Division of Christian Education of the National Council of the Churches of Christ in the United States of America. Used by permission. All rights reserved.

To my wife, Donna, for your love, support, and encouragement throughout the years

Contents

Foreword by Steven A. Hunt | ix

1. Introduction to the Prophets/*Neviim* | 1
2. Joshua | 11
3. Judges | 23
4. Samuel (1 and 2) | 37
5. Kings (1 and 2) | 54
6. Isaiah | 73
7. Jeremiah | 103
8. Ezekiel | 118
9. Hosea | 131
10. Joel | 142
11. Amos | 151
12. Obadiah | 160
13. Jonah | 165
14. Micah | 173
15. Nahum | 182
16. Habakkuk | 189
17. Zephaniah | 199
18. Haggai | 207
19. Zechariah | 215
20. Malachi | 229

Glossary | 239
Bibliography | 243

Foreword

JEWS AND CHRISTIANS APPEAR to share a common Bible—what Christians refer to as the Old Testament, and what Jews call the Hebrew Scriptures or Jewish Bible. Paradoxically, it is and is not the same document. How can that be? Both works contain the same books, although the order of those books differs. Both a traditional Jewish Bible and a standard Christian version of the Old Testament begin the same way: Genesis, Exodus, Leviticus, Numbers, and Deuteronomy form the first section, what Jews term the Torah or Pentateuch. The next two books, Joshua and Judges, are also in the same order. Then, in a Christian version of the Old Testament, there is an abrupt change, for the next books are Ruth, Samuel, and Kings. Chronicles, Ezra, Nehemiah, and then Esther follow.

This order follows a kind of historical sequence, and reflects a tradition that goes back to the time of the Septuagint (Greek translation of the Hebrew Scriptures), about 250 BCE. In contrast, Jewish Bibles divide into three sections: the Teaching, Instruction, or Law (*Torah* in Hebrew), the Prophets (*Neviim* in Hebrew), and the Writings (*Ketuvim* in Hebrew). These divisions are sometimes abbreviated into the acronym Tanak or Tanakh (*Torah, Neviim, Ketuvim*). Jesus seems to be familiar with that threefold order, for in Luke 24:44 he says, "These are the words which I spoke to you while I was still with you, that all things must be fulfilled which were written in the Law of Moses and the Prophets and the Psalms concerning Me."

Jesus spoke to a Jewish audience, and most of the earliest Christians were Jews. Over the years of course that demographic changed. The church moved away from its Jewish roots. Yet the Jewish Bible (Old Testament) continues to be the bedrock of Christianity. The other testament in a Christian Bible, the so-called New Testament, is filled with quotations from the Jewish Bible. There, as well as in the teachings of the church fathers, the early church sought to understand and to teach its unique lessons and to discern God's purpose. At roughly this same period, the ancient rabbis were addressing the Jews of their time. The rabbis also quote from the Jewish Bible to teach their values and lessons, as they sought to understand its unique lessons and discern God's purpose.

In this introduction to the Bible's Prophets (*Neviim*), the second part of the traditional Jewish Bible, Rabbi David J. Zucker offers the reader an overview of each book in this section: Joshua, Judges, Samuel, Kings, Isaiah, Jeremiah, Ezekiel, Hosea, Joel, Amos, Obadiah, Jonah, Micah, Nahum, Habakkuk, Zephaniah, Haggai, Zechariah, and Malachi.

For each of these works he devotes two segments to the historical context of and major ideas found within it, taking the reader section by section, and often chapter by chapter. In addition he enhances our understanding of each book by showing how it was utilized or reflected in the teachings of the New Testament writers. Then he provides a list of parallel teachings by the rabbis, showing how post-biblical Judaism understood those same writings. For many Christians these rabbinic materials will offer new and wonderful insights into biblical interpretation. For Jews, the selections from the New Testament will explain how Christianity, through a different set of lenses, saw and reinterpreted Jewish Scripture. A short study section completes the fivefold approach to these sacred biblical writings.

I have known Rabbi Zucker for several years. He is both a scholar and a teacher. His love of the Bible is reflected in his many articles, books, and chapters, often written with an interfaith Christian-Jewish audience in mind. One of my colleagues, Marvin Wilson, has written, "Rabbi Zucker is one who cares deeply how Jews perceive Christians and how Christians perceive Jews" (Foreword to *The Torah: An Introduction for Christians and Jews*). This volume, filled with insights and nuggets of wisdom, and written for both Christians and Jews, enhances mutual understanding and provides valuable lessons for all of us to learn from and about each other.

It is said that Winston Churchill once quipped that the United Kingdom and the United States are two nations separated by a common language. Indeed, language can be the glue that binds us together or the barrier that separates us. As his observation holds true for these two nations, so it is also true of the Scriptures of Judaism and Christianity.

This volume provides an opportunity for both religious traditions to learn about the other, and to appreciate more deeply how we both share a common Scripture, and how at the same moment there are significant differences in the ways in which we understand it. In the best possible sense, the wisdom contained in this fine book reflects on two scriptural texts: "In my Father's house there are many rooms" (John 14:2 NIV), and God's "house will be called a house of prayer for all nations" (Isa 56:7). The prophets spoke beautifully of a time of universal restoration, a time when the Creator of the universe would set things right. I imagine that's when we'll finally see his house, the one with many rooms for all the nations.

Steven A. Hunt
Professor of Biblical Studies
Gordon College
Wenham, MA

1

Introduction to the Prophets/*Neviim*

THIS VOLUME IS THE second work in a series that is an introduction to the Bible, written specifically for Christians and Jews. It offers a comprehensive, section-by-section and often a chapter-by-chapter overview to the world's most widely read book: the (Hebrew) Bible. This volume is unique in that a major feature offers examples how the Christian Scriptures utilized the Hebrew Bible to further the ideas and ideals of Christianity; as well as offering examples where the ancient rabbis in roughly a parallel time period utilized the Hebrew Bible to further the ideas and ideals of Judaism.

The Bible is read by millions of people, year by year. It is a sacred document, one that links Christians and Jews. Yet even the term "Bible" means one thing to Jews and something else to Christians. For Christians the Bible divides into two sections, the "Old Testament" followed by the "New Testament."

When Jews refer to a Bible, they mean a different—although in some ways very similar—set of books. For Jews the "Bible" is synonymous with the *TANAKH*, the threefold sacred scripture made up of the *Torah* (i.e., Teaching, Instruction, Law), the *Neviim* (Prophets), and finally the *Ketuvim* (Writings). The books that make up those three sections, beginning with Genesis, Exodus, Leviticus, Numbers, and Deuteronomy are the same books that Christians would find in their version of the Old Testament. Yet, as shall be explained later in this chapter, the books in the Christian Scriptures are set out in a different order than that found in the Hebrew Bible (*TANAKH*).

In the Hebrew Bible, the Prophets/*Neviim* are composed of twenty-one books: Joshua, Judges, 1 and 2 Samuel, 1 and 2 Kings, Isaiah, Jeremiah, Ezekiel, Hosea, Joel, Amos, Obadiah, Jonah, Micah, Nahum, Habakkuk, Zephaniah, Haggai, Zechariah, and Malachi. The third section of the

Hebrew Bible, the Writings/*Ketuvim*, is composed of thirteen books, in this particular order: Psalms, Proverbs, Job, Song of Songs, Ruth, Lamentations, Ecclesiastes, Esther, Daniel, Ezra, Nehemiah, 1 and 2 Chronicles. These differences in the order of the books between a Jewish Bible and a Christian Bible are explained in a section later in this Introduction.

The Overall Structure of This Book

This volume, while it stands on its own, is also the second section of a three-part set. The previous work in the series is *The Torah: An Introduction for Christians and Jews* (Paulist, 2005), and the third and final volume is *The Bible's WRITINGS: An Introduction for Christians and Jews* (Wipf and Stock, 2013). The present volume is an introduction to the Prophets/*Neviim*, those books in the Hebrew Bible that directly follow the Torah (i.e., the Pentateuch, the first five books of the Hebrew Bible).

Each chapter in this volume deals with one particular biblical book, and divides into five sections:

1, 2. An Introduction and then various matters including geopolitical background, significant events, personalities, and concepts and divisions found in that particular book;

3. The particular book in the Christian Scriptures;

4. The book in rabbinic literature (see section below on "Rabbinic Literature");

5. Text study.

On occasion an asterisk (*) follows certain words. This indicates that the word appears in the glossary at the close of this work.

Translations used for this book (unless specifically otherwise noted) come from the New Revised Standard Version (NRSV*).[1] This is a modern translation with inclusive, gender-neutral language. Occasionally there are differences in the verse numbers in the Hebrew Bible* (TANAKH) and a Christian Bible. Verse numbers were added to the biblical text during the Middle Ages. No one knows with certainty why there are occasional discrepancies between the two versions. When there are variations in a particular verse quoted, the NRSV translation will be followed by the Hebrew* tradition, set apart in parentheses and marked with an "H." Examples include Isaiah 9:2–7 (9:1–6 H) and Zechariah 1:18–21 (2:1–4 H). The standard

---

1. As published in the *New Oxford Annotated Bible with the Apocryphal/Deuterocanonical Books* (1991), hereafter abbreviated *NOAB*.

English version of the traditional Hebrew Bible (Masoretic Text)* is the New Jewish Publications Society translation, NJPS/*TANAKH*.*

I try to use gender-neutral language in terms for God. God cannot be described in terms of gender. God is neither a he nor a she. Yet the Hebrew language, like romance languages (French, Spanish, etc.), does not have a neutral case, only masculine and feminine nouns and pronouns. Unlike English and German, there is no "it." The default pronouns in the NRSV, as in this volume, when referring to God are "he," "him," and "his." While in the Bible God is most often described with masculine pronouns, feminine imagery is also used in the Bible. Isaiah explains that God says, "As a mother comforts her child, so I will comfort you" (Isa 66:13; cf. Isa 42:14; 49:15; 66:9). Since the word "Lord" has masculine overtones in most cases, unless quoting directly from a text this book uses the neutral term "God."

Further, the last quarter of the twentieth century saw a flowering of woman-authored scholarship that continues to flourish in the twenty-first century. All people, women and men alike, are indebted to their contributions, many examples of which also have influenced and are included in this volume.

Throughout North America, women and men share a common experience. When they rent a hotel/motel room, oftentimes they will find a copy of the Bible. Usually it will be a King James Version (KJV). These people may be Christians, Jews, Muslims, Buddhists, Hindus, or of no particular religious persuasion. They may be avowed atheists, or fully secular in their approach to life.

When Christians pick up this Bible, it is familiar to them. They understand that it has two parts. It begins with the "Old Testament,"* which is followed by the "New Testament."* The Christian Scriptures* (New Testament) begin with the Gospels*; next follows Acts; and the Epistles*; and they conclude with the book of Revelation. For Christians, "Old" and "New" are more than merely synonyms for "former" and "latter." Broadly speaking, Christians understand the "Old Testament" to be God's original words to the Jews, and the "New Testament" to be the New Promise, an updated covenant or a revised contract. Old and New, therefore, take on a "value."

When Jews pick up the Christian Bible, they have a different reaction. They recognize that there are two parts. It is only the first section, however, which is sacred for them. The New Testament does not inform the Jewish religious experience. Most Jews have never read the New Testament. Many

Jews would be surprised to learn that the New Testament often quotes from or alludes to the Hebrew Scriptures.*[2]

Jews recognize that for Christians there is another scripture in addition to the Hebrew Bible. Jews understand that Christians regard this later scripture as holy and as a record of God's continuing relationship. For a Jewish understanding of the Christian Scriptures, see the recently published excellent volume, *The Jewish Annotated New Testament—New Revised Standard Version.* Edited by Amy-Jill Levine and Marc Zvi Brettler. New York: Oxford University Press, 2011.

Jews nonetheless continue to believe that for Jews the original contract articulated in the Hebrew Scriptures is still binding. It continues to remain in place. For Jews the Hebrew Scriptures, as distinguished from the Christian Scriptures, continue to be the major source for understanding the ongoing covenant with God.

―――――◦―――――

In the Hebrew Bible (the Jewish Scriptures), Christians and Jews share a common sacred literature. For Jews, this Bible is the foundation for the ongoing and unbroken covenant with God. For Jews, it is not the "Old" Testament, having been succeeded by the "New" and improved Testament. It is *the* irreplaceable Testament.[3]

Jews appreciate that Christians understand the Christian Scriptures (New Testament) as God's new promise.[4] The authors of the Christian Scriptures write with a stated purpose: to convince people that the Messiah has come in the form of Jesus. "The gospels, like the other New Testament books . . . are the literary productions of a believing community. . . . They are written with the aim of changing the reader or of building up the community's faith. In the Fourth Gospel, John says clearly, these things are 'written so that you may come to believe that Jesus is the Messiah, the Son of God, and that through believing you may have life in his name' (Jn 20:31)."[5]

Christians read the Hebrew Bible ("Old Testament") as the foundation stone of their own faith. "The first disciples and Christian writers . . . searched the Old Testament for passages that would throw light on

---

2. In this book, the terms Jewish Bible,* Jewish Scriptures,* Hebrew Bible,* and Hebrew Scriptures are used synonymously.

3. Brueggemann, *Introduction*, 2–3; see also Boadt, *Reading the Old Testament*, 4, 8–9; Signer, "Searching the Scriptures"; Greenspahn, *Scripture in the Jewish and Christian Traditions*.

4. In the Christian Scriptures of Rom 9:2ff. and 11:1ff., Paul clearly states that God's covenant with the Jewish people is unbroken. Yet also look at Rom 9:14ff. and Heb 8:13; 9:15–20.

5. Metzger, "Narrative Books—Gospels and Acts," in *NOAB*, NT, ix.

the events of Jesus' life, death and resurrection. Matthew's Gospel is a case in point. It is filled with quotations from the Old Testament to explain each major step in Jesus' life.... Even the church fathers ... cited the Old Testament far more often than they did the Gospels."[6]

The first disciples and early Christian writers quote the Hebrew Bible as a source to teach new lessons and to explain God's purpose. Their writings parallel the teachings of the early rabbis, who often draw upon the Hebrew Bible to instruct and edify, and to understand God's purpose (see the section "Rabbinic Literature," below).

As mentioned earlier, most Jews have never read the Christians Scriptures. They often are unaware that quotations from the Jewish Bible appear in the Christian Scriptures. In like manner, most Christians are completely unfamiliar with the teachings found in rabbinic literature. They would be surprised to learn that the early rabbis often quote from the Hebrew Scriptures to support their Jewish teachings in a similar way as the writers of the New Testament support their Christian teachings in the Christian Scriptures.

The Order of the Books of the Bible

Another term for the Jewish Bible is the *TANAKH*. *TANAKH* (sometimes *TANAK*) is an acronym; the letters T, N, and KH (or K) each refer to a word. These three words are *Torah** (Teaching), *Neviim** (Prophets), and *Ketuvim** (Writings). They refer to the three sections of the Jewish Bible. This is the order of the books of the Hebrew Bible* (Hebrew Scriptures,* Jewish Scriptures,* Jewish Bible,* TANAKH).

1. The Teaching/*Torah* contains Genesis, Exodus, Leviticus, Numbers, and Deuteronomy.

2. The Prophets/*Neviim* has two sections, the Former Prophets and the Latter Prophets. In order they are: (Former Prophets) Joshua, Judges, 1 and 2 Samuel, and 1 and 2 Kings; (Latter Prophets) Isaiah, Jeremiah, Ezekiel, Hosea, Joel, Amos, Obadiah, Jonah, Micah, Nahum, Habakkuk, Zephaniah, Haggai, Zechariah, and Malachi.

3. The Writings/*Ketuvim* consist of the Psalms, Proverbs, Job, Song of Songs, Ruth, Lamentations, Ecclesiastes, Esther, Daniel, Ezra, Nehemiah, and 1 and 2 Chronicles.

The Protestant Bible reflects the divisions of the Jewish Bible, but rearranges the order of the books in the second and third sections. Broadly

---

6. Boadt, *Reading the Old Testament*, 468.

speaking, the Torah (Pentateuch*) is followed by the "historical books," Joshua, Judges, Ruth, 1 and 2 Samuel, 1 and 2 Kings, 1 and 2 Chronicles, Ezra, Nehemiah, and Esther. Next come the "poetical books," or "Writings," made up of Job, Psalms, Proverbs, Ecclesiastes, and Song of Songs. This set concludes with the "prophetical books," Isaiah, Jeremiah, Lamentations, Ezekiel, Daniel, Hosea, Joel, Amos, Obadiah, Jonah, Micah, Nahum, Habakkuk, Zephaniah, Haggai, Zechariah, and Malachi.

The Roman Catholic Bible, in such versions as the Jerusalem Bible, New Jerusalem Bible, and New American Bible, follows a different order: Genesis, Exodus, Leviticus, Numbers, and Deuteronomy; then Joshua, Judges, Ruth, 1 and 2 Samuel, 1 and 2 Kings, 1 and 2 Chronicles, Ezra, Nehemiah, Tobit, Judith, Esther, 1 and 2 Maccabees, Job, Psalms, Proverbs, Ecclesiastes, Song of Songs, Wisdom of Solomon, Ecclesiasticus (Sirach), Isaiah, Jeremiah, Lamentations, Baruch, Ezekiel, Daniel, Hosea, Joel, Amos, Obadiah, Jonah, Micah, Nahum, Habakkuk, Zephaniah, Haggai, Zechariah, and Malachi. In the Catholic Bible, what is termed in the Protestant Bible as the Apocrypha appears as part of the Deuterocanonicals. The Roman Catholic Church shares this tradition with the Greek and Russian Orthodox Churches.

Terms of Reference: BCE, CE

"Before the Common Era" (BCE*) and "Common Era" (CE*) refers to *exactly the same periods* as "Before Christ" (BC) and "Anno Domini" (In the year of our Lord, AD). Thus 150 BCE is the exact same year as 150 BC, and 1000 CE is the exactly the same year as 1000 AD. The terms "Christ" (Messiah or Savior) or "In the year of our Lord" are certainly appropriate for Christians, but the more neutral and inclusive terms BCE and CE are rapidly becoming standard usage.

Prophets

What, Who, and When?

In the Bible, a prophet is a spokesperson for God. The prophet comments on life. As a prophet he (sometimes she) might chastise, moralize, advise, and speak of the present and of the future. "The prophet's eye is directed to the contemporary scene; the society and its conduct are the main theme of his speeches. Yet his ear is inclined to God." The phrase "Thus says the LORD" is characteristic of the language of the prophets. Yet prophets are much more than the persons who convey God's message. The "prophet is not a mouthpiece, but a person; not an instrument, but a partner, an associate of God."[7]

Israel's prophets preach to a contemporary audience. The prophets are concerned with the here and now. Their audience understands the prophets' allusions. The prophets fully expect to see God's role in shaping history. It will happen shortly. Their prophecies apply to their own time. It might be in a matter of months or years, perhaps as much as a decade, but usually earlier. Punishment, and latterly repentance and salvation, are *near-time* events. The prophets and those they address do not envision that their remarks are to be applied to a far-off future period.

The most common term used for the word "prophet" in the Bible is *navi* (sometimes spelled *nabi* (*nun-bet-alef*); the plural is *neviim* (or *nebiim*). It is found in many books and applied to a broad range of people, from Genesis (referring to Abraham, Gen 20:7) to the book of Malachi (referring to Elijah, Mal 4:5 [3:23 H]). The term *navi* is used over three hundred times and in various contexts.[8]

The term "prophet" is used to describe very different figures. These range from Abraham to Aaron (Exod 7:1) to Elijah (1 Kgs 17–19, 21). There are true prophets and false ones (1 Kgs 22; Jer 4:9–10; 23:16, 21). There are prophets who speak plainly (1 Sam 10), those who are more sophisticated (the Isaiahs), and those who are visionaries (Ezek 1–2). Prophets speak either as critics from outside of the community (Amos) or as very engaged within it (Jeremiah).

In the books of Samuel and Kings, the most prominent prophets are Samuel, Nathan, Ahijah, Elijah, Micaiah, and Elisha. They are all part of the section known as the Former Prophets (see above). The Latter (or Literary, because their names form the title of their books) Prophets are, in order, Isaiah, Jeremiah, Ezekiel, Hosea, Joel, Amos, Obadiah, Jonah, Micah, Nahum, Habakkuk, Zephaniah, Haggai, Zechariah, and Malachi. Note that in the Jewish Bible, Daniel is not considered a prophet. The books of Lamentations and Daniel are part of the Writings/*Ketuvim*, not the Prophets/*Neviim*.

Sometimes the Latter Prophets are termed the Written (or Writing) Prophets. This is misleading. The prophet spoke; he was a preacher. It was only later that the prophet's words were set down and collected.

The books of the Former Prophets (Joshua, Judges, Samuel, and Kings) cover over six hundred years, c. 1200–586 BCE, from Joshua to the captivity in Babylonia. The books of the Latter Prophets cover from the mid-eighth century to the fourth or third century BCE.

---

7. Heschel, *Prophets*, 21, 25.
8. For a much fuller description, see "What Is a Prophet" in Zucker, *Israel's Prophets*, 7–35.

Do the Prophets Predict the Coming of a Messiah?

Do any of the prophets of the Hebrew Bible predict the coming of the Messiah? The term "messianic" refers to the idea of a Messiah, a Savior or Redeemer. These are all good Jewish words, as are the terms salvation, redemption, and resurrection. They are, naturally, good Christian words as well!

Judaism* clearly has concepts about messianism, as does Christianity. The actual "word Messiah derives from the Hebrew *mashiah*, anointed. . . . The Messiah of the future, the one who will bring peace and glory to Israel, will be the anointed one, the chosen descendant from the house of King David."[9] According "to the Hebrew Scriptures God will establish, through a descendant of David, called the Anointed or 'Messiah,' his everlasting reign on earth. This will be characterized by perfection in the material and moral realms."[10]

The Messiah, and the future coming of the Messiah, are clearly mentioned in the Jewish prayer book, and in certain Jewish rituals. An example is the weekly *Havdalah** (Hebrew for "Separation") ceremony, which acknowledges the separation from the holiness of the Sabbath day to the ordinary time of the weekdays. Within Judaism, historically there have been tensions between the idea of a personal Messiah and the coming of the Messianic Age. "Jewish messianism, like so many other theological concepts in Judaism, is complex, contradictory, and confusing." Yet it is also clear that messianism is an idea that comes into its own *after* the period of the close of the Jewish Bible, some time later than the middle of the third century BCE. Indeed, "there is no *personal* messiah in the [Jewish] Bible. Rather, we detect in this notion *soteriology*, human messengers or mortal agents, who carry out God's will and pave the way for salvation. In the [Jewish] Bible, God *alone* is the king-redeemer: Moses, Joshua, Gideon, Saul, David, Hezekiah and others were merely his mortal messengers."[11] This is not the place to review the massive amount of material written on Judaism's views on the Messiah. One place to delve further would be the article on "Messiah" in the *Encyclopedia Judaica* (first or second edition) or in its predecessor, the *Jewish Encyclopedia*, as well as to references in the article by Gilbert Rosenthal

---

9. Angel, "Messiah -Jewish View," 133; see also Horbury, *Jewish Messianism*, 7–13.
10. Lacocque, "Messiah-Christian View," 135.
11. Rosenthal, "Messianism Reconsidered," 552, 553.

(see Bibliography). Two exceptional works, both mentioned by Rosenthal, might here be highlighted: Joseph Klausner's *The Messianic Idea in Israel* and Gershom Scholem's *The Messianic Idea in Judaism*.

This section begins with the question, "Do any of the prophets of the Hebrew Bible predict the coming of the Messiah?" The clear answer to this question is "no." The idea of a personal Messiah, or even of a Messianic Age, is one that develops after the period of the Hebrew prophets.

Rabbinic Literature

There is a vast corpus of writings known as "rabbinic literature." There is the Babylonian Talmud* as well as the Jerusalem Talmud. Much of this is legal material. In addition, there are many collections of rabbinic homilies, collectively termed Midrash.* These were compiled c. 400–1550 CE. Whenever the Bible is not explicit or specific, the early interpreters of the post-biblical world (i.e., the rabbinic period), and their successors as well, sought to provide new insights for the context of given passages. Alongside the Bible, the rabbis developed a supplement, an additional way to understand what God desires of humans. The generic term for this exegesis or interpretation is *midrash* (plural, *midrashim**). The Hebrew for "sermon," *derasha*, is based on the word *midrash*. Through midrash, "a Scriptural passage yielded far more than could be discerned on the surface. The sacred words became an inexhaustible mine . . . of religious and ethical teaching."[12] As the *Babylonian Talmud* suggests, "One biblical statement may carry many meanings."[13] Tales and allegories, ethical reflections, epigrams and legends are all different ways in which midrash can be expressed.

Through their midrashim, the rabbis teach about the values of their time, such as the nature of God, opposition to idolatry, proper modesty, the importance of studying sacred texts, generosity, hard work, chastity, and loyalty. They also comment on differences between the Jewish community and other communities.

Midrash always develops out of, and is grounded in, the biblical text.[14] Midrashic literature was first spoken, and later compiled by rabbis. For the

---

12. A. Cohen, *Everyman's Talmud*, xviii.

13. *Babylonian Talmud, Sanhedrin* 34a. All quotations from and references to the Babylonian Talmud refer to the Soncino edition; see bibliography.

14. "Midrash is a type of literature, oral or written, which has its starting point in a fixed canonical text, considered the revealed word of God by the midrashist and his audience, and in which this original verse is explicitly cited or clearly alluded to." Porton, "Midrash," 4:819; see also Signer, "Searching the Scriptures."

purposes of this volume, even though composed and compiled over many different centuries and under different conditions, these midrash examples are offered as general rabbinic teachings based on biblical verses. The rabbis often disagree amongst themselves. To say that something is *a* rabbinic view, or even *the* rabbinic view, does not mean that all rabbis support that position or that interpretation.[15]

15. A specific midrash may respond to certain social/cultural/religious/political/economic issues of its time. Such detailed analysis is beyond the purview of this book. Not only are there differences of opinion among the rabbis, but also there may be variations in some of the details of a given midrash from one midrash collection to another. Some midrash collections repeat a midrash that appeared earlier in that same volume. Although I quote a specific midrash, there may be variations found in the literature.

2

Joshua

Introduction

THE ESSENTIAL MATERIAL OF the book of Joshua focuses on the conquest of the land of Israel, and the distribution of that land. The period of Joshua is about 1200 BCE.

Joshua is the sixth book in the Hebrew Bible. It also is the first book in the second section of the Hebrew Bible, the Prophets/*Neviim* (see Introduction: "The Order of the Books of the Bible"). In both Hebrew and English, its name is Joshua (Hebrew: *Yehoshua*). A literal translation of Joshua/*Yehoshua* is "YHVH is salvation / the LORD is salvation."

The books of Joshua, Judges, Samuel, and Kings comprise the Former Prophets.[1]

The events in the book of Joshua continue the narratives in the closing books of the Torah. The tribes of Israel are poised along the eastern edge of Canaan, the Promised Land.* Moses leads the people for forty years. He confronts Pharaoh in Egypt. He is the human agent who announces the ten plagues. Moses presides over the exodus from Egypt. He takes the people to Mt Sinai. There Moses receives the Ten Commandments, and brings them

---

1. As noted in the Introduction, the Prophets/*Neviim* divides into two sections. The Former Prophets (sometimes termed the Pre-Literary or Early Prophets) is constituted by the books of Joshua, Judges, Samuel, and Kings. The Latter Prophets (sometimes termed the Literary or Later Prophets) contains the books of Isaiah, Jeremiah, Ezekiel and the twelve Minor Prophets ("minor" here meaning shorter texts), Hosea, Joel, Amos, Obadiah, Jonah, Micah, Nahum, Habakkuk, Zephaniah, Haggai, Zechariah, and Malachi.

to the people of Israel. Throughout the forty years of the desert experience, Moses is the leader, the lawgiver, and the teacher.

At the close of the book of Deuteronomy, Moses dies and is buried (Deut 34). There is an orderly transition of leadership. Moses publicly endorses Joshua as his successor (Deut 34:9, cf. Num 27:18). The generation that left Egypt dies during the forty-year desert sojourn. The only exceptions are the leaders Joshua son of Nun and Caleb son of Jephunneh. In Deuteronomy, God is very explicit. Moses will see the Promised Land, but he will not enter it. That task, both the joys and the responsibilities of taking the Israelite tribes westward across the River Jordan, and then conquering the land, will fall on Joshua's shoulders.

Reading the book of Joshua conveys the notion of a unified, well-disciplined army achieving immediate and powerful victories. In reality, this was a slow process with successes as well as defeats, achieved over many years. The book of Joshua is a historical narrative, but it is history with a purpose. It is sacred history (see the section below, "Is Joshua 'Real' History?"). The book of Joshua, like the book of Deuteronomy, has a theological message. Joshua is best understood as a continuation of some of the ideas expressed in Deuteronomy. Most scholars today believe that Joshua is part of the Deuteronomistic corpus of literature.[2] Deuteronomy explains that Israel is on a journey. Its goal is the Promised Land, the area promised by God to Abraham, Isaac, and Jacob (also named Israel). There the descendants of Israel will spread abroad to the west, to the east, to the north, and to the south (Gen 28:14). The country is fertile and rich. It is "flowing with milk and honey" (Deut 6:3; 11:9; 26:9, 15). There are flowing streams with springs, a land of wheat and barley, vines, fig trees, and pomegranates, olive trees and honey. Filled with natural resources, it has stones, and iron and copper (Deut 8:7ff.) This land is a wonderful gift from God. Yet, Israel's possession of the land is conditional on her following God's commands. If she fails to obey God, Israel is told, "you shall be plucked off the land. . . . The LORD will scatter you . . . from one end of the earth to the other" (Deut 28:63–64). Stated briefly, this Deuteronomistic view, or Deuteronomistic history, explains that for Israel to hold on to the Promised Land she must follow God's laws; if she departs from the covenant, God will turn from her (cf. Deut 8:1, 18–20). For further details, see the sections on "Deuteronomistic History" that appear in the chapters on Judges and Kings later in this volume.

---

2. Concerning the term "Deuteronomistic history" or "corpus," see the relevant section in the chapters on Judges and Kings later in this volume. For a brief description of the Deuteronomistic history, see Cottrill, "Joshua," 103.

The Book of Joshua

Divisions in the Book of Joshua

The book divides into four sections:

Joshua 1	Joshua's induction
Joshua 2–12	Conquest of the land
Joshua 13–22	Division of the land
Joshua 23–24	Concluding matters

Joshua 1; Joshua's Induction

The first chapter follows directly upon the concluding words of Deuteronomy. The Torah closes with Moses' death and burial. Joshua commences with an announcement of Moses' death and God's command to Joshua to proceed now to cross the Jordan and conquer the land. God says to Joshua, "Every place that the sole of your foot will tread upon I have given to you. . . . From the wilderness and the Lebanon as far as . . . the river Euphrates . . . to the Great Sea in the west. . . . No one shall be able to stand against you all the days of your life" (vv. 3–5).

God instructs Joshua to be strong and courageous, stalwart and faithful. He is to act in accordance with the teaching given to Moses. This first chapter divides into two equal sections: verses 1–9, God's word to Joshua, and verses 10–18, Joshua's address to the people and their commitment to his leadership. As noted above, the twelve tribes are encamped to the east of the Promised Land. They are at the plains of Moab at Shittim (cf. Num 33:49; Josh 2:1; 3:1) In modern geopolitical terms, this is northwest Jordan. The Israelites are headed in a westward direction.

Joshua 2–12; Conquest of the Land

Chapters 2–12 feature the conquest of the land and its eventual distribution. Although several cities will fall into Israelite hands, the best known is the capture of Jericho. Chapter 2 describes the initial part of that campaign. It relates the adventures of the two spies sent to reconnoiter Jericho. (See the Text Study at the close of this chapter, "Rahab and the Spies.") The actual capture of Jericho comes later. The tribes first must traverse the Jordan River. They need to establish themselves on its western bank. (See the Text

Study at the close of this chapter, "Twelve Stones and the Jordan River.") The next few chapters in Joshua deal with the crossing of the Jordan. They explain how the priests take the ark of the covenant before the people. Chapter 5 mentions that the kingdoms to the west, the Amorites and the Canaanites, hear about the exploits of the Israelites. They are fearful of these new invaders. The rest of the chapter explains that the conquering Israelite army has to pause to circumcise all its males. This covenantal rite has not been followed during the forty-year desert experience (Josh 5:5ff.; cf. Gen 17:11).

Jericho's fall appears in chapter 6. "The people shouted, and the trumpets were blown . . . and the wall fell down flat; so the people charged straight ahead into the city and captured it" (6:20). The Israelites then plan to capture the town of Ai. There is a setback when Achan son of Carmi steals some booty. The matter is rectified and the conquest continues. By chapter 9, the inhabitants of the Canaanite town of Gibeon fear that they will be overrun. Their leaders carry out a ruse. They don worn-out clothing and visit Joshua at Gilgal. The Gibeonites pretend to come "from a very far country." They successfully establish a treaty with the Israelites. The next chapters detail successes over the Amorites and other tribal units. God-inspired miracles aid Joshua and the Israelite forces. In one instance, large hailstones fall on the enemy. This is between Beth-horon and Azekah. At Gibeon and the valley of Aijalon, in response to Joshua's plea to God, the sun stands still and the moon does not move, so that the Israelite army can press its advantage (10:11–14) (see the Text Study at the close of this chapter, "The Day the Sun Stood Still.") Chapter 12 lists some thirty-one kings that fall to the Israelite onslaught.

Joshua 13–22; Division of the Land

Chapters 13–22 feature the distribution of the captured land to various tribal units. By this point, Joshua is old and advanced in years. The country has yet to be conquered completely, much less subdued. Territory nonetheless is ceded out among the people. Most of the land is west of the Jordan. Yet, half the tribe of Manasseh and the tribes of Reuben and Gad will possess an area east of this marker. There are considerable details listed in these chapters. Of particular note is that the tribe of Judah is not able to vanquish the Jebusites, who continued to hold Jerusalem (15:63). Mention is made of the daughters of Zelophead (see Num 27:1ff.) They are allocated land that had been promised to them.

The distribution of the conquered territory is not without controversy. At one point, the double tribe of Manasseh-Ephraim asks for more area because they are particularly populous. It is clear that the allotment of land is time consuming (ch. 18). Seven tribes still need to be assigned their specific holdings. Joshua chastises them for their lack of action. He asks for three representatives from each tribe, who are then sent to map out the land. Joshua casts lots to see who will inherit which area. It states specifically that the tribe of Levi is not to own land. Rather, "the priesthood of the LORD is their heritage" (18:7).

Earlier, in the Torah, in Numbers and Deuteronomy (Num 35:9–34; Deut 19:1–13), God commands that there are to be cities of refuge. Persons may seek asylum in these specific areas if they cause an accidental death. Chapter 21 modifies a previous statement about the Levites not owning any land. They are allocated forty-eight cities and the surrounding pastureland for their livestock. The final part of this section, chapter 22, describes a misunderstanding between a coalition made up of the tribes of Gad, Reuben, and half of Manasseh, which dwell east of the Jordan, and the nine-and-a-half tribes west of the Jordan. The former group sets up an altar as a kind of memorial to remind them of their common Israelite traditions. The latter group assumes that these tribes are committing apostasy. They are prepared to attack them. The matter is resolved amicably.

Joshua 23–24; Concluding Matters

Chapters 23–24 present closing materials for the book of Joshua. In chapter 23 Joshua delivers a farewell address patterned on precedents set by Jacob and Moses (Gen 49; Deut 29–30). In tone, Joshua's remarks reflect the teachings of Deuteronomy: if you follow God's laws it will go well for you; if you turn from God's laws expect swift retaliation. Chapter 24 continues in a similar vein. It begins with a short history that remembers the time of the patriarchs. It briefly recalls the life and times of Moses. The chapter concludes with a covenant at Shechem, and Joshua's subsequent death and burial. Final sentences note the burial of the bones of Joseph (cf. Gen 50:25; Exod 13:19) and the death and burial of the priest Eleazar.

Is Joshua "Real" History?

The settling of Canaan takes many decades. Some territory is captured later. Some areas will be reconquered. The account found in the book of Joshua is a telescoping of actual events. It also is an idealized version of what takes place. Joshua's leadership achieves an impressive foothold in the land. In time, nonetheless, individual tribes will take up arms again (cf. Judg 1:3ff.)

Archeological evidence challenges the claim that Jericho and Ai were captured at the time of Joshua.

The descriptions in Joshua follow a logical routing, in terms of geography and topography. This does not mean that settlement follows literally in that order. It is more likely that individual tribes make inroads into Canaan. At times they achieve their goals. At other moments they regroup and try again later.

Violence in Joshua

Conquering land is a violent enterprise. In the mind of the ancients, these acts of war are a means to an end. They achieve what God promised earlier to the patriarchs and matriarchs. This is explained in Deuteronomy. "It is not because of your [Israel's] righteousness or the uprightness of your heart that you are going in to occupy their land; but because of the wickedness of these nations the LORD your God is dispossessing them before you, in order to fulfill the promise that the LORD made on oath to your ancestors, to Abraham, to Isaac, and to Jacob" (Deut 9:5). The book of Joshua does not minimize the horror of battle. When Jericho is captured, the warriors "devoted to destruction by the edge of the sword all in the city, both men and women, young and old, oxen, sheep, and donkeys" (6:21). When Joshua takes Makkedah, he "struck it and its king with the edge of the sword; he utterly destroyed every person in it; he left no one remaining." At Hebron "they assaulted it, and took it, and struck it with the edge of the sword, and its king and its towns, and every person in it; he left no one remaining, just as he had done to Eglon, and utterly destroyed it with every person in it." Earlier, Joshua killed five kings and hung their bodies on trees until evening (10:28, 36–37; 10:26).

Some scholars take a different approach. They suggest that the actual conquest and settlement of the land was more peaceful. They posit that while some of the tribes did come out of Egypt with Moses and Aaron, and subsequently attacked Canaan from the east, others infiltrated from the south via Beersheba and Hebron. Still others moved into the north around Galilee. There also is a theory that a few tribes never left the land to dwell in Egypt, but rather joined the invading forces upon their arrival.[3]

---

3. On violence in Joshua: Brueggemann, *Divine Presence amid Violence*. The conquering of Canaan may have been over a longer period of time, and more peaceful: Boadt, *Reading the Old Testament*, 165–67, 170–74. Perhaps the tribe of Ephraim never went to Egypt: Shinan and Zakovitch, *From Gods to God*, 157–63.

The Role of Joshua: A Life Patterned on Moses

Joshua is best known as the figure that spearheads the successful invasion of Canaan. Undoubtedly, he comes into his own in the book named for him. Joshua first appears, however, in the Torah, as Moses' assistant. He is a member of the tribe of Ephraim. Not long after the miracle at the Reed Sea (Sea of Reeds*), Moses appoints Joshua to lead the battle against the tribe of Amalek at Rephidim (Exod 17:8ff.) This is during the initial months of the desert experience of the exodus. There is a hint that Joshua in time will succeed Moses (Exod 17:14). The Bible explains that originally Joshua was named Hoshea (Hosea), son of Nun, but God gave him a new name (Num 13:16).[4]

Joshua accompanies Moses on the ascent and descent of Mount Sinai (Exod 24:13f.; 32:17f.) Along with Caleb son of Jephunneh, Joshua is one of the twelve spies sent to reconnoiter the Promised Land. He and Caleb favor an immediate invasion. The other ten spies overpower their voices. For their loyalty to God, Caleb and Joshua are permitted to enter the Promised Land (Num 13:8; 14:6ff.) As mentioned earlier, Moses appoints Joshua as his successor (Num 27:15ff.; Deut 1:38). Joshua's commission is to capture and divide the land among the tribes (Num 34:17, Deut 31:7ff.)

Joshua is not the exemplary teacher; that was Moses' role. It is clear, nonetheless, that the Bible regards Joshua as a leader in the image of his mentor. Joshua's authority comes because Moses publicly appoints him. Joshua is "full of the spirit of wisdom, because Moses had laid his hands on him; and the Israelites obeyed him, doing as the LORD had commanded Moses" (Deut 34:9; cf. Num 27:18). Moses is termed a "servant of the LORD," and this term is also applied to Joshua (Deut 34:5; Josh 24:29). A very common phrase in the Torah is, "The LORD spoke to Moses, saying . . ." (*Vayedaber Adonai el Moshe leimor*). That same phrase is used with Joshua (Josh 20:1). The waters of the Reed Sea part for Moses, allowing the Israelites to cross safely (Exod 14:21ff.), and the waters of the Jordan River part for Joshua, allowing the tribes to pass through on dry land (Josh 3:14ff.). God directly explains to Joshua that this miracle is for the express purpose that the tribes "may know that I will be with you as I was with Moses" (Josh 3:7). Moses was told to remove his sandals because he was on holy ground. A similar event takes place in Joshua's life (Exod 3:5; Josh 5:15).

Moses dies at the venerable age of 120. Joshua dies at 110, the same age as Joseph in Genesis—still a significant age in its own right.

---

4. Renaming someone is a significant event; see Gen 17:5, 15; 32:28–29.

As noted earlier, both Moses and Joshua deliver final addresses to the people before they die, challenging them to follow God's laws and be faithful to the covenant.

Joshua in the Christian Scriptures

Joshua in Hebrew is *Yehoshua* (*yud-hey-vav-shin-ayin*). Morphologically, this word is very close to the Hebrew term for Jesus, *Yeshua* (*yud-shin-vav-ayin*). A number of the church fathers see Joshua as a "type" (a symbolic representation) of Jesus. He leads the children of Israel into the Promised Land, thereby succeeding Moses, in the same way that the church succeeds Judaism.[5] In that sense, just as Joshua son of Nun is Moses' assistant, so in the same way Jesus of Nazareth is Moses' assistant and successor.[6] "The Fathers of the Church saw in him a foreshadowing of Jesus: both bore the name 'saviour' and both led their followers through the waters (the one of Jordan, the other of baptism) to a promised land, while the conquest and division of the territory are an image of the progressive expansion of the Church."[7]

Joshua does not bring a perfect rest for the people; but Jesus does do so (see Heb 4:1ff., esp. vv. 8–9).

The fall of Jericho is spoken about in the Epistles. There is praise for the prostitute Rahab for protecting the two spies who have come to check out the defenses of Jericho. Rahab abets the spies' escape (Heb 11:30–31). Using a rope, she lets them down from the window of an outside wall. This is echoed in an episode about Paul (Acts 9:25; 2 Cor 11:33; Josh 2). Rahab's works, along with her faith, are commended in the Epistle of James; in Hebrews, it is her faith that is noted (Jas 2:24f.; Heb 11:31; Josh 2).

As Joshua and the elders put dust on their heads as a sign of mourning; a similar image is portrayed in the book of Revelation (Rev 18:19; Josh 7:6).

Joshua's admonition to the wrongdoer Achan to "give glory to the LORD God of Israel and make confession to him" is directly reflected in the Gospel of John (John 9:24; Josh 7:19).

Joshua is mentioned by name in Acts (7:45).

---

5. On Joshua as a type, see Irenaeus, *Against Heresies*, xix, 549; see also MacKenzie. *Irenaeus' Demonstration*, 151–52.

6. Origen, *Homilies on Joshua*, Homily 2, 39.

7. Jones, "Introduction," 269.

Joshua in Rabbinic Literature

Joshua and the chain of tradition. Joshua is revered because he is the next link in the chain of tradition. This succession directly connects the rabbis to the teachings and the traditions of Moses. "Moses received the Torah from Sinai, and transmitted it to Joshua; Joshua to the Elders; the Elders to the Prophets; the Prophets to the Men of the Great Assembly" (*Mishnah Avot* 1.1).[8]

Joshua compared to Moses. "While Moses' face shone like the sun, Joshua's face was like the moon." *Babylonian Talmud Baba Batra* 75a. Compared to the brilliance of Moses, Joshua's accomplishments pale in significance. Yet, on the other hand, the laws of nature are suspended for Joshua, as they are for Moses and Naqdimon ben Gurion (*Babylonian Talmud Ta'anit* 20a).

Joshua seeks to make peace. The descriptions of the aggressive and brutal conquest of Canaan disturb the rabbis. To soften that image, they explain that before laying siege to a city, Joshua makes them an offer of peace. "Whoever desires to go, let him go; and whoever wants to make peace, let him make peace; and whoever wants to make war, let him make war. The Girgashites departed, and so were given a land of their own . . . the Gibeonites made peace. The thirty-one kings [Josh 12] waged war, and were defeated" (*Midrash Deuteronomy Rabbah* 5.14).[9]

Joshua a descendant of, and marries, a proselyte. Joshua is himself a descendant of a proselyte, and he marries a proselyte, Rahab, who converts after she joined the Israelite community (*Midrash Numbers Rabbah* 8.4; *Babylonian Talmud Megillah* 14b; *Midrash Exodus Rabbah* 27.4). Rahab also was a particularly virtuous proselyte (*Midrash Deuteronomy Rabbah* 2.26–27).

The many faces of Rahab. Rahab and her professional life intrigue the rabbis. On one hand, it seems that the text is clear: she is labeled a prostitute (*zonah*). On the other hand there is a tradition that she is the ancestress of eight prophets, including Jeremiah and Jeremiah's contemporary, the female prophet Huldah (*Babylonian Talmud Megillah* 14b). The medieval biblical commentator *par excellence* Rabbi Shlomo Itzhaki (Rashi, eleventh-century

---

8. According to tradition, the Men of the Great Assembly (or the Great Synagogue) are the direct forebears of the rabbis, a group of 120 sages who laid the foundation of the liturgy, edited several scriptural books, and served as a spiritual and legislative institution. They are credited with developing the major fields of *midrash, halakhah,** and *aggadah.**

All quotations of the Mishnah are from the Blackman translation; see bibliography.

9. All references to *Midrash Rabbah* in this volume come from the Soncino edition; see bibliography.

France), in a comment on Joshua 2:1, claims that the term *zonah* derives from the same word as for "food" (*mazon*). Therefore, she really is an innkeeper. His interpretation is based on the Targum's* translation of the word "prostitute" (*zonah*) to *pundaqit*, which can mean "innkeeper." It is possible that the translation "innkeeper" is a double entendre in the minds of the Targum translators, or that of Rashi.

Rahab is extraordinarily beautiful, one of the four most stunning women of all time. The mere mention of her name causes sexual excitement. She is immensely popular. She has a large clientele, including the nobility of many lands. Consequently, Rahab has wide-ranging and strategically important knowledge (*Babylonian Talmud Megillah* 15a; *Babylonian Talmud Zebahim* 116b).

Rahab sets a good example; Israel does not do likewise. Rabbi Abba bar Kahana said . . . Let the son of the wanton woman [Rahab] who had mended her ways present himself and reprimand the son of the virtuous woman who turned to wantonness [the people Israel]. You find that all those words of Scripture, which are used in tribute to Rahab, contain a reproach of Israel. Thus Rahab says, "Now then, since I have dealt kindly with you, swear to me by the LORD that you in turn will deal kindly with my family" (Josh 2:12); and of Israel it is said, "They swear falsely" (Jer 5:2). Rahab says, "Spare my father and mother" (Josh 2:13); but to Israel it is said, "Father and mother are treated with contempt" (Ezek 22:7). Of Rahab it says, "She . . . brought them up to the roof" (Josh 2:6); but of Israel it is said, "Those who bow down on the roofs to the host of the heavens" (Zeph 1:5); Rahab says, "[She had] hidden them with the stalks of flax [lit the tree of flax]" (Josh 2:6); but of Israel it is said, "Who say to a tree, 'You are my father'" (Jer 2:27). Rahab says, "Go to the hill country" (Josh 2:16); but of Israel it is said, "They sacrifice on the tops of mountains" (Hos 4:13). Rahab says, "Give me a sign of good faith" (Josh 2:12); but of Israel it is said, "No one speaks the truth" (Jer 9:5 [4 H]). You thus see that all those words in Scripture, which are used in tribute to Rahab, contain a reproach of Israel (*Pesikta de-Rab Kahana, Piska* 13.4).[10]

---

10. See fn. 9 in *Pesikta de-Rab Kahana, Piska* 13.4 for the comments by Leon Nemoy regarding the translation of "Let the son of the wanton woman."

Text Study

Joshua 2:1–24; 6:22–25; Rahab and the Spies

The events surrounding Rahab, the honorable and God-fearing prostitute, are contained in the larger narrative of Joshua. Joshua sends spies to check out the land. Their primary mission is to evaluate the fortifications at Jericho. They spend the night with a local prostitute, Rahab. Someone reports the presence of these foreigners to the king of Jericho. The king sends a message to Rahab to turn over the men. Instead of doing so, she hides them on her roof. She falsely informs the king that the men had left via the city gate. She urges the king to send soldiers to pursue them. Naturally, they are not found out in the countryside. That night she goes to the men. She tells them that all Jericho is in fear of the Israelites. There is "no courage left in any of us, because of you. The LORD your God is indeed God in heaven above and on earth below" (2:11). She promises to help them escape. She dwells on the outer side of the city wall. She will let them down by a crimson rope through an outward-facing window. Rahab asks that she and her family be spared when Jericho is taken by the Israelites. The men agree on a plan. She is to hang the crimson rope in her window. Then she is to gather her family with her. As long as they stay in her apartments they will be safe (2:17ff.) The crimson color of the rope, or perhaps a thread of red woven into the rope, both hints of danger and is a common folk motif in terms of avoiding danger.

In chapter 6 Jericho is taken. Rahab and her family are saved. They choose to dwell among the Israelites.

Rahab's "character traits are . . . generally speaking, greatly lauded—in both the Jewish and Christian traditions."[11]

Joshua 4; Twelve Stones and the Jordan River

In chapter 4 there are two intertwined stories. Each focuses on twelve stones found in the Jordan River. The twelve stones symbolize the twelve tribes. In both narratives, the stones serve as a memorial to the crossing of the Jordan. Like the Sea of Reeds (Exod 14–15), the Jordan splits to allow the Israelites to pass through on dry land. In one version the stones are taken *from* the

---

11. Robertson, "Rahab and Her Interpreters," 111. Nonetheless, it is also true that "Rahab is the epitome of the outsider. She is a woman, a prostitute, and a foreigner. As a prostitute she is marginal even in her own culture, and her marginality is symbolized by her dwelling in the city wall, in the very boundary between the inside and the outside. Yet it is Rahab who understands best the nature of Yahweh." Fewell, "Joshua," 66.

Jordan River and set up in Gilgal. In the second version, Joshua places the stones *in the river*, where, it is purported, they are to this very day.

Sentences in the Hebrew Bible generally have a pause point (something like a comma) about halfway through a verse. Scholars designate the first part of these sentences with pause points as the *a* section of the verse; the second part is the *b* section. Joshua 4:4–5, 8a, 9, 15–19 represent the "stones in the bed of the river" tradition. Joshua 4:1–3, 6–7, 8b, 20 correspond to the tradition that has these twelve stones set up at Gilgal.

Joshua 10:12–14; The Day the Sun Stood Still; the Book of Jashar

The Israelites are battling the Amorites, one of the tribal groupings in Canaan. Joshua feels that his troops need more time to complete their task. He appeals to God to hold the sun in its place. The text explains, the "sun stopped in midheaven, and did not hurry to set for about a whole day" (v. 13). In the mind of the biblical narrator, there has been no day like this before or since, when God responds in such a way to a human request.

Verse 13 mentions a mysterious "Book of Jashar." In this book further details of this miracle are recorded. The selfsame book is also mentioned in 2 Samuel 1:18. There David laments the death of Saul and Jonathan. Scholars think that this may have been a collection of war songs, or a book of poetry celebrating Israelite military victories. The references to this work appear only in Joshua and Samuel. Nothing more is known of it.

3

Judges

Introduction

THE BOOK OF JUDGES bridges the time from the death of Joshua to the institution of the monarchy. Scholars debate the exact period of Judges. In approximate terms, it would be about 1200–1020 BCE.

Judges is the seventh book in the Hebrew Bible. It is the second book in the second section of the Hebrew Bible, the Prophets/*Neviim* (see Introduction: "The Order of the Books of the Bible"). In Hebrew the title is *Sefer Shoftim*, "Book of Judges." The Hebrew for "judge" is *shofet* (plural, *shoftim*).

The term "judges" is somewhat misleading. These people are not judges in a judicial sense, but charismatic, inspired leaders that lead an individual tribe, or more often several tribes, in military battles to free Israel from foreign domination. (Exceptions include Deborah, who is both a judge and a military leader, and Samuel, who is a judge, priest, and prophet). Their rule is impermanent. No one judge holds the allegiance of all of the tribes. "The picture that emerges from the book shows an Israelite confederation of twelve tribes still struggling to find unity among themselves while at the same time fighting for footholds in different parts of the Canaanite territory. It was a time of small local wars and defensive fighting against desert nomads. The Song of Deborah in Judges 5 reveals that often one or more of the tribes would not come to the aid of others . . . it was like the wild west of American folklore."[1]

---

1. Boadt, *Reading the Old Testament*, 168; see also Matthews, *Judges and Ruth*, 3–6; Niditch, *Judges*, 1–6.

Deuteronomistic History, Part 1

As noted in the chapter on Joshua, scholars refer to a "Deuteronomistic history." This set of writings includes the books of Deuteronomy, Joshua, Judges, Samuel, and Kings. Many of the concepts that stand behind the view of history presented in Deuteronomy likewise stand behind the view presented in Joshua, Judges, Samuel, and Kings. Stated succinctly, the perspective is one of a "militant monotheism." According to the thinking of the Deuteronomists, all is dependent upon the actions of the people. If they are faithful, they will know great blessings; if they turn from God's word, they will experience defeat, exile, or pestilence, panic, terror, and drought.

Although the book of Deuteronomy is ascribed to Moses, in its concepts it reflects a much later time. Many scholars date the composition of Deuteronomy to the eighth or seventh century BCE (see the section on Deuteronomy in the companion volume, Zucker, *The Torah: An Introduction for Christians and Jews*). The message of Deuteronomy is that obedience to the one God of Israel brings blessings, while disobedience leads to hardship and defeat. Deuteronomy presents a highly developed and articulate theology unmatched by any other single book in the Torah.

> See, I have set before you today life and prosperity, death and adversity. If you obey the commandments of the LORD your God . . . you shall live and become numerous . . . in the land that you are entering to possess. But if your heart turns away . . . to bow down to other gods and serve them . . . you shall perish; you shall not live long in the land that you are crossing the Jordan to enter and possess (Deut 30:15–18).

The school of thought that supports the Deuteronomistic viewpoint continues to be a part of the leadership of Israel. They are not the monarchs, but perhaps a mixture of priests and prophets. This Deuteronomistic group or school of thought edits and sets down the history of the people of Israel, probably completing their work in Babylonia as part of the exilic community about 550 BCE.

"Formed under the impact of the great disaster of 722 [the defeat and exile of Israel, the northern kingdom, by the Assyrians] and further developed under the shadow of that of 587 BCE [the defeat and exile of Judah, the southern kingdom, by the Babylonians], the Deuteronomistic ideology taught that the people fully deserved what occurred to them because of their failure to live up to the covenantal obligations." The books of Joshua, Judges, 1 and 2 Samuel, and 1 and 2 Kings are composed by the Deuteronomistic writers in the mid-sixth century during the Babylonian Exile. . . . Sometimes the Deuteronomists themselves summarized a particular era; other times they put their ideas in the mouths of historical figures or added them to older speeches. The historical books [Joshua, Judges, Samuel, and Kings] are intended to be a balance sheet of Israel's religious behavior, the people's successes and failures (mainly failures) in constructing a society according to the principles of the covenant.

Each book has its own dominant mood . . . portraying a periodic ascent and descent of Israelite religious fidelity to [God]. . . . The book of Judges is the counterpart of the people's repeated failures of faith during the wilderness wanderings under Moses. . . . Another important theme of Judges is persistent lawlessness, which even leads to fighting between Israelite tribes (12:1–6, chap. 20). The [biblical] editors note, 'In those days there was no king in Israel; every man did what was right in his own eyes' (17:6, 21:25, [18:1; 19:1]). Civil anarchy and military weakness set the stage for the formation of the kingdom, the subject of 1 and 2 Samuel, which reflect, in the final version, an ambivalence toward Israel's acquiring a king 'like all the nations' (1 Sam. 8:5).[2]

A monarchy means a rejection of God's rule. At the same time, it is a gift from God, ideally to provide effective leadership.

A further discussion of the Deuteronomistic history appears in the section "Deuteronomistic History, Part 2," in the chapter on Kings.

The Book of Judges

There are twelve judges, six major figures and six minor ones.

The book of Judges presents a regular pattern of cyclical behavior: apostasy leads to oppression; which leads to relief/rebellion against the oppression; which leads to periods of righteousness; which in turn are followed by recurring periods of apostasy. The book explains that the Israelites turn from God. They worship idols. Consequently, God is angry with them. After a time, God is moved by their cries of oppression and persecution. God then inspires certain leaders who rally the tribes and allow them, for a time, to regain their independence. The tribes eventually return to apostasy.

---

2. Seltzer, *Jewish People, Jewish Thought*, 98–100. "Modern scholarship's conclusion concerning Joshua . . . is the statement that, before anything else . . . the book is part of the Deuteronomic corpus of literature." Boling and Wright, *Joshua*, 41. Concerning the term "Deuteronomistic history" or "corpus," see also the section in Kings in this volume. See also McConville and Williams, *Joshua*, 3–8.

This predictably brings oppression. "Then the LORD raised up judges, who delivered them out of the power of those who plundered them. . . . But whenever the judge died, they would relapse . . . following other gods, worshipping them and bowing down to them. . . . So the anger of the LORD was kindled against Israel" (Judg 2:16, 19–20; cf. 10:5–7; 12:15—13:1).

Divisions in the Book of Judges

The book divides into three major sections:

Judges 1:1—3:6; Incomplete Conquest; Why Judges Are Needed

Judges 3:7—16:31; Careers of the Judges: Major and Minor Judges

3:7–11	Othniel	Major Judge
3:12–30	Ehud	Major Judge
3:31	Shamgar	Minor Judge
4:1—5:31	Barak/Deborah	Major Judge
6:1—8:35	Gideon	Major Judge
9:1–57	Abimelech	Minor Judge
10:1–5	Tola and Jair	Minor Judges
10:6—12:7	Jephthah	Major Judge
12:8–15	Ibzan, Elon, Abdon	Minor Judges
13:1—16:31	Samson	Major Judge

Judges 17–21; Incidents in the Tribes of Dan and Benjamin

Judges 1:1—3:6; Incomplete Conquest; Why Judges Are Needed

Unlike the narrative in the book of Joshua, this is not an integrated and unified Israelite campaign against the indigenous groups living in Canaan. In Judges, we learn about various tribal units pursuing military objectives, either individually or in tandem with other Israelites. In the opening verses, the tribes of Judah and Simon band together. Later in the chapter other tribes are mentioned, but not all twelve. Some of this history is fanciful. Judges 1:8 speaks of the capture of Jerusalem. This will not take place until the time of David (cf. 2 Sam 5:6–9). Further, in Judges occasionally material essentially repeats incidents in Joshua (cf. Judg 1:11–15 and Josh 15:15–19).

Chapter 2 commences with the warning that the Israelites are not faithful to God's covenant. Evil is going to befall them. Verses 6–9 recap the final days of Joshua and his influence (cf. Josh 24:28–31). By mid-chapter apostasy is rife. The Israelites "abandoned the LORD, and worshipped Baal and the Astartes." (Baal is the generic male fertility God of the Near East, whose consort is Astarte. Asherah is another female goddess associated with Baal.) "So the anger of the LORD was kindled against Israel, and he gave them over to . . . the power of their enemies all around, so they could no longer withstand their enemies" (2:13–14). Still worse, the Israelites intermarry with the local populace and worship their gods (3:6).

Judges 3:7—16:31; The Careers of the Judges: Major and Minor Judges

3:7-11; OTHNIEL; MAJOR JUDGE

Othniel is the first judge/charismatic military leader. He rises to power after the Israelites fall into apostasy. They serve King Cushan-rishathaim of Aram (or Aram-naharaim) for eight years. The name of this king translates as the phrase "Cushan—Double Trouble." Then the spirit of God comes upon Othniel. He defeats this oppressor. Othniel remains in power; the Bible uses the phrase "the land had rest" for forty years. Then he dies. This figure of forty years is a generic unit. It often is used in a formulaic way in Judges, meaning many decades (cf. 3:11, 30; 5:31; 8:28).

3:12-30; EHUD; MAJOR JUDGE

Following Othniel's death, Israel relapses into apostasy. It is subject to the rule of King Eglon of Moab for eighteen years. Israel cries out in despair. God raises up Ehud, a Benjaminite. In what appears to be cryptic, if not superfluous information, the Bible mentions two items: Ehud is left-handed, and King Eglon is very obese.

At one point Ehud is sent to bring tribute to King Eglon. By way of preparation, Ehud makes himself a double-edged sword. He fastens it to his right thigh, secreting it under his clothes. Ehud presents the payment to King Eglon of Moab. He then explains that he has a secret message for the king. Eglon silences his courtiers. He orders them from his presence. Apparently, King Eglon received Ehud in the royal privy. One interpretation suggests that the king did this to show his disdain, his lack of respect for the Israelites. In any case, the biblical text is unmistakable.

> Ehud came to him, while he was sitting alone in his cool roof chamber, and said, "I have a message from God for you." So he rose from his seat. Then Ehud reached with his left hand, took the sword from his right thigh and thrust it into Eglon's belly; the hilt also went in after the blade, and the fat closed over the blade, for he did not draw the sword out of his belly; and the dirt came out (3:20–22).

Ehud leaves and closes the doors behind him. Eglon's servants have no idea what is going on. When they see "that the doors of the roof chamber were locked, they thought, 'He must be relieving himself in the cool chamber.' So they waited until they were embarrassed. When he still did not open the doors of the roof chamber, they took the key and opened them. There was their lord lying dead on the floor" (3:24–25).

Ehud then rallies the Israelite troops. They defeat the Moabites. The land has rest for eighty years.

3:31; Shamgar; Minor Judge

One verse describes the minor judge Shamgar, who prevailed against the Philistines.

4:1—5:31; Barak/Deborah; Major Judge

Chapters 4–5 relate the narrative of the woman judge/prophet Deborah. King Jabin, who reigns at the important city of Hazor, cruelly oppresses the Israelites for twenty years. He is well armored, with nine hundred chariots of iron. Sisera is the general of these Canaanite forces.

Deborah invites Barak, a local commander from the tribe of Naphtali, to engage Sisera in battle. Barak says he will not go unless she accompanies him. Deborah speaks plainly. She replies that she, not Barak, will earn glory that day. God will hand over Sisera into the power of a woman (4:9). The Israelites are unexpectedly successful against the might of the better-equipped Canaanites. They are aided by a thundershower that renders their enemies' chariots ineffective (5:20–21). The enemy is completely subdued. (See the Text Study at the close of this chapter, "Deborah, Jael, and the Death of Sisera.") Scholars regard the "Song of Deborah" (ch. 5) as a very ancient poem. It evokes powerful images, describing well the perilous conditions of that time and the surprise victory of the Israelites. This battle is dated around 1125 BCE.

6:1—8:35; GIDEON; MAJOR JUDGE

The narrative describing Gideon covers three chapters. It contains interesting details about this judge and his campaigns. Gideon is a very appealing character. Chapter 5 concludes with the familiar words that the "land had rest forty years." The opening words of chapter 6 commence with the formulaic note that the "Israelites did what was evil in the sight of the LORD, and the LORD gave them into the hand"—in this case the hand, i.e., the power, of the Midianites. Every time the Israelites plant crops or pasture their livestock, the enemy comes and lays waste to the land. The Israelites are impoverished. An angel appears to Gideon, a member of the tribe of Manasseh. The angel tells Gideon, "The LORD is with you, you mighty warrior." Gideon is incredulous. He wonders why God has turned from Israel. The angel seeks to commission Gideon. Gideon replies that his clan is the smallest in the tribe, and he the least of his family. God reassures Gideon that he will be successful. Still doubtful, Gideon asks for a sign that he really has been chosen for this task. A miracle occurs. When Gideon realizes he really has seen an angel of God he fears for his life. God reassures him, "Peace be to you; do not fear, you shall not die." Gideon builds an altar and calls it "The LORD is peace" (6:1, 12, 23–24).

Gideon, sometimes called Jerubbaal, acts decisively. Occasionally, however, he seeks confirmation from God that he still has divine blessing for his campaigns. The Israelites ask Gideon to create a dynasty, but he refuses and tells them that only God rules over them (8:22–23).

9:1–57; ABIMELECH; MINOR JUDGE

Abimelech is Gideon's son by a concubine from Shechem (8:31). Chapter 9 explains how Abimelech usurps power. He kills all but one of his brothers, Jotham who manages to escape. Abimelech attempts to set up a dynasty, something that Gideon refused to do. He first allies with his kinsfolk the Shechemites. He rules for three years. Then there is a falling out. Abimelech attacks Shechem and destroys it. He then goes to attack Thebez, and falls in battle. A fascinating section of this chapter is a parable spoken by Jotham. Jotham is Gideon's surviving son, Abimelech's half-brother. A common interpretation is that Jotham is mocking Abimelech's attempt to set up a monarchy. (See the Text Study at the close of this chapter, "Jotham's Parable of the Trees.")

10:1–5; Tola and Jair; Minor Judges

The opening verses of chapter 10 relate the histories of two minor judges, Tola and Jair.

10:6–12:7; Jephthah; Major Judge

Among the judges, only the narrative about Jephthah is set east of the Jordan River. Jephthah is the son of Gilead by a prostitute. His stepbrothers drive him away. They refuse to let him inherit any of their property. Jephthah, however, is a successful warrior. When the Ammonites attack the people of Gilead, he is recalled. Jephthah becomes a judge/charismatic military leader. Jephthah attempts to use diplomacy to settle the conflict with Ammon. He is unsuccessful (11:12ff., 27–28). Jephthah decides to go to war. He vows a vow to God that will have a disastrous personal effect on his life. He says: "If you will give the Ammonites into my hand, then whoever [alternatively: whatever] comes out of the doors of my house to meet me when I return victorious . . . shall be the LORD's, to be offered up by me as a burnt offering" (11:30–31). When he returns victorious, his only child, a daughter, comes out to greet him. The daughter accepts her lot but asks for a reprieve of two months to bewail her virginity, which she does, accompanied by female friends. The closing words explain that the daughters of Israel would, year by year, go out to mourn her for several days. (See the Text Study at the close of this chapter, "Jephthah's Daughter.")

12:8–15; Ibzan, Elon, Abdon; Minor Judges

Chapter 12 closes with references to three minor judges, Ibzan, Elon, and Abdon.

13:1–16:31; Samson; Major Judge

Chapter 13 commences with the statement that Israel once again does what is offensive to God. This time they are delivered into the power of the Philistines. The narrative of Samson from the tribe of Dan is that of a tragic hero.[3] He is a man of great strength and good will. He also is flawed and, at times, foolish. The four chapters devoted to Samson contain special materials. These include folk motifs and riddles. Early on the text

---

3. Bakon, "Samson."

explains that Manoah was married to a woman unable to conceive. One day an angel appears and tells her that she shall bear a son. This son is to be raised according to the traditions of the Nazirites. No razor is to come upon his head (cf. Num 6:2ff.). She is to avoid wine or other intoxicants. She is not to eat anything unclean. She is told further that her son will save Israel from the Philistines. The woman then goes and tells her husband that a "man of God came to me, and his appearance was like that of an angel" (13:6). Manoah is incredulous. He asks God for further instructions. The angel reappears to Manoah's wife. She goes again to find her husband, who joins them and asks for further instruction. After speaking with them the angel ascends in a fiery flame.

As chapter 14 begins, Samson now grown, seeks out a wife, a woman from the Philistine town of Timnah. This is the first of three Philistine women in Samson's life. His parents are dismayed at Samson's choice. They "did not know that this was from the LORD; for he was seeking a pretext to act against the Philistines" (14:4). Samson goes to Timnah. During the weeklong wedding celebrations, as part of a wager he poses a riddle to the men of the town. They are unable to answer. They then persuade Samson's fiancée to cajole the answer from him. She does so. When he hears their correct reply, he is very upset. He goes to the Philistine town of Ashkelon, kills thirty men, and brings back their garments as payment for losing his bet. Still angry, he returns to his parents' home, and his wife is given to another man.

Samson returns to Timnah in chapter 15. He finds out that his wife has been given to someone else. He wreaks revenge on some Philistine territory. Later in the chapter he kills a thousand[4] additional Philistines.

Chapter 16 commences with Samson visiting a prostitute in Gaza. The Philistines unsuccessfully try to capture him. A few verses on, he falls for a third Philistine woman, Delilah. Samson does not seem to learn from his experiences with women. The Philistine leaders offer to pay her a large sum if she can find out the secret of his strength. She pesters him continually until he reveals the source of his power: he is a Nazirite. Were his hair to be cut, he would lose his physical strength. He would be like any other person. Delilah shares this information with the Philistines, who pay her off. When Samson is asleep someone comes and cuts his hair. He loses his power. Samson is captured, blinded, and imprisoned. The Philistines celebrate their success. They bring him out of prison to a large indoor gathering. They do not realize his hair has grown back. In the banqueting hall he is able to reach

---

4. It is likely that the Hebrew word for "thousand," *elef*, may be likewise a term for a contingent or a unit. See Mendelhall, "Census Lists," which proposes that *elef* does not mean "thousand" but "unit" or the like.

out for some supporting pillars and pull them down. Samson dies along with all those in attendance.

Judges 17–21; Incidents in the Tribes of Dan and Benjamin

Chapter 17 relates the story of a man named Micah who lives in the hill country of Ephraim. By chance, he meets an itinerant Levite from Bethlehem in Judah. Micah invites the Levite to settle in Ephraim and serve there as the priest. In chapter 18, some five members of the tribe of Dan seek to relocate their tribal holdings. They chance upon the Levite serving Micah's family. In short order, six hundred well-armed members of their tribe join the five. They invite the Levite to join them. He agrees, preferring to serve a tribe rather than merely one family. They steal ritual objects from Micah's family. They end up settling in the north of Israel.

A grisly and gruesome tale of rape and its aftermath constitutes chapter 19. A Levite from the hill country of Ephraim marries a concubine from Judah. There are some marital differences. She returns to her home. In time he pursues her. They reconcile. Traveling back northward to his home, they plan to spend the night at Gibeah. This is a town in the tribal area of Benjamin. They stay in the town square. An older resident invites them to share his home for the night. In an episode clearly reminiscent of the perverse actions of the citizens of Sodom (Gen 19), some of the rowdy locals in Gibeah come to the old man's home. They demand that he give up his guest, so that they "may have intercourse with him." The old man refuses. He offers his virgin daughter and the concubine in place of his guest (cf. Gen 19:8). The men refuse this request. The Levite takes his concubine and pushes her out of the door. Throughout the night she is raped and abused, and finally left for dead. The next morning the Levite finds her body on the threshold of the house. He takes her back to his home. In anger he cuts her body into twelve parts and sends the pieces throughout the tribes of Israel, seeking revenge.

Chapter 20 finds all of the other tribes arrayed against the tribe of Benjamin. A bitter series of battles take place. The Benjamites take heavy losses both in terms of people killed and towns devastated.

In the final chapter of Judges, the tribe of Benjamin initially is isolated. There are no marriage alliances with their fellow Israelites. In time, this policy changes. Peaceful relations are restored. The final line in the book both describes the lawlessness of the time of the judges and sets the stage for the events portrayed in the books of Samuel: "In those days there was no king in Israel; all the people did what was right in their own eyes" (21:25).

Judges in the Christian Scriptures

A number of the judges are mentioned specifically by name in the Epistle to the Hebrews. "And what more should I say? For time would fail me to tell of Gideon, Barak, Samson, Jephthah, of David and Samuel and the prophets —who through faith conquered kingdoms, administered justice, obtained promises, shut the mouths of lions, quenched raging fire, escaped the edge of the sword, won strength out of weakness, became mighty in war, put foreign armies to flight" (Heb 11:32–34). These categories could apply to several of the judges above. The reference to lions refers to Samson (Judg 14:5ff.)

In Judges, an angel approaches Manoah's wife. The angel announces that she will give birth to a son who will bring salvation to Israel. Her husband Manoah is incredulous. A variation of this narrative is found in Luke's Gospel. An angel approaches Zechariah and announces that his wife Elizabeth will bear a son who is to do great things. In both cases the child is not to drink wine or strong drink (Luke 1:11ff.; Judg 13:3ff.)

Judges in Rabbinic Literature

Judging judges. A place that has a judicious judiciary fares well. Likewise, if the judiciary is corrupt, trouble ensures. The Midrash observes, "Woe to the generation which judges its judges," and by inference, woe to the generation whose judges are in need of being judged (*Midrash Ruth Rabbah* 1.1).

People are recognized for their good deeds. Phineas, the son of Eleazar and grandson of Aaron, is still serving as a prophet and judge in the time of Deborah. The question is raised, why then is she called a prophet and a judge (4:4)? The answer is, "I call heaven and earth to witness that whether it be a heathen or a Jew, whether it be a man or a woman, a manservant or maidservant, the holy spirit will suffuse each of them in keeping with the deeds he or she performs" (*Tanna Debe Eliyyahu* [9] 10, p. 48 [112–13]).[5]

Deborah is one of seven female prophets. Deborah is one of seven female prophets. The others are Sarah, Miriam, Hannah, Abigail, Huldah and Esther (*Babylonian Talmud Megillah* 14a).

Obsessive pride can lead to tragedy. Jephthah is criticized for his rash vow to offer up whatever/whoever came out of his house when he returned from war. He should have gone to the high priest Phineas and had his vow revoked. He

---

5. See this title in the bibliography.

stands on his dignity, refusing to go. Phineas likewise is criticized for failing to intervene in this tragic matter (*Midrash Genesis Rabbah* 60.3).

There is a divine reckoning in kind. Samson rebelled with his eyes. Consequently, he is blinded. "Samson said to his father, 'Get her [the Philistine woman] for me, because she pleases me [lit. "is pleasing in my eyes"].'" Accordingly, he is punished through his eyes, for it says, "So the Philistines seized him and gouged out his eyes" (14:3; 16:21) (*Midrash Numbers Rabbah* 9.24).

Means to an end. A transgression with good intent is more meritorious than the performance of a commandment with no intent. The example is Jael's killing Sisera (*Babylonian Talmud Horayot* 10b).[6] She is praised for her act, for in doing so she saved the lives of the Israelites (*Midrash Genesis Rabbah* 48.15).

Text Study

Judges 4–5; Deborah, Jael, and the Death of Sisera

Many more male than female figures are named in the Bible; more is written about men than about women. Deborah and Jael are rare exceptions. They truly are heroes of the first order. Deborah is a female judge. She shows that women are perfectly capable of taking needed action. King Jabin reigns in Hazor. His chief commander Sisera has subjugated Israel. Deborah sends a message to Barak (presumably another judge living at this time). She says God has explained this is the time to overcome and subdue their enemy. Barak answers that if she will go, he will accompany her. He himself will not go alone. Deborah speaks plainly. She replies that she will lead the troops in battle. She says though that it is her name that will shine, "for the LORD will sell Sisera into the hand of a woman" (4:9). Deborah organizes the troops. Although the Israelites are inferior in terms of armaments, they prevail over the Canaanites. A violent storm prevents the enemy from using their chariots.

Deborah says that the general Sisera will fall into a woman's hands. This is true both in its generalization and in its specific context. Deborah's tactics defeat Sisera's forces. A woman subsequently slays the general. After his defeat, Sisera leaves his chariot. He attempts to flee by foot. He comes to the tent of Jael, the wife of Heber the Kenite. Jael greets Sisera. She offers him refuge.[7] She gives him food. She allows him to sleep, promising him

---

6. See Bronner, "Valorized or Vilified?," 89.

7. Reis, "Uncovering Jael and Sisera," makes a compelling case that Jael seduced Sisera. See also Niditch, "Eroticism and Death."

her protection. When he is asleep, Jael takes a tent peg and a hammer. She drives the peg through his temple, killing him. When Barak comes looking for Sisera, Jael shows him the fallen enemy.

Chapter 4 concludes with a note that the Israelites go on to destroy the kingdom of King Jabin of Canaan.

Chapter 5 is a poetic version of chapter 4. Numerous scholars regard this as one of the oldest sources in the Bible. Many feel the author is a woman.[8]

Judges 9:7-21; Jotham's Parable of the Trees

Jotham offers a parable about the trees that seek to appoint a tree to rule over them. This story appears to be a bitter denunciation of the concept of a monarchy. In verse 8, "the trees" approach the olive tree and ask it to reign over them. The olive tree claims it is too involved in producing rich oil that is appreciated by gods [or possibly God] and mortals, to take on this task. A similar dismissive answer is offered to the trees by the fig tree, and then the vine. Only the bramble (alternative: thornbush) replies in the affirmative, "If in good faith you are anointing me king over you, then come and take refuge in my shade; but if not, let fire come out of the bramble and devour the cedars of Lebanon" (9:15).

If this is a denunciation of Abimelech and the monarchy, the message is clear: little good would come from Abimelech's rule. Brambles do not offer shade. Often brambles are used for kindling. Fire would come from Abimelech and destroy Shechem, and that fire might destroy Abimelech.

There are difficulties with this interpretation. The fable does not explicitly condemn the monarchy. Abimelech approached the Shechemites; they did not seek him out. No mention is made of the violent murder of Jotham's seventy brothers. A case can be made that the olive, fig, and vine each choose to shirk responsibility, and then because nature abhors a vacuum, an inferior element takes advantage of the situation, bringing disastrous results.

Judges 11; Jephthah's Daughter

The narrative of Jephthah and his unnamed daughter is a troubling text. It runs counter to the spirit and religious traditions of Israel. Child sacrifice is abhorred and expressly prohibited (cf. Lev 18:21; 20:2-5). Jephthah feels unable to revoke his vow and repent of his words. This is an enigma. The

---

8. Liver, "Deborah," 1431; see also Bledstein, "Is Judges a Woman's Satire?," 34; Stewart, "Deborah, Jael," 128-32.

Talmudic rabbis condemned Jephthah for his actions (see earlier in this chapter, "Judges in Rabbinic Literature.") This is not the first example of what would have been a child sacrifice. In Genesis 22, God expressly asks Abraham to sacrifice Isaac. God then relents. A more parallel case is 1 Samuel 14 where Saul rashly vows a similar vow to Jephthah's vow. In the event, the people intervene and prevent Jonathan's death (1 Sam 14:24f., 43–45).

It is questionable what Jephthah really means by this vow. The Hebrew verb used (*ha-yotzey,* Judg 11:31) in this context could mean equally "the one that comes out," "whatever comes out," or "whoever comes out." It is likely that Jephthah assumes it will be an animal, and not a person that will come out to greet him. Perhaps he expects that his daughter would know about his vow, and will stay indoors.

A careful reading of this text raises some interesting issues. Jephthah finds that it is his daughter who greets him. He says to her, "Alas, my daughter! You have brought me very low; you have become the cause of great trouble for me. For I have opened my mouth to the LORD, and I cannot take back my vow" (Judg 11:35). This is a classic case of blaming the victim, and indeed the female victim!

Words kill, but "they can also heal. The destructive power of language is counterbalanced in this tale by its sustaining capacity . . . After her death, the women of Israel commemorate Jephtha's daughter in a yearly ritual . . . Jephthah's daughter finds life through communal recollection."[9]

Commentators over the ages have interpreted this episode differently. Some offer various explanations for the actions taken, others condemn human sacrifice, and still others hold up the daughter as an exemplar of faithfulness.[10]

---

9. Exum, "Murder They Wrote," 54.

10. Stewart, "Jephtha's Daughter and Her Interpreters," 133. See Brown, "Jephtha's Daughter," 128n2. One interpretation suggests that Jephthah's daughter purposely took on this role. She did so to challenge and pass "judgment on her father's willingness to bargain for glory with the life of another." Fewell, "Judges," 71. Trible regards this as an example of blaming the victim. Trible, *Texts of Terror*, 101–2. Violence done to women and men is a theme in the book of Judges. Yet here, as in the sexual violence depicted in Judges 19, one needs "to interrogate structures of societal domination and not to limit sexual violence to an individualized problem, as if it were unrelated to society in general." Scholz, "Judges," 124.

4

Samuel (1 and 2)

Introduction

IN THIS SECTION OF Israelite history, the books of 1 and 2 Samuel, the tribes slowly coalesce into one kingdom. They select their first two monarchs, Saul and David. The narratives are quite detailed. Parts have the feel of a contemporary writer. The period covered in these books is under one hundred years, from the time of the judge/prophet/priest Samuel to the close of the reign of King David, about 1050–960 BCE.

The books of Samuel are the eighth and ninth books in the Hebrew Bible. They are the third and fourth books in the second section of the Hebrew Bible, the Prophets/*Neviim*. In Christian versions of the Bible, the eighth book is Ruth. It follows Judges and precedes Samuel. In the Hebrew Bible, Ruth is part of the Writings/*Ketuvim* (see Introduction: "The Order of the Books of the Bible"). In Hebrew this book is termed *Shmuel*, Samuel, or *Sifrei Shmuel*, the Books of Samuel.

Originally, these two books of Samuel were regarded as one complete book. Then in the early sixteenth century, some five hundred years ago, when the first Hebrew Bible was printed, editors divided the one book into two sections, 1 Samuel and 2 Samuel. This reflected the tradition of the Septuagint* and the Vulgate.*

Biblical scholars debate which sections come from this period, and which reflect later writing and redaction. "Many scholars argue . . . that 'David's Rise' and the 'Court History' were put into writing in the tenth century BCE within or very close to the lifetime of David . . . the basic biblical narrative as a work . . . to provide a persuasive explanation of the legitimacy of the Davidic dynasty." The contemporary scholars Israel Finkelstein and Neil Asher Silberman contest this idea in their work, *David and Solomon: In Search of the Bible's Sacred Kings and the Roots of the Western Tradition*.[1]

The books of Samuel are part of the Deuteronomistic history.[2] See the "Deuteronomistic History" sections in the chapters on Judges and Kings.

The chapters in the books of Samuel provide more information about this period than any other time in Israel's history. Because of the external threats by other tribes, primarily the Philistines, it becomes clear why Israel needs a more unified, centralized government. Yet, some people oppose setting up a monarchy. The books of Samuel reflect two distinct and opposing traditions: an anti-monarchical viewpoint and a pro-monarchical viewpoint. Both traditions are woven into the text of the books. They are particularly evident in the chapters that deal with Samuel and Saul.

The Books of Samuel

Divisions in the Books of Samuel[3]

1 Samuel

    1 Samuel 1–7   Samuel

    1 Samuel 8–15   Samuel and Saul

    1 Samuel 16–31; 2 Samuel 1   Saul and David

2 Samuel

    Samuel 2–20 (Completed in 1 Kings 1–2)   David

    2 Samuel 21–24   Appendices

---

1. Finkelstein and Silberman argue that these narratives initially are composed two centuries after the time of David and Solomon, during the late eighth century BCE. Finkelstein and Silberman, *David and Solomon*, 122. In contrast, Halpern argues "large parts of our information on the United Monarchy stem from roughly contemporary sources." Halpern, *David's Secret Demons*, 226; see also Brooks, *Saul and the Monarchy*, 1–21.

2. The idea of a "Deuteronomistic history" has been challenged, but as McKenzie notes, Martin "Noth's model for the composition of the DH is still the most useful." McKenzie, *Trouble with Kings*, 19; see also 1–18.

3. There are different ways to divide these chapters. An alternative view is: "Three distinct but overlapping cycles of stories unfold in 1–2 Samuel: (1) a Samuel cycle (1 Samuel 1–25); (2) a Saul cycle (1 Samuel 9–2 Samuel 2); and (3) a David cycle (1 Samuel 10—2 Samuel 24). Interlaced ark, Jerusalem, and house themes run through the stories giving them continuity and vibrance." Flanagan, "Book of 1–2 Samuel," 5:962.

1 Samuel 1–7; Samuel

The books of Samuel commence with the birth and early life of Samuel. Readers familiar with biblical texts, in particular Genesis, Exodus, and Judges, will recognize a familiar motif. A married couple has trouble producing progeny, or there are difficulties surrounding a pregnancy. Then a child who will be significant in the life of Israel is born (cf. Gen 18, Isaac; Gen 25, Jacob; Gen 30, Joseph; Exod 2, Moses; Judg 13, Samson; 1 Sam 1, Samuel.) The prayer of Hannah, Samuel's mother, in chapter 2 is particularly poignant.

Samuel is reared in the home of the priest Eli, who serves at Shiloh. Samuel is still a child when he receives a call from God. God tells Samuel that Eli's sons are acting in a blasphemous way, and because Eli did not intervene, they will be punished.

Years pass. As Samuel grows up it becomes clear that he is an important leader. The Bible explains, "the LORD was with him and let none of his words fall to the ground. And all Israel from Dan to Beer-sheba knew that Samuel was a trustworthy prophet of the LORD" (3:19–20). Not long thereafter (around 1050 BCE), serious conflict erupts with the Philistines, a country to the southwest of the Israelite tribal holdings. The Philistines' five main cities, Ashdod, Gaza, Ashkelon, Gath, and Ekron, are situated near to the Mediterranean Sea, along the southwestern coast of Canaan. The Philistines have mastered the use of iron, a skill that the Israelites lack (13:19–22). The Philistines decide to expand their territory eastward into Israelite territory. They move into the Shephelah, east of the central plain and west of the Judean hills. The Israelites band together and battle the Philistines at Aphek. The Israelites lose this battle. The Philistines capture the ark of God. Eventually they will return the ark to the Israelites.

During this period, Samuel serves as a judge in the sense of military leader, as a judge-magistrate, as a prophet, and as a priest (3:20; 7:5–17).

1 Samuel 8–15; Samuel and Saul

Samuel is a both a king maker and a king breaker. As mentioned, the books of Samuel reflect both a pro-monarchical and an anti-monarchical viewpoint. The pro-monarchical view suggests that Israel needs a central ruler that can unite the tribes in common purpose. A monarch would lead them in battle against their enemies. The anti-monarchical view reflects different thinking. Kings would unify the country; they would also assess taxes and often have building projects that demand ever more taxes.

When Samuel is an old man, the people clamor for a monarch just "like other nations." Samuel is personally appalled and theologically resistant to this idea. God, however, tells him, "Listen to the voice of the people . . . for they have not rejected you, but they have rejected me from being king over them . . . only—you shall solemnly warn them, and show them the ways of the king who shall rule over them" (8:7, 9). Samuel lists in some detail the various demands a monarch will make: taxation, conscription, appropriation of property, and more. The people refuse to listen. Once again, they demand a human ruler.

Saul first appears in chapter 9. He is tall and handsome. One day he meets Samuel. Samuel takes Saul aside. He tells Saul that he has been chosen to lead Israel. Saul is skeptical, but Samuel insists. Samuel privately anoints Saul, telling him he will rule over Israel (10:1).[4] Saul's appointment does not seem to take immediate effect. Later Samuel convenes the tribes at Mizpah and rails against them for demanding a human sovereign. Nonetheless, he acquiesces to their demand. Saul is chosen king. The people recognize him in that role, but no further action takes place.

Saul faces a threat from the Ammonites. He is successful in this military campaign. Chapter 12 features the viewpoint of the anti-monarchical tradition (cf. ch. 8; 10:17–25). It also contains the view of the Deuteronomistic historian, telling the people as long as they obey God it will go well for them. If they rebel against those teachings the hand of God will be against them and their human ruler. In a series of skirmishes, Saul and his son Jonathan engage the Philistines and other tribes in several battles. They generally fare well. Samuel has been a reluctant supporter of the monarchy, and specifically of Saul. Nonetheless, Samuel brings a message to the king. God says, avenge the Amalekite attack against the Israelites when they were in the desert with Moses (Exod 17:8–14; Deut 25:17–19). Go and destroy them. Utterly wipe them out, people and animals alike. Saul attacks this perennial enemy of Israel. He triumphs, but saves the life of the Amalekite king, Agag. Saul takes the best of their flocks as booty. Samuel comes to meet Saul. He berates the monarch. Samuel condemns Saul for his actions with words that anticipate the call of the prophet Hosea (cf. 1 Sam 15:22ff.; Hos 6:6). Samuel then personally takes a sword and hacks Agag to death.

---

4. The Septuagint and Vulgate add the words that Saul will not only rule over Israel, but also that he will save them from their enemies all around. These words are found in some Christian versions of the Bible, but not in Jewish texts. Cf. NRSV, NAB,* and NJPS/*TANAKH*.

1 Samuel 16–31; 2 Samuel 1; Saul and David

God tells Samuel that Saul needs to be replaced. Samuel is to anoint a new king. Samuel fears that Saul will kill him if he does this. Nonetheless, Samuel secretly anoints David, Jesse's son. Yet David's time has not yet come.

Beginning with 1 Samuel 16, the Bible features several long and colorfully detailed chapters. These include the narratives of David entering Saul's service, and his playing the lyre for the king to soothe the monarch's spirit. They also mention David slaying the giant Goliath, David's close friendship with Jonathan, Saul's son, and David's marrying Michal, Saul's daughter. They portray David as favored by God, and God turning from Saul.

These chapters compare and contrast David's successes with Saul's failures. At one point, the women of the towns of Israel come out to meet Saul, singing and dancing. They say to one another, "'Saul has killed his thousands, and David his ten thousands.' Saul was very angry, for this saying displeased him. He said, 'They have ascribed to David ten thousands, and to me they have ascribed thousands; what more can he have but the kingdom?'" (1 Sam 18:7–8).

> One can hardly fail to note that once David appears in the accounts Saul's personality deterioration begins.... Saul's later years were marked by manic states of fitful depression and paranoia, described in the language of the times as "an evil spirit from the Lord" (16:14). Perhaps the loss of Samuel's favor, together with the popularity that young David enjoyed with the masses, was too much of a strain for the aging Saul.... The several attempts on David's life and the latter's magnanimous refusal to retaliate in kind may reflect the pro-David slant of the sources.[5]

In the meantime, the Philistines are mounting their attacks on the Israelites' communities. First Samuel 27 sets out David's choices. With whom shall he ally? He faces difficult decisions. King Saul is actively trying to kill David; he is a hunted man. If David stays in Judah, eventually Saul will catch him and annihilate him as well as the six hundred men who are part of his band of warriors. In addition, David now has two wives, Ahinoam of Jezreel and Abigail of Carmel. Yet, if he actively goes over to the Philistines and joins them, he will be regarded a traitor to his people. Then he will never attain the monarchy.

Given these possibilities, David opts to leave Judah. He becomes a vassal to one of the Philistine monarchs, Achish the king of Gath. David

---

5. West, *Introduction*, 231.

will be in exile for sixteen months. He is granted the fortress at Ziklag, located between Gath and Judah. David and his men go on forays against the Amalekites and other tribes. They send deceptive reports to Achish. They say that they are attacking Judah or Judah's allies. Meantime, Saul faces an attack from the Philistine armies. Saul is rightfully fearful for his future. He consults a necromancer. He learns that he will fail. (See the Text Study at the close of this chapter, "Saul and the Witch of Endor.")

David's patron, King Achish of Gath, explains that he expects David to join the Philistine forces in their attack on Israel. David has no choice but to agree to this request. Yet, the other Philistine commanders tell Achish they do not want David to accompany them. They are suspicious about his true loyalties. David and his men return to Ziklag. When they get there, they find that in their absence Amalekites have attacked his camp. The Amalekites carried off the families living there and burned the camp to the ground. David and many of his men pursue and overtake the Amalekite raiding party. They rescue their families, and capture a fair amount of valuables. When David returns to Ziklag, he shares some of this plunder with various allies in Judah and the surrounding areas (1 Sam 29–30).

First Samuel closes with the death of Saul and Jonathan. The first chapter in 2 Samuel relates how the news of Saul and Jonathan's death reached David. It also contains the heartrending words of David's lament for them, which includes the phrases, "Tell it not in Gath, proclaim it not in . . . Ashkelon," and "How the mighty have fallen in the midst of the battle!" (2 Sam 1:20, 25).

2 Samuel 2–20 (Completed in 1 Kings 1–2); David

Initially David reigns in Hebron as the ruler of Judah for seven years. Ishbaal, one of Saul's sons rules over the other tribes, with Abner as his chief commander. There are skirmishes between the two kingdoms. David's forces fare well. Eventually there is a falling out between Ishbaal and Abner. Abner defects to David's side. Not long thereafter, Joab kills Abner, for Abner had killed Joab's brother. In chapter 4, two brothers attack and kill Ishbaal. They bring his head to David. They expect to be rewarded for assassinating David's rival. Wisely, David executes them. He thus makes it clear that he did not authorize their activities. David accords Ishbaal a special funeral. The northern tribes then come and pledge their loyalty to David. "David was thirty years old when he began to reign, and he reigned forty years. At Hebron he reigned . . . seven years . . . [and] over all Israel and Judah thirty-three years" (5:4–5).

David's next feat is to capture Jerusalem and make it his capital. This is an astute move. Like Washington, DC, Jerusalem is neutral territory; it has no previous connections to any of the twelve tribes. David then fights several successful battles against the Philistines. His next task is to bring the ark of God to Jerusalem (6:1–19). David does so with great fanfare, and he literally dances in front of the ark as part of the procession, an event that irritates his wife Michal (6:20–23), and causes dissent between them.[6]

David intends to build a proper house for the ark. The prophet Nathan advises him that this undertaking will fall to David's successor.

David is a victorious warrior. He can be a magnanimous friend. Overall, he is a capable ruler. David also has a shadow side. He can be extremely ambitious and unprincipled. He murders Uriah to get his beautiful wife Bathsheba (ch. 11). One of his own sons leads a revolt against him, and receives widespread support, which suggests many were unhappy with his despotic rule, especially among the northern tribes (chs. 15–18). His forced labor gangs (20:24) as well as the establishment of a military draft after taking a census (ch. 24) become hated elements of the monarchy.

A large part of 2 Samuel constitutes a segment in its own right. It is termed the Court History of David, or the David-Solomon Succession Narrative. Beginning with 2 Samuel 9, it reaches through 1 Kings 2, with several appendices inserted at 2 Samuel 21–24. (See the Text Study at the close of this chapter, "David and Bathsheba.")

2 Samuel 21–24; Appendices

The appendices contain varied material. There is reference to an outstanding vendetta from the time of Saul. There also is a notation that Saul and Jonathan's bones are finally interred in their family tomb. Several of David's heroic warriors are lauded in this section. Chapter 22 is a psalm attributed to David. It reappears with some variations as Psalm 18. David's "last words" form the opening verses of chapter 23, followed by some further mention of David's warriors. As noted earlier, chapter 24 explains that David orders a census of the Israelites. He does this against the advice of his generals, and later he regrets his actions. (See the Text Study at the close of this chapter, "Speaking Truth to Power: Joab Challenges David.")

---

6. Exum, "Michal, the Whole Story." The Michal-David relationship probably was doomed from the start. "To her father [Saul], Michal was a snare to entrap David; to David, she is a political convenience" which by this point had achieved its goal. Consequently, now "Michal is David's wife in name only; her bed and womb remain empty." Rosenblatt, *After the Apple*, 139, 144.

David: Lights and Shadows

Much of the books of Samuel chronicle the life of David from his youth to old age. In times to come, both biblically and in the post-biblical world, David is characterized as the exemplar of Israelite rule and leadership. In the words of the prophet Jeremiah, just as God will not change the forces of nature, so God will not sever the divine eternal covenant with David (Jer 33:19–26). Many of the psalms are attributed to David. In Jewish as in Christian religious tradition, the Messiah is to be a descendant of David. Liturgically, David is lauded as one of God's favored individuals.

> David's reign not only established the broad patterns for Israel's four centuries of monarchical rule, but produced as well significant and lasting concepts of the divinely appointed rule of the king, the nation, and the city of Jerusalem in the future destiny of world history . . . David took a place alongside Abraham and Moses as the recipient of a covenant with Yahweh which assured for his descendants an everlasting kingdom.[7]

The prophet Nathan explains to David that God has appointed David as monarch, and that he will establish a dynasty. God has said, "Your house and your kingdom shall be made sure forever . . . your throne shall be established forever" (2 Sam 7:16).

David is a complex figure, a complicated character. In his long history, he is portrayed as caring, compassionate, and considerate. He is also cunning, conniving, and crafty. David is ambitious, and he is ruthless. He can be a loyal friend, and an implacable enemy. He can be generous, and he can be shortsighted. "From bitter wives to a ravished princess, to cold-blood killers and traitors; from secret lovers to betrayed confidants to out-and-out scoundrels—there is perhaps no more fascinating cast of characters in the Bible than the close circle that surrounded King David in his court in Jerusalem."[8]

David's rise to the monarchy and his forty-year reign are catalogued in the books of Samuel. Given the many examples of David's publicly recognized, and self-admitted failures as a leader and as a man (a husband, a father), his popularity is nothing short of amazing.

Yet, perhaps that is exactly what turns the day for David. He is a curious mix of lights and shadows. He colossally fails in some aspects of the moral arena, and shines in others.

---

7. West, *Introduction*, 240.

8. Finkelstein and Silberman, *David and Solomon*, 91; see aso Halpern, *David's Secret*, 18–53.

- David is immoral (2 Sam 11).
- David repeatedly admits his faults, repents or recants (2 Sam 12:13–23; 24:10ff.).
- David is respectful of Saul as God's anointed (1 Sam 24).
- David is a successful warrior (2 Sam 8).
- David is a generous leader, treating his troops fairly and equitably (1 Sam 30:21ff.).
- David grieves when his children disappoint him (2 Sam 13:37; 18:33 [19:1 H]).

Samuel in the Christian Scriptures

The opening words of the Christian Scriptures, literally the first verse refers to Jesus as the Messiah (the anointed one), the son of *David*. Jesus' royal descent is also mentioned elsewhere (Matt 1:1; 22:41–45; Mark 12:35–37; Luke 3:23–38; Rom 1:3; 2 Tim 2:8).

Samuel, Saul, and David as historical figures are mentioned at various points (Acts 13:20–22; Heb 11:32; Mark 2:25f.; John 7:42).

According to a note in the *New Oxford Annotated Bible*, the "stories of the birth and childhood of Samuel were in the mind of Luke as he began the writing of his Gospel."[9]

Likewise, the "Magnificat"—termed such from the first word in the Latin translation of Mary's prayer in Luke 1:46–55—is based on Hannah's prayer in 1 Samuel 2:1–10.[10]

As discussed in the Text Study at the end of this chapter, "Speaking Truth to Power: Joab Challenges David," one of David's sons, Absalom, leads a revolt against his father, forcing David to leave Jerusalem for a time. A number of the episodes in this period of David's life are used in the Christian Scriptures to describe Jesus' life, mission, and suffering: John 18:1, Jesus crosses through the Kidron Valley during his passion (2 Sam 15:23); Luke 22:39, Jesus, weeping and praying, ascends the Mount of Olives (2 Sam 15:30); Luke 23:35, Jesus accepts curses from the people (2 Sam 16:5–13); and Revelation 21, Jesus returns to Jerusalem (2 Sam 20:2).

---

9. *NOAB*, 345 [1 Sam], n. 3.1—4.1a.
10. Jobling, *1 Samuel*, 137.

Samuel in Rabbinic Literature

Samuel

There is continuity in leadership. Before Eli's sun sets, Samuel's sun rises (*Midrash Genesis Rabbah* 58.2).

Samuel and Moses. Samuel and Moses are valued equally. Psalm 99:6 states, "Moses and Aaron were among his priests, Samuel also was among those who called on his name." Another interpretation: Samuel's virtue was greater than that of Moses. Moses sat and people came to seek his judgment, Samuel went from place to place to spare people the trouble of coming to him. "Samuel judged Israel.... He went on a circuit year by year ... he judged Israel in all these places" (1 Sam 7:15f.) (*Midrash Exodus Rabbah* 16.4).

Samuel as a biblical author. Samuel wrote the books of Judges, Samuel, and Ruth (*Babylonian Talmud Baba Batra* 14b end).

Samuel prophesies in his life, and after he dies. Samuel prophesies both in life and after he dies. Samuel appears to Saul after his death. (See the Text Study at the close of this chapter, "Saul and the Witch of Endor") (*Pirke de Rabbi Eliezer*, ch. 33[11]).

Samuel taught humility by God. In 1 Samuel 9:18f., Samuel acknowledges that he is a seer. God explains to him that nonetheless his powers are limited. When it comes time to anoint one of Jesse's sons, Samuel does not know which one to choose (*Sifre, Deuteronomy, Piska* 17[12]).

Samuel's death. When Samuel dies, all Israel mourns (*Midrash Ecclesiastes Rabbah* 7.1.4).

Saul

Why Saul's dynasty ends. Because Saul is brazen, he is slain and his royal line cut off. He goes against the express wishes of God in not completely destroying the Amalekite forces (1 Sam 15: 3, 20). He also does what he is not commanded to do. He orders the killing of the priests of Nob (1 Sam 22:13, 18–19) (*Tanna Debe Eliyyahu* [31] 29, p. 159 [346]).

Do not overdo justice. The rabbis in the Talmudic period voice concern at the divine order for complete annihilation of the Amalekites, including

---

11. See this title in the bibliography.
12. See *Sifre* in the bibliography.

children and cattle. They portray Saul protesting God's command. A divine voice supports him, (quoting Eccl 7:16) "Do not overdo justice"[13] (*Babylonian Talmud Yoma* 22b).

Forgiveness for sins. If one is ashamed of sinning, those sins are forgiven. This applies to Saul. He accepts his fate when he speaks to Samuel at Endor. The prooftext is ". . . never open your mouth again because of your shame, when I forgive you all that you have done, says the Lord GOD" (Ezek 16:63). (See the Text Study at the close of this chapter, "Saul and the Witch of Endor.") (*Babylonian Talmud Berakhot* 12b).

David

David is revered as the ideal ruler, and as the ancestor of the Messiah. There are literally dozens of rabbinic statements that praise him for his many virtues.[14]

David possesses six attributes of perfection. David possesses six attributes of perfection. Among them he is able to ask pertinent questions and answer them; he has the intelligence to deduce one thing from another and to give and take in intellectual discussions (*Midrash Numbers Rabbah* 13.10).

David and Moses share good qualities. God tests both Moses and David in similar ways. God sees that they are good shepherds. As they pasture their flocks well, so will they take care of my flock Israel (*Midrash Exodus Rabbah* 2.2, 3).

David both studies and prays. Up to midnight David studies Torah. From midnight on he recites songs and praises (*Babylonian Talmud Berakhot* 3b).

David as biblical author. David wrote the book of Psalms (*Babylonian Talmud Baba Batra* 14b).

David involves himself with laws dealing with menstruation. He is ready to consult about his decisions with other scholars. Other monarchs are concerned with feasting. David is concerned about marital purity laws. He

---

13. The Hebrew word *tzadiq* (NRSV: "righteous") is interpreted by the rabbis as "justice."

14. See the section "In Rabbinical Literature" in the entry for David in the *Jewish Encyclopaedia*, and the "In the Aggadah" in the entry for David in the *Encyclopaedia Judaica*. See also the indexes of such midrash collections as *Midrash Rabbah* (Soncino ed.), *Midrash on Psalms* (trans. Braude), and *Pirke de Rabbi Eliezer* (trans. Friedlander).

also is not ashamed to seek advice from his teacher (*Babylonian Talmud Berakhot* 4a).

David's virtues. David displays the virtues of strength, Torah, and humility (*Midrash on Psalms*, Ps 18.28).

David's monarchy is eternal. God says David's reign will be for all time (*Midrash Genesis Rabbah* 88.7)

David lives. David, king of Israel, lives and endures (Hebrew: *David melekh yisrael, hai vekayam*) (*Babylonian Talmud Rosh Hashanah* 25a).

Yet David is fallible. David is fallible. David is castigated for the seduction/rape Bathsheba. He is penalized for conducting a census. Among his punishments are the death of his first child by Bathsheba, the rape of his daughter Tamar by her half-brother Amnon, and the rebellion and death of Absalom. David also is afflicted with a skin disease (*Babylonian Talmud Yoma* 22b). Yet in another Talmudic source, David's actions are rationalized. It suggests that Uriah gave Bathsheba a bill of divorce before he went out to battle (*Babylonian Talmud Ketubot* 9b beginning). Elsewhere, it claims that David *desired* Bathsheba, but did not actually sin. That same source seeks to malign Uriah as a rebel against royal authority (*Babylonian Talmud Shabbat* 56a; cf. *Babylonian Talmud Kiddushin* 43a).

With greatness comes temptation. The greater the person, the greater the evil inclination (*Babylonian Talmud Sukkah* 52a end). Although the Talmud does not associate this saying with David, it applies to him.

Liturgical references. The Jewish liturgy contains many references to David. He is glorified as the author of many psalms and praises to God.

David's name is featured in many prayers, including the blessings after meals, and the prayers that close out the Sabbath and greet the weekdays (*Havdalah*). There is mention of the Davidic dynasty, and with it undertones of the messianic age. In the blessings following the additional biblical readings on Sabbaths, Festivals, and the High Holy Days, there is a reference to the House of David.

God is praised as the Shield of David.

Text Study

1 Samuel 28; Saul and the Witch of Endor

Desperate situations create desperate people. Saul has reason to feel vulnerable. The Philistine armies are massing against him. It is clear that a fearful and fateful battle will rage at Mt. Gilboa, in the hill country of Israel, just southeast of the Jezreel Valley. Samuel has died. When Saul inquires of God, he is not answered, neither directly nor by dreams, by Urim, or by prophets. Following Levitical tradition, Saul has expelled mediums and wizards from the land (1 Sam 28:3; Lev 19:31; 20:6, 27). Feeling he has no other recourse, Saul seeks out a necromancer, someone who can communicate with the dead.

One night, wearing a disguise, he visits a woman whom he is told is a medium. When he asks her to consult a spirit, she fears that this is a trap. She retorts that King Saul has forbidden this kind of wizardry. Saul, still disguised, swears by God she will not be harmed. The woman brings up the deceased spirit of Samuel. Samuel is vexed at being disturbed! He tells Saul that he and his sons will die on the next day. Saul falls to the ground, faint with hunger and filled with fear and foreboding. At the urging of his servants and the woman, he takes some nourishment. Saul and his servants then leave.

This is a fascinating passage. Saul is portrayed sympathetically. Yet, events have overtaken him. Samuel, who never was a strong supporter of the monarchy, and certainly had reservations about Saul, is merciless in his remarks to the king. He taunts Saul. "The LORD has torn the kingdom out of your hand, and given it to your neighbor, David. Because you did not obey the voice of the LORD" (vv. 17–18).

Samuel is pictured as "coming up out of the ground . . . wrapped in a robe." Samuel then says to Saul, "Why have you disturbed me by bringing me up?" Although the text does not state so explicitly, the inference is that Samuel has been brought up from Sheol, the biblical abode of the dead, a place of darkness and silence (cf. Gen 37:35; Ps 88:3–7 [88:4–8 H]).

2 Samuel 11; David and Bathsheba

David has many admirable qualities. In both Judaism and Christianity the Messiah is described as his direct descendant. Nonetheless, there are serious shadow sides to David's life. The Bathsheba affair is among his most appalling acts. To the credit of the editor of Samuel, this shameful story of misplaced royal privilege and naked lust is not excised from the narrative.

One day David, from the vantage of his palace, sees a beautiful woman bathing herself. She is Bathsheba, the *wife* of one of his most successful warriors, Uriah the Hittite. He inquires who she is. Then he has her brought to his bed. In short order she becomes pregnant. Bathsheba informs David of her condition. David then tries to cover up his betrayal by insuring that Uriah will cohabit with Bathsheba. Uriah explains he is on active duty. He will refrain from privileges not accorded to his own men. David then has his trusted general Joab place Uriah in the front lines of battle. Expectedly, Uriah is killed by the enemy. Bathsheba then marries David. In the next chapter, Nathan the prophet reprimands David. The child of this adulterous union dies. David mourns the child. David impregnates Bathsheba again, and Solomon is born.

David's actions are unconscionable. They are an embarrassment. Centuries later, some in the rabbinic tradition sought to whitewash David's actions (see the source for "*Yet David is fallible*" in "Samuel in Rabbinic Literature" above).

The fact is that David acted improperly. This is a sordid tale of rape and murder. The chasm of power differential between David and Bathsheba is momentous. No manner of rationalization can deny that David was the *ruler*. Bathsheba was a *subject* of the king, and she was a woman. He acted in bad faith. She had little choice but to acquiesce to his demands. Bathsheba's affection for her husband, or his for her, is not discussed in the text. "Bathsheba is pictured as almost entirely passive in this episode." Further, the "narrative does not seem to hold her responsible for her actions with David."[15] There likewise was a huge power differential between David and Uriah. Again, David was the ruler, and nominally in charge of the armed forces. Uriah, presumably a professional mercenary at the king's hire, also served at the king's will. It is to Uriah's credit that he stood up to David to the extent that he would not take leave of his men during an active military campaign.

Or, is there more to this episode? Broadly, there are two schools of thought on the David/Bathsheba affair. Some scholars, both male and female, suggest that Bathsheba is at least as interested in David as he is interested in her. They suggest that it is unclear whether any force or just minimal persuasion was exerted on the part of David. "Bathsheba's complicity in the sexual adventure" may be her desire to bear a child, for she seems to have been childless before her encounter with David—"rather than merely participation in an adulterous (lustful) act."[16] Did Bathsheba plan or agree to

---

15. Hackett, "1 and 2 Samuel," 159.
16. Klein, "Bathsheba Revealed," 49. Perhaps there is the "possible element of female

this liaison; thus is she equally guilty of adultery? Did she not know that the king could see her bathing from his roof? Why would she stand naked and bathe potentially in sight of the king if he were on his roof? Might it be considered that she seduced him?

Those who see her complicit in this affair follow the reasoning that the text "suggests a woman who has her eye on the main chance, and it is possible that opportunism, not merely passive submission, explains her behavior here."[17]

While it could be that there "is no evidence that she is ever less than a willing participant in their adultery,"[18] there remains the power differential between David and Bathsheba.

Other scholars, often feminists both female and male, see the early Bathsheba as someone caught up in an intrigue not of her own making. David exploited his power as ruler, and simply took Bathsheba because he could do so. In short, he sexually exploited and raped Bathsheba.[19] As one scholar noted, "David is hardly passive: He is a *taker*. . . . The king who *takes* is the king of I Sam 8,11–17, about whom the prophet Samuel warned the people."[20] Put another way, "Bathsheba [is] a casualty of David's sexual imperialism."[21] She is a victim of "power rape."[22]

The Hebrew of 2 Samuel 11:4 is ambiguous; either explanation is possible. As has been suggested, there are "an elaborate system of gaps between what is told and what must be inferred [and this] has been artfully contrived to leave us with at least two conflicting, mutually complicating interpretations of the motives and states of knowledge of the principal characters."[23]

---

flirtation." Hertzberg, *I and II Samuel*, 309.

We do not know how long Bathsheba had been married to Uriah, but she appears to have been a childless woman until David. Klein, *From Deborah to Esther*, 56.

17. Alter, *David Story*, 251. Perhaps she was working toward a "political marriage" and so was "a willing and equal partner to the events which transpire." Bailey, *David in Love and War*, 88. Parallels between the David/Abigail narrative in 1 Sam 25 and the David/Bathsheba narrative in 2 Sam 11 are explored in Shinan and Zakovitch, *From Gods to God*, 250–58.

18. Nicol, "Alleged Rape of Bathsheba," 50.

19. Bach, *Women, Seduction, and Betrayal*, 149–50. Jobling writes of "David's rape of Bathsheba, a married woman, and his murder of her husband." Jobling, *1 Samuel*, 160.

20. McCarter, *II Samuel*, 290; emphasis original.

21. Bach, "Pleasure of Her Text," 36.

22. That Bathsheba is the victim of a "power rape" is argued convincingly by Davidson, "Did King David Rape Bathsheba?"; see in particular 82, 87.

23. Alter, *Art of Biblical Narrative*, 18. See also Sternberg, *Poetics of Biblical Narrative*, 190–222; Bach, *Women, Seduction, and Betrayal*, 134–45; Huwiler, *Biblical Women*, 55–58.

Later, in Kings 1–2, Bathsheba will exercise great power to assure the succession of their son Solomon. Over the twenty years, Bathsheba certainly finds her voice. The mature woman presented in Kings is very politically astute. While a good case can be made that the early Bathsheba was innocent or, at worst, a bit naïve, the Bathsheba of the book of Kings is someone who knows how to make her way through the corridors of power. She clearly has friends, and knows how to influence events. One motivating factor for her was that she understood that if she did not act for her son Solomon, and for herself, their very lives were in danger. It likely was a choice between acting or being killed so that they would not be a threat to another faction who desired the throne.

2 Samuel 19:1–8 (19:2–9 H); 24:1–4; Speaking Truth to Power: Joab Challenges David

If being the ruler is difficult, serving as the advisor to the monarch is equally a challenging position. If one is going to be effective, and ethical, at times this requires great discretion. On occasion, the advisor needs to confront the decisions made by the superior. David's long-term general, Joab, often walks a difficult line. He serves at the pleasure of the king. At times he acts as David's "hatchet man." On other occasions, he finds it necessary to challenge David's actions.

In 2 Samuel 13, one of David's sons, Amnon, rapes his half-sister, Tamar. Tamar's full-blood brother Absalom eventually kills Amnon, but then he flees the country. David grieves his estrangement from Absalom, but he does not know how to effect a reconciliation with his son. In 2 Samuel 14 Joab devises an elaborate, although successful scheme to reunite David and Absalom. Some years later, Absalom turns traitor. He leads a revolt against David. He forces David and his followers literally to decamp from Jerusalem. Absalom then sets up power there (chs. 15–17). David eventually counterattacks. Absalom is defeated. David expressly asks for Absalom's life to be spared. Nonetheless, Joab himself takes weapons and personally kills Absalom. When he learns of Absalom's death, David is overwhelmed with grief. He becomes effectively incapacitated (Sam 2 19:1f. [19:2f. H]). At this moment, Joab speaks truth to power. Mincing few words, he berates David for his lack of leadership. He questions David's failure to support those who loyally have supported the king (2 Sam 19:5–7 [19:6–8 H]). To his credit, David follows Joab's advice; he does not argue, much less punish his general.

In 2 Samuel 24:1–4, Joab advises David not to conduct a census. David ignores Joab's suggestion, and lives to regret it (24:10ff.)

Although Joab was loyal to David, David did not repay that loyalty. Joab supports another of David's sons in the succession controversy. David's dying instructions then urge Solomon to assassinate Joab—advice that he follows (1 Kgs 2:5ff., 28ff.)

5

Kings (1 and 2)

Introduction

THE PERIOD FEATURED IN these books is nearly four hundred years, c. 966–586 BCE. This covers from the time of the final years of the reign of David to the destruction of the Temple, the fate of Judah's king and the aftermath in Jerusalem. If, broadly speaking, the book of Samuel recounts the "waxing of the ancient Israelite monarchy, then the book of Kings recounts its waning. The 'glory days' of David are over" and the book depicts the slow decline of the monarchy due to apostasy from the God of Israel. Kings will conclude with the destruction of Jerusalem and the exile to Babylon.[1]

This is also the time of the classical prophets, Isaiah, Jeremiah, Ezekiel, Hosea, Amos, and others.

The books of Kings are the tenth and eleventh books in the Hebrew Bible. They are the fifth and sixth books in the second section of the Hebrew Bible, the Prophets/*Neviim*. In Hebrew, this book is termed *Melakhim*, Kings, or *Sifrei Melakhim*, The Books of Kings.

Originally, these two books of Kings were regarded as one complete book. Then in the early sixteenth century, some five hundred years ago, as with the books of Samuel, when the first Hebrew Bible was printed editors divided the one book into two sections, 1 Kings and 2 Kings. This reflected the tradition of the Septuagint and the Vulgate.

---

1. Howard, "1 and 2 Kings," 164. The exact dating of the rulers of Judah and Israel are notoriously difficult to ascertain. The dates in this chapter follow the suggestions in NRSV based on the research of Albright, "Chronology Tables of Rulers," *NOAB* 338–39.

The document that we now have as the books of Kings is the result of years of collecting and editing. The final redacted copy reflected both oral and written traditions that were set down as part of the Deuteronomistic history.[2]

Kings includes the period of the divided monarchy. This means that there are separate rulers in Judah, the southern kingdom, and in Israel, the northern kingdom. The narrative in Kings shifts from one country to the other, and then back again. Each of the monarchs' reigns is coordinated with that of the parallel ruler in the other kingdom.[3]

The book of Kings uses a set formula to demark the years that a monarch rules. (1) It begins with the date the king ascends to the throne, which is then synchronized with the reign of the rival monarch. (2) This is followed with the length of his administration. (3) Next comes the narrator's judgment about this reign. In the case of the kings of Judah, the text provides two additional features: (4) the age of the king when he came to power, and (5) the name of the king's mother. There also is a closing formula consisting of three parts: (1) a reference to further sources of information about the king, (2) a notice of his death and burial, and then, in addition, (3) the successor's name.

Each of the monarchs, for Judah as for Israel is either praised or condemned by the rigor to which the ruler was faithful to God's commands. All of the northern kings are judged wanting. This is also true of the southern monarchs, with the exception of Hezekiah and Josiah, who were well regarded as religious reformers. Stated simply, every monarch is judged by the ruler's fidelity to the legislation found in Deuteronomy 12, which centralizes worship at Jerusalem and orders the destruction of the high places. Using these criteria, all the kings of Israel are denounced for doing evil in God's sight, by not rejecting the sin of Jeroboam I, who made Dan the capital of the northern kingdom and set up a national sanctuary at Bethel.

---

2. *NOAB*, 423.

3. Coordinating reigns between two kingdoms is an imperfect process.

"A few minutes' labor with a hand calculator will convince the reader not only of serious discrepancies between tallies of the individual regnal years of the kings of Judah and Israel but of outright contradictions between different citations of the same chronological event. For example, 143 years and seven months is the total for the reigns of the Israelite kings from Jehu through Hoshea; for the corresponding reigns in Judah, the tally is 166 years . . .

"Although chronological information useful for ordering events and determining length of reigns is found in Kings, efforts to comprehensively convert the dates in Kings to absolute dating (B.C.E.) yield results which are approximate at best. A fact lost sight of in most studies of chronology in Kings is the nature of the text: it is a *theological* history; a precise and accurate exposition of historical events was not the primary concern of the authors." Holloway, "Book of 1–2 Kings," 4:74–75.

These histories of the monarchy—united, north, and south—find parallels in the final books of the Jewish Scriptures, 1 and 2 Chronicles (for a more detailed, chapter-by-chapter analysis of Chronicles, see the companion volume *The Bible's WRITINGS*).

Deuteronomistic History, Part 2

The Deuteronomistic history is initially discussed in a preceding chapter in the book of Judges. There it notes that the term "Deuteronomistic" refers to a group of leaders who teach and pass on their traditions and philosophy over several hundred years, c. 750–550 BCE. Among the Deuteronomists are priests and prophets, probably including, in his time, Jeremiah. The Deuteronomistic historians are responsible for editing and setting down the history of the people of Israel. This group or school is well aware of the defeat and dissolution of the northern kingdom. They live through the destruction of the temple and the devastation of Judah. Many among this group go into exile to Babylon.

The Deuteronomistic "ideology taught that the people fully deserved what occurred to them because of their failure to live up to the covenantal obligations." Joshua, Judges, 1 and 2 Samuel, and 1 and 2 Kings were composed by the Deuteronomistic writers in the mid-sixth century during the Babylonian exile. These historical books are intended by the Deuteronomists "to be a balance sheet of Israel's religious behavior, the people's successes and failures (mainly failures) in constructing a society according to the principles of the covenant. . . . Each book has its own dominant mood . . . portraying a periodic ascent and descent of Israelite religious fidelity to [God]"[4]

Five stages characterize the Deuteronomistic history:[5]

- The first stage is the conquest of Canaan under Joshua. There is an initial enthusiasm, but this soon dissipates.

- The second stage or period is that of the judges. This is a time of successes, backsliding, and frequent anarchy. "In those days there was no king in Israel; all the people did what was right in their own eyes" (Judg 21:25).

- The third stage is the rise of the monarchy. More specifically, the reign of David constitutes the high point of fidelity to God. The Deuteronomists could well relate to the sentiments expressed in Psalm 89. There the text

---

4. Seltzer, *Jewish People, Jewish Thought*, 98–99.
5. Developed from Boadt, *Reading the Old Testament*, 330–32.

explains that God said, "I have made a covenant with my chosen one, I have sworn to my servant David: 'I will establish your descendants forever, and build your throne for all generations.' . . . My faithfulness and steadfast love shall be with him; and in my name his horn shall be exalted. . . . He shall cry to me, 'You are my Father, my God, and the Rock of my salvation!'" (Ps 89:3–4, 24, 26 [4–5, 25, 27 H]).

- The period of the Kings is the fourth stage. The time of the monarchy after David is a mixture of many rulers who fail to live up to the Deuteronomistic expectations, and a few who do. It ends with the destruction of both the northern and southern kingdoms.
- The fifth stage is the time of the exile. Although it is not the last line in 2 Kings, it summarizes well the situation: "The LORD said, 'I will remove Judah also out of my sight, as I have removed Israel; and I will reject this city that I have chosen, Jerusalem, and the house of which I said, My name shall be there'" (2 Kgs 23:27).

Although there is no stated sixth period, the underlying hope of the Deuteronomists was that eventually there would be a restoration of the Davidic monarchy. They could not envision this as a living reality c. 550 BCE. In their hearts, however, they longed for a return to Jerusalem and the glory days of David.

The Books of Kings

Division in the Books of Kings

1 Kings

1 Kings 1:1—2:12	Death of David; Enthronement of Solomon
1 Kings 2:13—11:43	Reign of Solomon
1 Kings 12–22	Divided Kingdoms; Ahab of Israel; the Prophet Elijah; Jehoshaphat of Judah

2 Kings

2 Kings 1–17	The Prophets Elijah and Elisha; Reigns of Ahaziah and Jehu of Israel; Various Rulers of Judah and Israel; Fall of Israel
2 Kings 18–25	Kingdom of Judah; Capture of Jerusalem; Aftermath

1 Kings 1:1—2:12; Death of David; Enthronement of Solomon

Several years passed since the close of the book of Samuel. King David has aged. He is near death. Supported by David's general, Joab, and the priest, Abiathar, David's eldest son, Adonijah, makes a premature bid for the throne. In the meantime, Nathan the prophet and Benaiah the priest support Solomon, another one of David's many sons. Nathan advises Bathsheba, Solomon's mother, to intervene lest the throne slip away from her son. She does this. David pronounces Solomon his successor.

In his final words to Solomon, David urges him to walk in God's ways. Ironically, he then asks his son to avenge some old grudges that David had never settled. Adonijah attempts to usurp Solomon's power. Adonijah is killed; Joab likewise is assassinated. Solomon brutally but effectively consolidates his power.

1 Kings 2:13—11:43; Reign of Solomon

In a dream, God appears to Solomon. God asks Solomon what he would like to receive. Solomon asks for an understanding mind to govern, and wisdom to discern between good and evil (3:9). Solomon then sets out to build the temple for God. He orders cedars from Lebanon. Building the temple is quite an undertaking. He conscripts a forced labor pool of 30,000 men from Israel (5:13 [5:27 H]; see also 9:15ff.) The temple has a rectangular floor plan. It is about 90 feet in length by 30 feet in width, and about 45 feet in height (30 meters, by 10 meters, by 15 meters). The temple is decorated inside and outside. It takes seven years to build.

Solomon also builds a magnificent palace and an administrative building. Chapter 8 describes the dedication of the temple, including Solomon's prayer. This prayer is described in verses 22–53. The latter section, verses 41–53, however, is appended at a later point. The reference to being "carried away captive to the land of the enemy" (v. 46) is written by an author during the Babylonian exile.

The Bible lauds Solomon's successes. It claims that the whole earth seeks his presence and wisdom. Sadly, in his later age Solomon turns from God. He commits apostasy. He "did what was evil in the sight of the LORD" (11:6). At the same time, various local nations rise up against his hegemony. Solomon's apostasy impels the prophet Ahijah to approach a local leader, Jeroboam son of Nebat. Ahijah urges Jeroboam to lead a revolt against Solomon. This is conditional on the premise that Jeroboam will follow God's commandments (11:29ff.)

1 Kings 12-22; Divided Kingdoms; Ahab of Israel; the Prophet Elijah; Jehoshaphat of Judah

After Solomon dies, Jeroboam and a group of northern tribal leaders come to Rehoboam, Solomon's son and successor. They wish to pledge their support to Rehoboam and to the united kingdom. This support, however, depends on a concession that they request. They ask Rehoboam to lighten the tax load, which Solomon had imposed. Some of Solomon's older advisors suggest that he acquiesce to this appeal. Rehoboam's contemporaries urge him to take a hard line. Rehoboam pledges no relief from taxes. Consequently, the ten northern tribes secede. Jeroboam leads this revolt.

To consolidate his power, Jeroboam sets up a capital in the north. He builds sanctuaries at Bethel and Dan. He revises the cultic calendar, and appoints non-Levitical priests. He offers incense at the altar even though he is not a priest.

Jeroboam reigns for over two decades. Despite warnings, he continues to worship idols (13:33; 14:15-16).

Jeroboam's counterpart in Jerusalem, King Rehoboam, now rules solely over Judah (made up of the two tribes of Judah and Benjamin). He reigns for seven years. In Judah, the populace also commits apostasy. They build high places, pillars, and sacred poles on every high hill and sacred poles under every green tree. They pollute the land with idolatry (14:22ff.)

Chapters 15-16 detail the lives of several kings of Israel and Judah. Each one in his turn does evil in the sight of God; each is condemned for it. All of the Judean kings are direct descendants of David. In the northern kingdom, there are a series of dynasties. In terms of military success, the most powerful dynasty is that of the family of Omri (876-42 BCE—the reigns of Omri, Ahab, Ahaziah, and Jehoram [of Israel]). Although there are continual skirmishes between the two kingdoms, Omri forces a peace that lasts for many years. Omri regains territory in Transjordan, which was lost to neighboring countries. Omri's son Ahab takes as his wife Jezebel of Sidon (Phoenicia). He introduces Baal worship and other forms of idolatry (16:29-33).

Elijah the prophet, a major figure in the ninth century, first appears in 1 Kings 17. Narratives about Elijah continue through the opening chapters of 2 Kings. Elijah's first public act is to confront King Ahab. Elijah announces to Ahab that there will be a drought for three years, and then the prophet flees away. In the third year of the drought, God sends Elijah back to Israel to confront Ahab once again. In the meantime, Queen Jezebel kills many of God's prophets. Ahab greets Elijah with the words, "Is it you, you troubler of Israel?" (18:17). Not surprisingly, the prophet denies this charge. Instead,

Elijah labels Ahab as the troubler of Israel. He accuses Ahab of forsaking God and introducing Baal worship. Elijah then challenges Ahab to a public contest to determine who is in the right. Elijah triumphs and Ahab retreats from the field. (See the Text Study at the close of this chapter, "Elijah and the Prophets of Baal.")

Ahab and especially his wife, Queen Jezebel, are furious. She is quite clear that she intends to kill Elijah. Elijah flees south to Beersheba. He continues a day's journey further into the wilderness. He travels to Mt. Horeb, where God speaks to Elijah. God tells Elijah that he still has great deeds to perform. He is to anoint Hazael as a future king over Aram (Syria), and anoint Jehu as a future king over Israel. Elijah also is to appoint Elisha son of Shephat as his own eventual successor.

Chapter 20 details both dialogues and battles between King Ben-Hadad of Aram and King Ahab of Israel. Ahab vanquishes the Arameans. The next chapter explains that Ahab wants to acquire a certain vineyard belonging to his neighbor Naboth. Naboth refuses to sell this ancestral property. Ahab is depressed that he cannot convince Naboth. Queen Jezebel intervenes. She arranges for Naboth's assassination. When Ahab takes possession of the vineyards, Elijah meets him. The prophet predicts that because of this vile act, disaster awaits Ahab. To his credit, Ahab repents and God recognizes his change of heart. God postpones the fall of Ahab's dynasty.

About three years pass. Then Ahab joins with King Jehoshaphat of Judah in an alliance against the Arameans. Together they form a powerful army. Just before the battle begins, King Jehoshaphat turns to King Ahab and suggests that it would be wise to check with God about the success of this venture. King Ahab gathers four hundred prophets. They claim that God has given approval for this war. Jehoshaphat wants further assurance. King Ahab mentions that there is another prophet, Micaiah son of Imlah. Ahab voices concern that Micaiah always has bad things to say about Ahab. Jehoshaphat insists, nonetheless, that they consult with Micaiah. The result is a kind of prophetic duel. (See the Text Study section at the close of this chapter, "Micaiah and the Kings of Israel and Judah.") In the ensuing battle, an archer kills King Ahab. Ahab's son Ahaziah then reigns in his place. Ahaziah worships the pagan god Baal.

King Jehoshaphat of Judah began his reign in the fourth regnal year of King Ahab of Israel. He reigns for well over two decades, and is succeeded by his son Jehoram.

The book of 1 Kings concludes at about the middle of the ninth century BCE.

2 Kings 1–17; The Prophets Elijah and Elisha; Reigns of Ahaziah and Jehu of Israel; Various Rulers of Judah and Israel; Fall of Israel

This section begins with the death of King Ahaziah, the son of King Ahab of Israel, c. 850 BCE. Another son of Ahab, Jehoram (Joram), succeeds him. Coincidentally, Jehoram of Israel has a brother-in-law with the same name, Jehoram. That Jehoram is king of Judah. Each Jehoram reigns for about seven years. Their rules overlap some of the same period. King Jehoram of Israel will be assassinated by one of his own generals, Jehu.

Much of the material found in the first nine chapters of 2 Kings focuses on the narratives of Elijah's designated successor, the prophet Elisha. Chapter 1, however, still focuses on Elijah. Chapter 2 describes the transition of leadership from Elijah to Elisha.

Several of the miracles associated with Elisha are prefigured in the life of Elijah. In chapter 4, Elisha's actions parallel that of his predecessor (cf. 2 Kgs 4:1–7 with 1 Kgs 17:14–16; and 2 Kgs 4:8–37 with 1 Kgs 17:17–24). "There are eight miracle stories in 1 and 2 Kings. Five of these involve the direct interaction of Elijah or Elisha and a woman [1 Kgs. 17:8–16; 17–24; 2 Kgs. 4:1–7; 8–17; 18–37]. . . . These female characters are best understood as generic rather than historical; that is they represent groups within the population . . . who were struggling for survival amid the political strife and agricultural hardships of mid-ninth-century Israel."[6]

Elijah is a king breaker. He announces the destruction of the reign of Ahab (1 Kgs 21:21–22). Elisha is a king maker. He arranges that one of his disciples secretly anoint Jehu as the next king of Israel (2 Kgs 9).

> Jehu, with the backing of [the prophet] Elisha and the prophetic party began a *coup d'état* that swept the Omrides from power in a bath of blood. Jehu's wholesale slaughter took the lives of both Hebrew kings [Jehoram of Israel, and] Ahaziah of Judah, who was . . . a descendant of Omri through his mother, Athaliah . . . as well as those of Jezebel and the northern Baal party. It was a thorough job of housecleaning, from which Baalism was not soon to recover. Its undue bloodletting, however, was to have a bitter burden on the Israelite conscience for years to come (cf. Hos. 1:4).
>
> Jehu's dynasty lasted five generations [842–745 BCE] . . . longer than any other royal house in northern history.[7]

---

6. Camp, "1 and 2 Kings," 97.

7. West, *Introduction*, 256. Jehu is the only Israelite monarch who is depicted in Near Eastern art. See comments below in this chapter. Matthews and Benjamin, *Old Testament Parallels*, 181.

Jehu's rise to the monarchy, and the "bloodbath/housecleaning" is dramatically presented (2 Kgs 8:25—10:36).

After Jehu assassinates King Ahaziah of Judah, Ahaziah's mother, Athaliah declares herself queen. She begins her reign with a bloodbath of her own. One of her first acts is to kill off any of the royal family who might be a threat to her. Unbeknownst to Queen Athaliah, one of her relatives takes Joash (Jehoash), one of (the late king) Ahaziah's young sons, and hides him away. Queen Athaliah reigns for about a half dozen years. Then there is a *coup d'état* in Jerusalem. The queen is killed, and Joash becomes king (for a detailed discussion see the chapter on 1 and 2 Chronicles in the companion volume *The Bible's WRITINGS*).

All of these changes in Judah and Israel take place in a wider world context. For three hundred years (c. 900-600 BCE) the dominant force in the ancient Near East is Assyria. In modern terms, it is the "superpower" of the day. Assyria is centered in northern Mesopotamia. It has major cities along the Tigris River. Although culturally connected to Babylonia, Assyria remains fiercely independent. In the ninth century under the leadership of several strong rulers, it begins to build its empire. Assurnasirpal II (883-59) and Shalmaneser III (859-24) are fierce conquerors. They use conscious cruelty in warfare as a means to subdue their enemies. The only Hebrew king depicted in Near Eastern art is Jehu of Israel. He is bowing before Shalmaneser (the Black Obelisk of Shalmaneser).

At various times both Judah and Israel will be, in effect, vassal states to Assyria. Some of the pagan shrines set up in both Israel and Judah may have been at the insistence of the Assyrians. That said, under the leadership of several strong kings (and coincidentally a weaker set of kings in Assyria), Israel and Judah do prosper and regain some territory c. 800-750 BCE.

Second Kings 15:29 explains that during the reign of King Pekah of Israel, the Assyrian king Tiglath-Pileser III attacks Israel. He carries away captives to Assyria. Later King Ahaz of Judah pays obeisance to Tiglath-Pileser (16:8ff.) This is about 735/734.

The final defeat of Israel (722) is described in chapter 17. For three years, the Assyrian forces, under the leadership of King Shalmaneser V, and then his brother and successor, Sargon II, besiege Samaria, the capital of the northern kingdom. Then they destroy the kingdom. They carry away the survivors, exiling them in Assyria. This is the end of the nation formed by the ten tribes over two hundred years earlier, the kingdom of Israel.

The ten tribes cease to exist as an independent entity. In the comment of the Deuteronomist, this "occurred because the people of Israel had sinned against the LORD their God. . . . They had worshipped other gods . . . they set up for themselves pillars and sacred poles on every high hill and under every green tree . . . they . . . did not believe in the LORD their God" (17:7, 10, 14; cf. 18:12). The Assyrian king then settles foreigners in the land of Samaria (17:24ff.)

2 Kings 18–25; Kingdom of Judah; Capture of Jerusalem; Aftermath

Judah now is the remaining kingdom. In less than one hundred fifty years, it too will be destroyed. During much of this period, the kings of Judah pay enormous tributes to the kings of Assyria. Judah often is a vassal state with little power. It is likely that the Assyrian rulers continue to demand that pagan shrines be set up in Judah. Often there is little resistance from the monarchy.

Of the last nine rulers of Judah, only Hezekiah and Josiah are regarded favorably in the mind of the Deuteronomist. Hezekiah comes to power in 715 and rules for close to three decades. Initially he remains subservient to Assyria. At one point he tries to regain independence. It is futile. Halfway through his reign, he pays additional levies to the Assyrians. At one point, Hezekiah goes to the prophet Isaiah and seeks advice (2 Kgs 19; cf. Isa 37).

In the book of Kings, Hezekiah's religious reforms are limited to one verse. It says, "He removed the high places, broke down the pillars, and cut down the sacred pole. He broke in pieces the bronze serpent that Moses had made" (2 Kgs 18:4). A much fuller account of Hezekiah's reforms are delineated in the book of Chronicles (2 Chr 29–31; the relationship between Kings and Chronicles is discussed in the chapter on Chronicles in the companion volume *The Bible's WRITINGS*).

Hezekiah's son Manasseh succeeds him. He reigns for well over four decades. As much as Hezekiah is revered, so the writer of Kings reviles Manasseh. The opening verses of chapter 21 catalog Manasseh's turn to idolatry. He negates all his father has done. "Manasseh misled them [the people of Judah] to do more evil than" had ever been seen before. "Moreover Manasseh shed very much innocent blood" (21:9, 16). Amon succeeds Manasseh. He follows his father's example. Josiah succeeds him and is the only king of Judah, aside from Hezekiah, who is favorably described. This is because of his religious reforms. About halfway through Josiah's reign, at the king's instigation, repairs are made to the temple in Jerusalem. One day the workers find what is purported to be a (or "the") lost book of the Torah, "the book of the law." (See the Text Study at the close of this chapter, "The Discovery of the 'Book of the Law.'") This spurs Josiah to initiate a thorough religious reform (chs. 22–23).

Toward the end of the reign of King Josiah, the Egyptians ally with their former foe Assyria, in an attempt to counter the rising power of Babylonia. Josiah attempts to head off the Egyptian army as they move northward. Josiah is killed at a battle at Megiddo.

There are several more kings of Judah (Jehoahaz, Jehoiakim, Jehoiachin, and Zedekiah). These kings are caught up in the various battles between the superpowers of that day: Egypt to the south, and Assyria and then Babylon, to the north. Judah is a pawn, a chess piece in the wider struggle between these nations. It is almost impossible to stay neutral in these conflicts. That said, a number of the kings make bad choices. They ally themselves with the losing side. In the event, by the early years of the sixth century, Babylon, now the greatest power of the day, lays siege to Jerusalem. There is an initial deportation of Judean notables, c. 597 BCE (ch. 24). A few years later, Judah rebels again against Babylonia. It is a fatal error. In the summer of 586 BCE, Jerusalem's walls are breached by the forces of Nebuchadnezzar of Babylon. As explained in chapter 25, the temple is destroyed, and the king and many people are exiled to Babylon.

The wealth of the temple is stripped, and taken to Babylon. Only the poorest people of the land are left to be vinedressers and tillers of the soil (25:12). Many of the remaining leaders in Judah are executed (25:18–21). With the abolition of the monarchy, Gedaliah is appointed governor over the territory. Gedaliah, who has been on good terms with the prophet Jeremiah (cf. Jer 39:14; 40:6), tries to encourage the remnant that remains. He urges them to be respectful of the Babylonians. Sadly, a member of the deposed royal family assassinates Gedaliah. His murderers flee to Egypt. The book of Kings closes with the information that King Jehoiachin of Judah, who has been imprisoned in Babylonia, is subsequently released, and is treated well by his captors.

The book of Kings does not describe the terrible conditions in Judah and Jerusalem in the months and years after the destruction of the temple. That subject, however, is at the center of the book of Lamentations.

Elijah and Elisha

Although not the exclusive prophets of their time, Elijah and Elisha are the major prophetic figures mentioned in the book of Kings. Curiously, their stories are not featured in Chronicles. Elisha will be Elijah's disciple, but the two men are very different. Elijah usually acts alone. Elisha often is portrayed with a group of prophets. Elijah appears hermit-like in rough-hewn clothing. Elisha probably comes from a wealthy family. Elijah often actively confronts his opponents. Elisha is more of a wonder-worker, and someone involved in the daily life of the people. Together, their primary mission covers about fifty years (c. 860–10 BCE).

Unlike such literary prophets as Isaiah, Jeremiah, Ezekiel, Amos, and Hosea, Elijah and Elisha leave no written records of their times. Rather narratives are written about them. These descriptions portray powerful figures that regularly perform miracles.

Without warning, Elijah abruptly appears in the opening verse of 1 Kings 17. He confronts King Ahab and announces the beginning of a drought. In the next verse, God instructs Elijah to escape and hide. He takes refuge in the Wadi Cherith, east of the Jordan. Miraculously ravens feed him day and night. Later in that chapter, he performs miracles for a widow at Zarephath, a town miles away from the kingdom of Israel. Zarephath is located on the Phoenician coast, near Sidon.

The next major Elijah narrative is found in 1 Kings 18. This is his confrontation with the prophets of Baal. (See the Text Study at the close of this chapter, "Elijah and the Prophets of Baal.") As noted earlier, following that event, Elijah flees for his life. He eventually takes refuge at Mt. Horeb, in the wilderness south of Beersheba. This episode, described in chapter 19, clearly echoes many events in the life of Moses. It takes Elijah forty days to get to Mt. Horeb, just as Moses was atop Mt. Sinai for forty days (1 Kgs 19:8; Exod 24:15ff.) Elijah dwells in a cave on Horeb, where God speaks to him, just as Moses was atop the mountain when God spoke to him (1 Kgs 19:9; Exod 33:22). As Elijah deals with apostasy just before this episode, so did Moses (1 Kgs 18; Exod 32). There are many other parallels.[8]

As explained above in the section, "1 Kings 12–22 Divided Kingdoms; Ahab of Israel; the Prophet Elijah; Jehoshaphat of Judah," King Ahab is resentful and sullen because he fails to purchase land belonging to Naboth. Ahab's wife Jezebel has Naboth killed. Elijah then predicts that disaster awaits both Ahab and Jezebel (1 Kgs 21:17ff.)

King Ahab's successor, his son Ahaziah, suffers an accident (2 Kgs 1). He is concerned about his recovery. Ahaziah sends messengers to seek an answer from a local pagan god in Ekron, Baal-zebub (lit. "Lord of the Flies"). An angel of God appears to Elijah. He tells Elijah to intervene. Elijah meets the king's messengers. Without identifying himself, he delivers a message that Ahaziah is going to die. When the messengers return to the king, Ahaziah asks them who said this. They describe him as a "hairy man, with a leather belt around his waist." The king immediately realizes it is Elijah.

8. See Zucker, *Israel's Prophets*, 43–44; Boadt, *Reading the Old Testament*, 262–63; *Pesikta Rabbati*, Piska 4.2.

The final scene involving Elijah describes the transition of leadership to his disciple Elisha.

When Elisha son of Shaphat first appears (1 Kgs 19:19ff.), he is plowing with twelve yoke of oxen. Elijah comes up to him and "appoints" Elisha by throwing his mantel over the younger man. Elisha takes leave of his parents. He slaughters the oxen, boils their flesh, and gives the meat to some people. At this period most of Israel was living at a subsistence level. That Elisha's family could afford to spare twelve pair of oxen indicates they must have been very wealthy.

Elisha's miracles are overshadowed by those of Elijah. Yet, he is a formidable presence in his own right. In contrast to Elijah who lives alone and in the wilds, Elisha dwells in the city (2 Kgs 6:13, 19). He seems to have his own house (v. 32). Elijah is a solitary figure who makes pronouncements and then retreats from the scene. Elisha often is accompanied by a group of prophets, and is more accessible to people. Elisha visits religious centers such as Gilgal, Bethel, and Mt. Carmel (2 Kgs 2:1; 4:38; 2:23; 2:25; 4:25).

Elisha is involved in the daily life of those around him. He performs miracles such as providing oil for a widow. He predicts that a barren woman will conceive. Later he saves the child when the young boy becomes unwell.

Elisha's concern for people is not limited to his fellow Israelites. He is instrumental in finding a cure for the skin ailments of Naaman, the commander of the forces of Aram (Syria), as delineated in the narrative of 2 Kings 5. Here, as elsewhere, the purpose of the miracle is to underscore God's concern for, and involvement within, the world of humans.

"Elisha's greatest work was on a political level. . . . As his master had been deeply involved in the politics of his day, so Elisha went on to complete the tasks assigned to Elijah (1 Kings 19:15–16; 2 Kings 8:7–15; 9:1–10) and became constantly involved in the affairs of the nation. He provided water to a thirsty army (2 Kings 3:4–20), was instrumental in routing the Moabites (3:21–27), warned the king of enemy plans more than once (6:8–12), helped avert disaster at the hands of the Syrians [6:13—17:20] . . . and from his deathbed prophesied Joash's defeat of the Syrians (13:14–19)."[9] He predicts the downfall of King Ben-hadad of Damascus, and sees to it that Jehu will be anointed king over Israel (2 Kgs 8:7ff.; 9:1ff.)

Kings in the Christian Scriptures

It is claimed "throughout the gospels, that Jesus was modeling his ministry not on one figure alone, but rather on a range of prophets from the Old

---

9. Bratcher, "Elisha," 259.

Testament. . . . Like Elijah or Jeremiah, Jesus was proclaiming a message from the covenant god, and living it out with symbolic actions. He was confronting people with the folly of their ways, summoning them to a different way, and expecting to take the consequences of doing so." In addition to Elijah and Jeremiah, this scholar mentions Elisha and Micaiah son of Imlah.[10] In Luke's Gospel, Jesus makes specific reference to Elijah and Elisha, and various miracles they performed. These include the ending of the three-year famine, the widow at Zarephath (Elijah), and the healing of Naaman (Elisha) (Luke 4:25ff.) Jesus' observation about the leaderless sheep evokes Micaiah's comment to King Jehoshaphat (Matt 9:36; Mark 6:34; 1 Kgs 22:17).

The prophet Malachi's statement that Elijah would be sent "before the great and terrible day of the LORD comes" (Malachi 4:5 [3:23 H]) is understood by later generations to be the person who would announce the coming of the Messiah! The Gospel writers place John the Baptist in this role. Jesus does not exactly identify John (Matt 17:9–13), but the disciples reckon that this *is* his meaning. Luke identifies John as the long-awaited Elijah (Luke 1:17). In the Fourth Gospel John the Baptizer actually denies he is Elijah (John 1:21). Nonetheless, many believe that he is Elijah. Others, including some of Jesus' contemporaries, see Jesus as the Elijah figure (Matt 16:14; Luke 9:8).

At one point during the episode of the transfiguration of Jesus, three of the disciples see Jesus actually speaking with Moses and Elijah! (Matt 17:1–8; cf. Mark 9:2–8 and Luke 9:28–36). These two powerful Jewish leaders give credence and stature to Jesus in the eyes of his disciples.

Elisha performs a number of miracles involving food (2 Kgs 4:38ff.), which are echoed in miracles performed by Jesus with loaves and fish (cf. Matt 14:13–21; 15:32–38).

Kings in Rabbinic Literature

Solomon

Like parent, like child. Many of David's merits are replicated in the life of Solomon (*Midrash Song of Songs Rabbah* 1.1.6.)

Solomon chooses wisdom. Solomon chooses wisdom knowing that from this choice, all would flow (*Midrash Song of Songs Rabbah* 1.1.9.)

---

10. Wright, *Jesus and the Victory of God*, 166, 167–68. See also Gospel references in Fritz, *1 and 2 Kings*, 184–85.

Solomon has great knowledge. Solomon understands the language of birds and beasts (*Midrash Ecclesiastes Rabbah* 1.1.1).

Solomon and the temple. Solomon builds the temple in Jerusalem with the help of humans and spirits (*Midrash Exodus Rabbah* 52.4). He also has the help of the *Shamir*, a miraculous worm that cuts through stone (*Babylonian Talmud Gittin* 68b).

Elijah

Elijah and the Messiah. Elijah will announce the coming of the Messiah (*Pesikta Rabbati, Piska* 35.4).

Elijah and resurrection. Elijah will help bring about the resurrection of the dead (*Mishnah Sotah* 9.15 end).

Elijah provides enigmatic answers. Elijah will settle certain business matters and harmonize disputes that had proved enigmatic for the rabbis (*Mishnah Eduyot* 8.7).

Elijah, Rabbi Joshua son of Levi, and the Messiah. At one point Rabbi Joshua son of Levi asks Elijah when the Messiah will come. Elijah's answer is that the Messiah would come today, if people would repent and obey God's teachings (*Babylonian Talmud Sanhedrin* 98a).

Elijah appears in disguise. Elijah often appears in disguise, doing good deeds and helping or healing people (*Babylonian Talmud Sanhedrin* 109a; *Midrash Genesis Rabbah* 33.3).

Elijah is a popular figure in Jewish folklore. The figure of Elijah is associated with hope for better times. At the *Havdalah* ceremony, the ritual that commemorates the weekly close of the Sabbath, Elijah is highlighted as the one who will announce the coming of the Messiah. Elijah's presence is noted as part of the *Seder* meal at Passover, again as the herald of the coming days of peace.[11]

Elijah is present at circumcisions. At a ritual circumcision, traditionally there is an "Elijah Chair."

---

11. "Elijah, Cup of," in *Encyclopaedia Judaica*, 645. Elijah's many roles are depicted in this and adjacent articles in the *Encyclopaedia Judaica*.

Elijah is the Messiah's active partner. Elijah is associated with Jewish eschatology and becomes not only the Messiah's precursor, but also the Messiah's active partner (*Midrash Leviticus Rabbah* 34.8).

Hezekiah

Hezekiah is a positive role model. Hezekiah is devoted to the study of Torah (*Midrash Song of Songs Rabbah* 4.8.3).

Manasseh

Manasseh's evil deeds. Manasseh sets up an idol with four faces so that whatever direction someone enters the temple, the person sees the face of an idol. He also cuts out God's name from the Torah (*Babylonian Talmud Sanhedrin* 103b).

Manasseh's punishment. Manasseh has no share in the World to Come because of his evil deeds (*Babylonian Talmud Sanhedrin* 102b). This, however, is a matter of contention for the rabbis. and contrary views are also expressed.

Jerusalem

Jerusalem is revered by the rabbis. It is the most beautiful place in the world (*Avot de Rabbi Natan*, ch. 28[12]). Jerusalem is the center of the world (*Pesikta Rabbati, Piska* 10.2). A person who prays in Jerusalem is reckoned as if praying before the throne of God's glory, for Jerusalem contains the gate of heaven (*Pirke de Rabbi Eliezer*, ch. 35). In future time, God will rebuild the temple in Jerusalem (*Pesikta Rabbati, Piska* 1.2). Further, in time to come, God will bring healing waters from Jerusalem to all who are ill (*Midrash Exodus Rabbah* 15.21).There is a heavenly Jerusalem corresponding to that of the earthly Jerusalem (*Babylonian Talmud Ta'anit* 5a). Eventually, God will bring this heavenly Jerusalem and have it descend, resting upon four mountains, Sinai, Tabor, Hermon, and Carmel (*Pesikta de-Rab Kahana*, Supplement 5.4; cf.*Midrash on Psalms*, Ps 87.3).

---

12. *Avot de Rabbi Natan* (trans. Goldin); see Zucker (with Jane Smith), "Jerusalem, the Sacred City."

Text Study

1 Kings 18; Elijah and the Prophets of Baal

Elijah and King Ahab have a long history of mutually confrontational behavior. At one point after three years of drought, the prophet challenges the king, saying to him, let us meet at Mt. Carmel—part of Israel's coastal range, overlooking the Mediterranean to the west, and the River Kishon to the north—and there we will see who is more powerful. Will it be those who follow the prophets of the pagan gods Baal and Asherah? Or will it be those who follow the LORD God? Ahab accepts this contest of wills. Detailed in 1 Kings 18:17–46, the competition between the pagan prophets and Elijah takes place publicly for a full day. Elijah sets down the rules. Each side has a sacrificial bull placed on an altar, but no fire is lighted. For a day, the pagan prophets call out to Baal. Nothing happens. Elijah mocks them. He urges them to try harder. Then Elijah calls the people who have come to witness this contest. Elijah takes twelve stones (reminiscent of the twelve tribes of Israel) and builds a new altar. He places a trench around it. Elijah then prepares his offering. He asks the people to fill four jugs of water and pour them on the burnt offering. He repeats this twice (so that a total of twelve jugs of water are poured—again reminiscent of the twelve tribes). Elijah then calls on God to demonstrate divine power. Fire falls from heaven and consumes the altar, the stones, and even the water that was in the trench. The people profess their belief in God. Elijah then commands them to annihilate utterly the four hundred prophets of Baal, which they do. The passage ends with the three-year drought coming to an end.

1 Kings 22; Micaiah and the Kings of Israel and Judah

Micaiah son of Imlah prophesies at the same period as Elijah. He too criticizes King Ahab. At a certain point Ahab joins with King Jehoshaphat of Judah in an alliance against the Syrian king. Their goal is to recapture Ramoth-Gilead. This is a piece of former Israelite territory east of the Jordan River. King Jehoshaphat is concerned about the outcome of the battle. He requests a divine oracle before the troops set out. Ahab obliges by calling upon his four hundred prophets. They support the military venture.

King Jehoshaphat is nonetheless skeptical. He requests a further opinion. Ahab says there is only one other person. It is "Micaiah son of Imlah; but I hate him, for he never prophesies anything favorable about me, but only disaster."[13] In the meanwhile, one of the four hundred prophets,

---

13. Zucker, "Cold Case."

Zedekiah son of Chana'anah, performs a kind of mimetic ritual wherein he suggests that the two kings will be victorious.

The kings send a messenger for Micaiah. This messenger instructs the prophet to prophesy favorably about the forthcoming military venture. Micaiah explains he will speak only what God tells him. Micaiah stands before Ahab and Jehoshaphat. He predicts that they will succeed. He says, "Go up and triumph; the LORD will give [the territory] into the hand of the king." Ahab is suspicious of this answer. He cautions Micaiah only to speak the truth. Micaiah then announces that the campaign is doomed to failure.

Micaiah goes on to explain to the two kings that he saw God in conference with the host of heaven. They were planning how to entice Ahab to Ramoth-Gilead. Finally, a certain spirit (*ha-rua<u>h</u>*) volunteered to be a false witness. This spirit would "be a lying spirit in the mouth of all [King Ahab's] prophets." God gave consent and sent the spirit on its way.

The two kings, Ahab and Jehoshaphat, ignore Micaiah's advice. They fail in this battle. Ahab is mortally wounded.

2 Kings 22–23; The Discovery of the "Book of the Law"

As noted earlier, in the book of Kings only Kings Hezekiah and Josiah of Judah are regarded as worthy successors of David. Each one is praised for bringing about religious reforms. Josiah rules from 640 to 609 BCE. Around 622, he authorizes repairs for the temple. In the midst of the construction work, the high priest Hilkiah reports that he has found a book. This is then termed the "the book of the law," or "the book of the teaching" (*Sefer haTorah*). King Josiah seeks the advice of Huldah, a female prophet living in Jerusalem.[14] "It appears . . . that prophecy was one religious vocation open to women on an equal basis with men. Certainly the narrator of Kings takes no notice whatsoever of Huldah's gender. . . . Huldah speaks in Yahweh's name with the authority of any other biblical prophet."[15] There is no mention of King Josiah going to consult with the prophet Jeremiah, who is also living and prophesying at this point. Huldah, in effect, confirms the authenticity of the book. She condemns the rampant idolatry of the time. Josiah then makes sweeping reforms. The exact nature of the book is unknown. Most modern scholars agree, nonetheless, that the center of that "book of the law" is at the core of what today is the book of Deuteronomy.

There are important links between Deuteronomy's legislation and Josiah's reforms.

14. Edelman, "Huldah the Prophet."
15. Camp, "1 and 2 Kings," 109.

- Deuteronomy prohibits serving other gods or worshipping them, and mentions specifically heavenly worship (sun, moon, and hosts of heaven). Josiah deposes idolatrous priests who made offerings to Baal, the sun, moon, constellations, and all the host of the heavens (Deut 17:2–3; 2 Kgs 23:5).

- Deuteronomy states that the observance of Passover is limited to the one centralized place, which God will make known. Josiah orders that Passover is only to be celebrated in Jerusalem—a tradition that, according to the narrative in Kings and Chronicles, had not been observed in four hundred (!) years (Deut 16:1–8, esp. vv. 2, 6–7; 2 Kgs 23:21–23; cf. 2 Chr 35:18).

- Deuteronomy calls for the demolition of the sacred places of worship where the previous inhabitants of the land had their shrines. Josiah actively destroys pagan shrines in Israel (Deut 12:2ff.; 18:9ff.; 2 Kgs 23:6ff., esp. vv. 15ff.)[16]

---

16. For a detailed analysis of Josiah's religious reforms, see Weinfeld, *Deuteronomy 1–11*, 65–84.

6

Isaiah

Introduction

THE OPENING VERSE OF Isaiah provides an historical context. His prophecies are spoken in Jerusalem, they overlap the reigns of four different kings of Judah. These monarchs are Uzziah, Jotham, Ahaz, and Hezekiah (c. 740–1 BCE).

Isaiah is the seventh book of the "second section" of the Hebrew Bible, the Prophets/*Neviim* (see Introduction: "The Order of the Books of the Bible").

The sixty-six chapters of Isaiah comprise *three different* voices and *three different* periods. These three divisions are: chapters 1–39, called "First Isaiah"; chapters 40–55, "Second Isaiah"; and chapters 56–66, "Third Isaiah." Each of these terms will be defined in the appropriate sections below.

How does one read the book of Isaiah? Isaiah cannot be read chapter by chapter as if the book were a novel with a beginning, middle, and an end. Isaiah is composed of a series of prophecies. Much of the book contains speeches that the prophet speaks at different times and for different occasions. His contemporaries collect these speeches and then set them down, some during his time, some later. That a number of Isaiah's prophecies were delivered orally is clear from their context (see 7:1ff.; 38:1ff.) Other prophecies are written down at God's command, as the text explains (8:1ff.; 30:8). The chapters in Isaiah are *not set out in chronological order*. In addition, when reading Isaiah, as with other prophets, the reader needs to distinguish between words of prophecy, words of biography, and words of autobiography.

The Book of Isaiah

Divisions in the Book of Isaiah

Isaiah 1–39; First Isaiah (Isaiah of Jerusalem)

First Isaiah lives in Jerusalem. He prophesies for about four decades toward the close of the eighth century BCE. "As the tradition has remembered him, Isaiah plays a role in political affairs without real analogy for contemporaries Amos, Hosea, Micah, and Zephaniah. Isaiah's closest counterpart is probably the prophet Nathan, who likewise had access to the royal house, wielding direct authority over the Davidic line (2 Sam 7; 12:1–15)."[1]

Geo-Political Background

Isaiah receives his call during the last year of King Uzziah. He specifically states this at the opening of chapter 6. In addition to being a prophet in Jerusalem, Isaiah may be a priest as well. (See the Text Study at the close of this chapter, "Isaiah's Commission.") Isaiah probably was from a prominent family. He has easy access to the monarchs and their entourages.

The renewed strength of the Assyrian Empire is the major factor in the geo-political background to Isaiah. During Isaiah's lifetime, Assyria expands westward aiming to challenge and, hopefully, conquer the other major political power of that time, Egypt. The route to Egypt passes right through ancient Israel. Throughout these years both the northern kingdom of Israel and the southern kingdom of Judah are threatened by the ongoing tensions between Assyria and Egypt. In the book of Isaiah, the kingdom of Israel often is termed Ephraim. Ephraim was one of the traditional tribes that made up Israel. The use of the term Ephraim as a synonym for Israel reflects the importance of that particular tribe's holdings and influence.

About 735, Israel (Ephraim) forms a military alliance with her neighboring country, Aram (Syria). They intend to oppose Assyria. Since the addition of another partner to this alliance would lend added strength, Aram/Syria and Israel/Ephraim invite the kingdom of Judah to join with them. King Ahaz of Judah refuses this invitation to join their coalition. Consequently, these two allies lay siege to Jerusalem. This is the Syro-Ephraimitic War of c. 735–32.

During the siege, Isaiah publicly meets with King Ahaz of Judah. The prophet explains that this attack on Jerusalem will fail. Isaiah urges King

---

1. Seitz, "Book of Isaiah," 3:477–78.

Ahaz to stay calm. He advises the monarch against joining in this rebellion against Assyria. Isaiah also tells Ahaz not to make an alliance with Assyria, but to simply trust in God. Isaiah's initial words to Ahaz include the famous "Immanuel" ("God is with us") passage. (See the Text Study sections at the close of this chapter, "Judah under Siege" and "The 'Immanuel' Passage." For a wider historical context, see the chapter on Chronicles in the companion volume *The Bible's WRITINGS*).

King Ahaz ignores Isaiah's advice of absolute neutrality. Instead Ahaz opts to become a vassal of Assyria (2 Kgs 15:37—16:9). The Assyrian ruler, Tiglath Pileser III (745-27), attacks and subjugates both Aram and Israel. About a dozen years later King Hoshea of Israel (732-24)—not be confused with the prophet Hosea—rebels against Assyria. It is a fatal error. For three years, the Assyrians lay a siege against Samaria, the capital city of the kingdom of Israel. This is led by the son of Tiglath Pileser III, Shalmaneser V, and then later by Shalmaneser's brother and successor, Sargon II (722-25). Sargon destroys the northern kingdom in 721. He exiles their population. This marks the *end* of the ten tribes as a separate entity (2 Kgs 17:5-23).

King Ahaz of Judah rules for two decades (735-15). His son Hezekiah succeeds him and rules successfully for nearly three decades (715-687). Vassalage to Assyria means difficult days economically for Judah. To pay the heavy tribute, the rich tax the poor.

Although Hezekiah brings about some religious reforms, nonetheless there also is a rise in pagan worship in the land.

In 705 Sargon II of Assyria is killed. Using his death as a pretext, a number of countries try to break free of Assyrian influence. Against Isaiah's advice (Isa 30-31), Hezekiah joins in this revolt against the new Assyrian ruler, Sennacherib. Hezekiah sides with Egypt. Politically it is an unwise decision. The Assyrians move to quell this rebellion. They attack Judah and its environs.

The Assyrians destroy dozens of Judah's fortified cities. Many Judeans are killed; others are deported. Jerusalem is besieged, and Hezekiah is forced to submit, and then to pay increased tribute. Much territory is lost (2 Kgs 18:13-16). The final prophecies of First Isaiah come toward the end of the eighth century, about 701, when Hezekiah submits. Coincidentally it is at this time that the famous underground tunnel is cut through nearly 1800 feet of rock to the spring of Gihon (2 Kgs 20:20; see also 2 Kgs 18-20 and Isa 36-39).

Central Ideas

- God is a deity who works in and through history. Consequently, Isaiah teaches trust in God and not in "foreign alliances" (Isa 7, 37).

- God directs Israel's history and that of the other nations as well (Isa 10, 13–23, 37).
- God is an exalted God, who at the same time demands faith and righteous living from the people (Isa 1–3, 5).
- God will call the people to repentance and demand that they change (Isa 1:18, 25–28). Isaiah is concerned with the inner state of the nation, its morality, not its foreign policy.
- The people will be punished for their wrongdoing, but in the end, a remnant shall be saved and Jerusalem shall stand (Isa 10:20–23, 27; 37:31–32). Isaiah suggests that the future will eventually be peaceful, and the Davidic dynasty will rule in justice and equity (Isa 11:1–13; 12:1–6).

Divisions[2]

Isaiah 1–12	Prophecies/pronouncements against rebellious Judah and Jerusalem
Isaiah 13–23	Prophecies/pronouncements against foreign nations
Isaiah 24–27	Prophecies/pronouncements of universal judgment
Isaiah 28–33	Oracles of woe against Judah and Jerusalem
Isaiah 34–35	Prophecies of Zion's restoration after judgment
Isaiah 36–39	Historical account concerning Isaiah and Hezekiah

Isaiah 1–12; Prophecies/Pronouncements against Rebellious Judah and Jerusalem

Isaiah criticizes Judah and Jerusalem for its religious hypocrisy. He faults it for abuses in terms of socio-ethical issues. The wealthy exploit the poor. "Ah, sinful nation, people laden with iniquity . . . who have despised the Holy One of Israel, who are utterly estranged. . . . Why do you continue to rebel? . . . Hear the word of the LORD. . . . What to me is the multitude of your sacrifices. . . . I have had enough of burnt offerings . . . bringing offerings is futile. . . . I will not listen; your hands are full of blood. Wash yourselves; make yourselves clean; remove the evil of your doings . . . cease to do evil, learn to do good; seek justice, rescue the oppressed, defend the

---

2. Adapted from Gitay (as are the divisions for Second and Third Isaiah), "Book of Isaiah," 426.

orphan, plead for the widow" (1:4–5, 10–11, 13, 15–17; cf. 10:1–4) (see the Text Study at the close of this chapter, "Social Justice.")

Isaiah criticizes many of his contemporaries. Yet, he also holds out hope. If they return and repent, God will forgive them. If they demonstrate righteous behavior, then God will favor them with able rulers. He warns them that should they continue to follow in their rebellious ways, destruction will follow. "If you are willing and obedient, you shall eat the good of the land; but if you refuse and rebel, you shall be devoured by the sword. . . . Zion shall be redeemed by justice, and those in her who repent, by righteousness. But rebels and sinners shall be destroyed together, and those who forsake the LORD shall be consumed" (1:19–20, 27–28).

Isaiah terms Assyria as the "rod of [God's] anger" (10:5). Assyria will come and punish Judah. It shall chastise the people for their wrongdoing. Yet, beyond this, following Judah's change of heart and actions, there will arise true and upright leaders. They will be moral and blameless. Isaiah explains that this leader (or these leaders) will bring "endless peace for the throne of David. . . . He will establish and uphold it with justice and with righteousness from this time onward and forevermore" (9:7 [9:6 H]). God's spirit will rest on this new ruler. The monarch will act morally. For "with righteousness he shall judge the poor, and decide with equity for the meek of the earth." There will be peace in Jerusalem and Judah. "The wolf shall live with the lamb. . . . They will not hurt or destroy on all my holy mountain; for the earth will be full of the knowledge of the LORD as the waters cover the sea" (11:4, 6, 9).

The reference to a figure named Immanuel ("God is with us") in chapter 7, and the projections of a future leader who would rule with righteousness (chs. 9 and 11) reflect Isaiah's basic optimistic thinking. Isaiah believes that within a short time Judah and Jerusalem *will* repent of their wrongdoing. Therefore, they will deserve a cadre of moral leadership. Isaiah is pointing to a leader (or leaders) who will come to rule *within a few years of his pronouncements*. It will be within the lifetime of his audience. Isaiah does *not* prophecy about some far-off future event (see the Text Study at the end of this chapter, "Two possible Messianic Passages").

Isaiah 13–23: Prophecies/Pronouncements against Foreign Nations

Isaiah focuses initially on Judah and Jerusalem. His concerns are broader. Non-Jewish nations both interest and trouble Isaiah. Chapters 13–23 contain condemnations of Babylon, Moab, Damascus, Ethiopia, Egypt, Assyria, Seir (Edom), Dedan and Tema (Arabia), and Tyre. A century later, similar prophecies against foreign nations will be made by the late-seventh-/early-sixth-century figure Jeremiah (Jer 46–51) and the early-sixth-century prophet Ezekiel (Ezek 25–32).

Many of Isaiah's verbal accusations begin with the word "utterance," "oracle," or "pronouncement." In Hebrew, the word is *massa* (*m-s-'a*, mem-sin-alef). This same phrase, "utterance"/"oracle"/"pronouncement," often becomes a hallmark of Israel's prophets (Nah 1:1; Hab 1:1; Zech 9:1; Mal 1:1).

A number of these national condemnations may have been written later, and then placed within the book of Isaiah. For example, in chapter 13 Isaiah inveighs against Babylon, but Babylon is not yet a world power. It will supersede Assyria about a hundred years later, in the closing years of the seventh century BCE.

Isaiah 24–27; Prophecies/Pronouncements of Universal Judgment

These chapters are an example of apocalyptic literature. They probably come from a later date than First Isaiah, perhaps from the late sixth to early fifth centuries. "These chapters, unrelated to their context, are frequently called the 'Isaiah Apocalypse' because of their use of eschatological themes found in later apocalyptic writings (universal judgment, eschatological banquet, heavenly signs and the like)."[3]

Isaiah 28–33; Oracles of Woe against Israel, Judah, and Jerusalem

Chapter 28 begins with a pronouncement against the northern kingdom of Israel, here termed Ephraim. Then, beginning in verse 7, Isaiah directs his wrath at Judah. Isaiah demonstrates powerful rhetoric and his love of language as he forms plays on words:

> Stupefy yourselves and be in a stupor, Blind yourselves and be blind,
> Be drunk, but not from wine; Stagger, but not from strong drink!
> (29:9)
>
> The wisdom of their wise shall perish,
> And the discernment of the discerning shall be hidden. (29:14)

Chapter 31 deals with the major political event late in Isaiah's career (705–1). King Hezekiah declares Judah free of Assyrian influence. Then, in 701, the ruler of Assyria, Sennacherib, comes with his army and lays siege

---

3. *NOAB*, 895, comment to chs. 24–27.

to Judah. Sennacherib captures much of the surrounding area. Isaiah urges Hezekiah to stand firm and not to make an alliance with Egypt. "Alas for those who go down to Egypt for help . . . but do not look to the Holy One of Israel" (31:1).

Isaiah 34–35; Prophecies of Zion's Restoration after Judgment

These chapters look forward to a time when Zion will be restored, and all her enemies vanquished.

Isaiah 36–39; Historical Account Concerning Isaiah and Hezekiah

The material here duplicates the narratives of 2 Kings 18:13—20:19, with the exception of the few verses in Isaiah 38:9–20, which is a song of thanksgiving for personal deliverance. This section concludes with Isaiah informing Hezekiah that, at a future time, Hezekiah's descendants will be carried off to Babylon (39:5ff.).

Isaiah 40–55; Second Isaiah (Deutero-Isaiah)

The prophecies of Second Isaiah (Deutero-Isaiah) are *different from* those of Isaiah of Jerusalem. Second Isaiah lives between one hundred fifty to two hundred years *after* the period that First Isaiah flourished. The time of Second Isaiah is c. 550–39 (520?).

> The historical context of chaps. 40–55 differs entirely from that of chaps. 1–39. The enemy of Israel is the Neo-Babylonian Empire (626–539 B.C.; cf. chaps. 46; 47; 48:20–21), not the Neo-Assyrian Empire of Isaiah (935–612 B.C.; cf. chaps. 10; 14:24–27), which collapsed with the destruction of Nineveh in 612 B.C. The gentile king in chaps. 40–55 is Cyrus of Persia (fl. 560–30 B.C.; cf. 41:2–3, 25; 44:24—45:13; 48:14), not the Assyrian king of Isaiah (10:5–19). The people are in Babylon, not in Isaiah's 8th-century Jerusalem; the message is to leave Babylon, cross the desert, and return to Zion.[4]

---

4. Clifford, "Book of Isaiah," 3:490.

Geo-Political Background

When the Babylonians destroy Jerusalem in 586, they take what remains of the cream of Judah's society and resettle them in Babylonia. A major deportation of Judah's notables occurs a decade earlier. Babylonia is more than a thousand miles distant. These refugees are devastated emotionally and psychically. Some false prophets claimed that this would be merely a temporary displacement (Jeremiah denounces these prophets, Jer 27:12–18). Nonetheless, the exile continues unabated for decades. Those people deported to Babylon have to live with a painful reality. Jerusalem is destroyed. It has been razed to the ground. The four-hundred-year-old Jerusalem temple built by Solomon no longer exists. The enemy has confiscated the temple's holy vessels. The monarchy that reached back to the time of David no longer exists. Psalm 137 describes well the trauma of those in exile: "By the rivers of Babylon, there we sat down and there we wept when we remembered Zion" (v. 1).

There is no reasonable expectation of a return to their homeland. Consequently, the community-in-exile makes the best of their situation. They follow the prophet Jeremiah's advice to build homes and gardens, and farm the land (Jer 29:5ff.) The prophet Ezekiel describes several Jewish communities (Ezek 3:15; 8:1; 33:30f.) The community-in-exile maintains a sense of its own distinctiveness. It forms a collective history and memory. No other ethnic or religious group of this period of the Assyrian and Babylonian era does something comparable following disasters that befall them.

Coincidentally, in this general period the former *Hebrew* community over a period of time reconstitutes itself as a *Jewish* community. This community will be based on common Jewish culture, history, and ethnicity. Judaism moves from a religious/ethnic group solely centered in the land of Israel to a religion/people international in scope. As discussed in the chapter on Ezra in the companion volume *The Bible's WRITINGS*, this era is a watershed in Jewish history. "The distinguishing mark of a Jew would not be political nationality, nor primarily ethnic background, nor even regular participation in the Temple cult (impossible for Jews of the Diaspora), but adherence to the law of Moses."[5]

In this general period, in terms being part of the chosen people, one's resolve is equal to one's birth. "Membership ceases to be based on birth." At this point, "the gates of the community which worships Yahweh are now open to the world. This is opposed to a priestly and legal tradition that seeks to limit the community to those who are Jews by birth."[6]

---

5. Bright, *History of Israel*, 390; see also Cohen, *Beginnings of Jewishness*.
6. Westermann, *Isaiah 40–66*, 305, 316. See McKenzie, *Second Isaiah*, 150–51.

Those who hold fast to God's covenant are welcomed; those who keep the Sabbath and do not profane it—those foreigners who do this—are welcomed into God house, for it is to be a place of prayer for all peoples. As shall be enunciated a bit later in the words of Third Isaiah,

> Do not let the foreigner joined to the LORD say, "The LORD will surely separate me from his people" ... the foreigners who join themselves to the LORD, to minister to him, to love the name of the LORD, and to be his servants, all who keep the sabbath, and do not profane it, and hold fast my covenant—these I will bring to my holy mountain, and make them joyful in my house of prayer; their burnt offerings and their sacrifices will be accepted on my altar; for my house shall be called a house of prayer for all peoples. (56:3, 6–7).

In Babylon, the Torah reaches its final shape. It is likely that there are some local Jewish cultic gatherings.

The synagogue, or the proto-synagogue, develops in this period. Second Isaiah addresses this very population.

The prophecies of Second Isaiah come about when they do because great changes are taking place on the world stage. Babylon has been at the height of its power under Nebuchadnezzar and his successors (605–539). Nonetheless, Babylon succumbs to Cyrus the Persian, who moves decisively beginning about 550. In 546, Cyrus attacks and conquers Lydia in Asia Minor. Next on Cyrus' list is Babylon, which he takes with surprising ease in 539. A year later in 538, Cyrus officially allows the Jews to resettle in Judah, and to restore their religious traditions (Ezra 1:1–11; 6:3–5). This decree clearly was promulgated in response to a petition from the community-in-exile.

In contrast to the Assyrians and Babylonians, Cyrus and his Persian successors are essentially benevolent rulers. They allow conquered nations to function in the old manner as long as they are loyal to their "masters."

There are no biographical details found in Second Isaiah. We know nothing about his life. This contrasts with the writings of First Isaiah, which contains some biographical information about that prophet. In like manner, in the books of Jeremiah, Ezekiel, Amos, and Hosea there are some biographical details relevant to each of those specific prophets.

On what basis, then, do scholars speak of a separate authorship for chapters 40–55, situated c. 550–39 (520?)? Several matters make it clear that this is a different author, and a different period.

Second Isaiah refers to Cyrus, the ruler of Persia. Cyrus lived in the sixth century, nearly two hundred years *after* the time of First Isaiah (Isaiah of Jerusalem). Second Isaiah is addressing a despondent community. He calls for a restoration of Judah and Jerusalem. The prophet's audience is invited to leave Babylon, to go to rebuild Jerusalem. God will bring the people to Zion (48:20; 51:11; 49:14–23; 40:1–11; 43:1–7). If Second Isaiah's audience is not living in Babylon, this prophecy makes no sense.

Unlike First Isaiah, whose legacy is in both prose and poetic form, Second Isaiah's utterances are all presented as poetry. They are a series of pronouncements, which do not necessarily fall neatly into chapters, for these divisions will come about many centuries later.

Central Ideas

- The exile in Babylon, and the soon-to-be-realized triumph of Cyrus, are *part of God's plan.*
- God has not forsaken Israel. A new era, Israel's redemption, is about to begin.
- The exiles will soon return. Judah and Jerusalem will be rebuilt.
- God is granting Israel a release from her past wrongdoing even if she is not fully deserving of these blessings. This is God's gratuitous act (43:25; 48:9, 11).[7]
- Israel has a new role: it is to proclaim the universal God's absolute rule over the earth, over all people and all nations.
- God is the one and only Creator of the world.
- Israel is the "servant of the LORD." Indeed, an important subsection of Second Isaiah is the Servant Songs (42:1–9; 49:1–13; 50:4–11; 52:13—53:12).

Second Isaiah is unique in that he is exclusively an *exilic** (as opposed to pre-exilic* or post-exilic*) prophet. The prophet presents a message of hope to the community of refugees. Some of his words address concerns articulated in the book of Lamentations—specifically, if and when Jerusalem will be restored. At points Lamentations questions God's purpose. It wonders if God has revoked the longstanding covenant with Israel. "Both the language

---

7. Paul, *Isaiah 40–66*, 221; McKenzie, *Second Isaiah*, lxiii.

and the ideas in the laments of the [book of Lamentations] influenced Deutero-Isaiah."[8] Second Isaiah counsels hopefulness!

> Second Isaiah intends to persuade his fellow exiles that the time has come to leave Babylon and return to Jerusalem (Zion). His is a program, not a theology; ideas are arranged to persuade, not to make a system.
>
> As an orator he gives his audience reasons to change their attitudes and to act. He must show that the ancestral traditions, to which all prophets appealed, contain an imperative for his day. For him, the tradition tells the people that Babylon with its false gods is doomed and Zion is about to be rebuilt and repopulated. Israel's journey to Zion will be a new Exodus-Conquest, a new participation in the defeat of chaos (= cosmogony).[9]

Second Isaiah stands apart from both prophetic predecessors and successors in his unabashed themes of hope and promise for the future. In his mind, the movement from judgment to salvation has been achieved. "Comfort, O comfort my people.... Speak tenderly to Jerusalem, and cry to her that she has served her term, that her penalty is paid" (40:1–2).

In Second Isaiah's mind, God's very presence is becoming acknowledged among the nations at large. It is a public fact. God says, "I will go before you ... level the mountains ... break into pieces the doors of bronze." God proclaims, "To me every knee shall bow, every tongue shall swear" (45:2, 23).

Second Isaiah's message is distinctive in its immediacy and personal sense. The individual and the people are as one. Together they are the object of God's love and concern. "The audience addressed by the prophet is the entire nation taken as a unit; nevertheless, the word of God given him to proclaim is meant to affect every individual member at the most personal and existential level."[10]

Second Isaiah often draws upon the theme of the exodus from Egypt (43:16–21; 51:10–11; 52:11–12). Dwelling in Babylon, separated from Judah by a vast desert wilderness, Second Isaiah sees parallels to the desert wilderness of the Sinai. That desert is to be traversed. Second Isaiah's "Zion" is a latter-day Sinai. At Sinai, God first proclaimed divine sovereignty and the divine contract with Israel-the-people. At Zion (the "second" Sinai), God will proclaim divine universal sovereignty and contract with the world. A

---

8. Paul, *Isaiah 40–66*, 57. Linafelt, *Surviving Lamentations*, 62–79.
9. Clifford, "Book of Isaiah," 3:497–98.
10. Westermann, *Isaiah 40–66*, 13.

messenger will proclaim to Zion that God reigns. All the ends of the earth shall see God's salvation (52:7, 10). The age-old promise of First Isaiah shall be realized, "For out of Zion shall go forth instruction, and the word of the LORD from Jerusalem" (2:3).

Second Isaiah draws upon the Psalms. There are parallels between Isaiah 40:31 and Psalm 103:5 (youth/eagles); Isaiah 41:18 and Psalm 107:35 (lakes/desert); Isaiah 45:2 and Psalm 107:16 (breaking bronze gates; cutting bars of iron.)

Divisions

Isaiah 40–48   The coming of salvation; God the only God; Babylon's fall; Cyrus as God's anointed

Isaiah 49–55   Promise of restoration for Zion/Jerusalem

Isaiah 40–48; The Coming of Salvation; God the Only God; Babylon's Fall; Cyrus as God's Anointed

Chapter 40 contains many of Second Isaiah's major themes. It begins with a combination of consolation and reassurance. "Comfort, O comfort my people . . . Speak tenderly to Jerusalem, and cry to her that she has served her term, that her penalty is paid" (vv. 1–2). This follows immediately with a reference to the desert experience. "In the wilderness prepare the way of the LORD, make straight in the desert a highway for our God" (v. 3). A few verses on he declaims, "Get you up to a high mountain, O Zion, herald of good tidings. . . . O Jerusalem, herald of good tidings . . . say to the cities of Judah, 'Here is your God!'" (40:9). Later in that same chapter, Second Isaiah asks rhetorically, "Have you not known? Have you not heard? The LORD is the everlasting God, the Creator of the ends of the earth" (v. 28).

Elsewhere one reads that Babylon shall be brought to its knees. "Come down and sit in the dust . . . Babylon! Sit on the ground without a throne, daughter Chaldea [a synonym for Babylon]. . . . Sit in silence, and go into darkness daughter Chaldea! For you shall no longer be called the mistress of kingdoms" (47:1, 5). The tool for God's will is Cyrus of Persia. "Thus says the LORD to his anointed, to Cyrus, whose right hand I have grasped to subdue nations before him . . . I have aroused Cyrus in righteousness, and I will make all his paths straight; he shall build my city and set my exiles free" (45:1, 13).

The first Servant Song (42:1–9) appears in this section. (See the Text Study at the conclusion of this chapter, "The Servant Songs.")

Isaiah 49–55; Promise of Restoration for Zion/Jerusalem

Israel is God's servant. Part of her task is to proclaim God's glory to the world. "You are my servant, Israel, in whom I will be glorified. . . . I will give you as a light to the nations, that my salvation may reach to the end of the earth" (49:3, 6). God tells Zion to "put on your strength. . . . Put on your beautiful garments, O Jerusalem, the holy city. . . . Break forth together into singing, you ruins of Jerusalem; for the LORD has comforted his people, he has redeemed Jerusalem" (52:1, 9).

The second, third, and fourth Servant Songs (49:1–13; 50:4–11; 52:13—53:12) appear in this section. (See the Text Study at the conclusion of this chapter, "The Servant Songs.")

"Isaiah 34–35 [chapters in First Isaiah], 40–55 . . . [Second Isaiah, and] 56–66 [Third Isaiah . . .] use a shared vocabulary of female imagery. [They] personify Jerusalem/Zion as a woman. Such a personification is hardly unfamiliar, as it is found already in First Isaiah (1:21–23; 3:25–26), but in First Isaiah the woman Israel was scorned as an apostate and a harlot. In the sixth century Isaianic [Second and Third Isaiah] materials the images of the woman Jerusalem/Zion are, with one exception (57:3, 6–13; cf. 47:1–15), positive."[11]

Isaiah 56–66; Third Isaiah (Trito Isaiah)

Although Cyrus grants permission, and even encourages Jews to restore Jerusalem, only limited numbers return. This prophet may live in Jerusalem in the early years following the restoration (c. 538–16 [?]), or perhaps still later.

Central Ideas

These chapters reflect the fact that the temple has yet to be built. The promise of a glorious salvation as suggested earlier by the Second Isaiah has not been realized. There is a sense of possible changes to come. Yet, these are tempered with a note of pessimism. Third Isaiah does not perceive of Israel being a "light to the nations." There is, therefore, a narrower focus. In these final chapters of the book, there is a considerably less "universalistic" image. The people's morale is low; there are doubts whether the restoration will succeed; the goals set were unrealistically high. The preaching of Second Isaiah did not match the facts facing the returning community.

---

11. Ackerman, "Isaiah," 166.

Divisions

Isaiah 56–58   Prophecies of judgment against the restoration community

Isaiah 59   Call to repentance and community response

Isaiah 60–62   Promises of salvation

Isaiah 63–64   God's statement and then a community lament

Isaiah 65–66   Further prophecies of judgment and promises of final salvation

Isaiah 56–58; Prophecies of Judgment Against the Restoration Community

The prophet argues that, in principle, God has said, "My house shall be called a house of prayer for all peoples" (56:7). Yet, the leadership in Jerusalem is without knowledge. It lacks understanding. He complains that the "righteous perish and no one takes it to heart" (57:1). Like the opening chapter of First Isaiah, this prophet condemns those who are religious hypocrites. They practice a ritual life, but not righteous living. "Is this not the fast that I choose: to loose the bonds of injustice, to undo the thongs of the yoke, to let the oppressed go free? . . . to share your bread with the hungry?" (58:6–7).

Isaiah 59; Call to Repentance and Community Response

In this chapter, Third Isaiah lays out the iniquity of the people (vv. 1–8). They claim their wrongdoing (vv. 9–15).

Isaiah 60–62; Promises of Salvation

These three chapters momentarily return to the optimistic call of Second Isaiah. Chapter 60 begins with the inspiring words, "Arise, shine, for your light has come, and the glory of the LORD has risen upon you." Chapter 61 contains the inspiring message that God has sent the prophet "to bring good news to the oppressed, to bind up the brokenhearted, to proclaim liberty to the captives, and release to the prisoners, to proclaim the year of the LORD's favor" (vv. 1–2).

Isaiah 63–64; God's Statement and Then a Community Lament

These chapters begin with a question, perhaps by a sentry or watchman (63:1-2), and then comes God's response (63:3-6). Israel's community lament follows (63:7—64:12 [64:11 H]).

Isaiah 65–66; Further Prophecies of Judgment and Promises of Final Salvation

In the previous chapter, the people voice their sense of estrangement from God. They ask that God not turn from them. "Do not be exceedingly angry, O LORD, and do not remember iniquity forever" (64:9 [64:8 H]). God now answers this call with divine rebuke, claiming that it is not God, but the people who are silent. God says, "I was ready to be sought out by those who did not ask, to be found by those who did not seek me. I said, 'Here I am, here I am,' to a nation that did not call on my name. I held out my hands all day to a rebellious people, who walk in a way that is not good . . . a people who provoke me" (65:1-3). The book then abruptly changes at the conclusion. Hope once more is proclaimed. "As a mother comforts her child, so will I comfort you; you shall be comforted in Jerusalem" (66:13).

Isaiah in the Christian Scriptures

Taken as a whole, the book of Isaiah is quoted or alluded to throughout the Christian Scriptures. It is found in the Gospels, Acts, many of the Epistles, and in Revelation.

First Isaiah

Paul refers to Isaiah in Romans, quoting images that suggest only a remnant will be saved (Rom 9:27-29; cf. Isa 10:22; 1:9). The Epistle 1 John speaks of walking with God in the light just as God is in the light. If "we walk in the light as he himself is in the light, we will have fellowship with one another." These words echo Isaiah's statement, "O house of Jacob, come, let us walk in the light of the LORD!" (1 John 1:7; Isa 2:5).

In the Gospels, Jesus offers the parable of the vineyard, basing his illustration on Isaiah's allegory of the song of the vineyard (Matt 21:33ff., Mark 12:1ff.; Luke 20:9ff.; Isa 5:1ff.)

In Revelation, a recurring image is the glory of God seated on the divine throne, ideas that reflect that author's familiarity with Isaiah (Rev 4:2, 9, 10; 5:1, 7, 13, et al.; Isa 6:1).

Isaiah's description of the Seraphim praising God with the words "Holy, holy, holy . . ." are paraphrased by Revelation's author (Rev 4:8; Isa 6:2–3).

The Gospel writers quote from Isaiah's commission. They contrast the inability of the people in his day to hear with the idea that those who are listening to Jesus do hear and understand (Matt 13:14ff.; Mark 4:12; Luke 8:10; Isa 6:9–10).[12] The closing lines of the book of Acts likewise refer to this section in Isaiah (Acts 28:26ff.; Isa 6:9–10).

The notion that "nation will rise against nation, and kingdom against kingdom" found in the Synoptic Gospels* (Matthew, Mark, and Luke) is based on Isaiah's pronouncements against the Egyptians where he says, "they will fight, one against the other, neighbor against neighbor, city against city, kingdom against kingdom" (Matt 24:7; Mark 13:8; Luke 21:10; Isa 19:2).

The most famous image from First Isaiah found in the Christian Scriptures, however, may be the prophet's confrontation with King Ahaz as recorded in Isaiah 7. In that passage, Isaiah gestures toward a young pregnant woman. He states that when her child is born, he will be named Immanuel/God is with us. (See the Text Study at the close of this chapter, "The 'Immanuel' Passage.")

Second Isaiah

In all of the Gospel accounts, the lead into the introduction of John the Baptist is based on Second Isaiah's imagery of a voice crying out in the wilderness (Matt 3:3; Mark 1:3; Luke 3:4–6; John 1:23; Isa 40:3–5). Jesus' ministry as recorded in Matthew (Matt 12:17ff.) includes an extensive quotation from the Second Isaiah's first Servant Song (Isa 42:1–9).

The Servant Songs were a source of inspiration to the writers of the Christian Scriptures. The "sequence of thought in the four Songs is reproduced in the ministry, death and resurrection of Jesus."[13] Christianity traditionally understands the Servant Songs to refer to Jesus. One of the most famous instances confirming this is the episode of Philip the Apostle and

---

12. "The disciples are more special than the prophets of old only because they live in a time when they can receive a greater revelation than the prophets of old, as Jesus' blessing on them makes clear, 'Happy are those who see' (God's long-awaited blessings on Israel; his Messiah; etc.)" Keener, *Commentary on Matthew*, 380.

13. Winward, *Guide to the Prophets*, 186.

the Ethiopian eunuch as recorded in Acts 8:26–35. In Matthew's Gospel, Jesus seems to refer to the Servant when he suggests that suffering is a necessary part of his life (Matt 16:21–23).[14]

In the second Servant Song, Isaiah describes God telling the servant, "I will give you as a light to the nations." In various forms, Luke, John, and the book of Acts reflect those words (Luke 2:32; John 8:12; 9:5; Acts 13:47; 26:23; Isa 49:6).

In John, Jesus paraphrases Isaiah. "If any man is thirsty, let him come to me" (John 7:37f.; Isa 55:1; see Isa 44:3). In James there is a paraphrase of the statement concerning "Abraham, my friend" (Jas 2:23; Isa 41:8).

The Epistle to the Romans reflects Isaiah's image of the one who brings good news (Romans 10:15: Isa 52:7).

Third Isaiah

Third Isaiah's prophecy that God will "create new heavens and a new earth" is alluded to in Revelation (Rev 21:1; Isa 65:17). Likewise, Third Isaiah's universalistic welcoming statement that God declares, "For my house shall be called a house of prayer for all peoples" is quoted by the Synoptics (Matt 21:13; Mark 11:17; Luke 19:46; Isa 56:7). Isaiah's follow-up sentence in that same chapter, that God will not only gather Israel's outcasts, but God also will "gather others to them besides those already gathered," is reflected in the writings of the Fourth Gospel. There Jesus says, "I have other sheep that do not belong to this fold. I must bring them also, and they will listen to my voice" (John 10:16; Isa 56:8).

Parts of Third Isaiah suggest apocalyptic times. This theme is taken up in Revelation. "And the city has no need of sun or moon to shine on it, for the glory of God is its light, and its lamp is the Lamb" (Rev 21:23; Isa 60:19). In a similar manner, the apocalyptic-like images in Revelation show a familiarity with Isaiah (Rev 19:13ff. and 14:19–20; Isa 63:1ff.)

Third Isaiah's statement about bringing "good news to the oppressed, to bind up the brokenhearted, to proclaim liberty to the captives, and release to the prisoners" has echoes in Matthew and Luke (Isa 61:1; Matt 11:5; Luke 4:16–20; 7:22), as well as affinities to Isaiah 29:18f.; 35:5f.

Finally, Romans 10:20–21 features a quote based on Isaiah 65:1–2.

---

14. "Jesus taught the Jewish view that sufferings precede the kingdom (cf. 24:8) . . . he also accepted the Jewish view, confirmed in John's death, that prophets are martyred." Keener, *Commentary on Matthew*, 432.

Isaiah in Rabbinical Literature

First Isaiah

Holy, holy, holy. Isaiah's commission contains the familiar words "Holy, holy, holy is the LORD of hosts" (6:3). This phrase forms part of the liturgies of both the synagogue and the church.

The Seraphim. The biblical text indicates that the Seraphim are six-winged. They fly with two wings, cover their faces with two wings, and cover their legs with the remaining two wings. Covering their eyes presumably protects them from seeing the heavenly appearance. Covering their "legs" or "feet" refers to their calf-like feet, for exposing such hooves would remind God of the blasphemy of the golden calf (Exod 32:1ff.) (*Midrash Leviticus Rabbah* 27.3, based on Ezek 1:7).

Standing and praising God is the sole role of the Seraphim. (*Midrash Exodus Rabbah* 25.2). They proclaim God's greatness three times. Therefore, Jews praise God in their daily service with the words "God of Abraham, God of Isaac, God of Jacob" to correspond to the angels' Trisagion (*Midrash Exodus Rabbah* 15.6).

As part of Isaiah's vision, in that same passage a Seraph takes a burning coal and touches it to Isaiah's lips to purify him. Isaiah is standing in the temple in Jerusalem (6:1, 6–7). Tradition links this passage to words in the Torah, "Surely, this commandment . . . is not too hard for you, nor is it too far away. It is not in heaven, that you should say, 'Who will go up to heaven for us, and get it for us so that we may hear it and observe it?'" (Deut 30:11–12) (*Midrash Deuteronomy Rabbah* 8.2).

God's words are exclusively for humans. Now that humans have God's instruction, they are responsible for following it and are able to receive the blessings that go with it. While the angels want to know God's laws and blessings, those traditions are too complicated for angels to understand (*Midrash Deuteronomy Rabbah* 8.2.)

God's characteristics are not like those of humans. God is not like humans. In the world of humans, one person is a prosecutor, another is a defense attorney. The prosecutor cannot be counsel for the defense, and the defense counsel cannot be the prosecutor. With God it is otherwise. God can be both prosecutor and defense counsel. The same mouth which says, "Ah, sinful nation" (1:4) also says, "Open the gates, so that the righteous nation that keeps faith may enter in" (26:2) (*Midrash Exodus Rabbah* 15.29).

The whole Torah rests on justice. Rabbi Elazar says, The whole Torah rests on justice. Therefore God gives enactments about justice (Exod 21:1ff.) immediately after the Ten Commandments, because people transgress justice and God punishes them. . . . Jerusalem is not punished until they disregard justice, [as it is said] "Your princes are rebels and companions of thieves. Everyone loves a bribe and runs after gifts. They do not defend the orphan, and the widow's cause does not come before them" (Isa 1:23) (*Midrash Exodus Rabbah* 30.19).

Moses and Aaron, David and Solomon. Isaiah says, "I will restore [to life] your judges as at the first, and your counselors as at the beginning. Afterward you shall be called the city of righteousness, the faithful city" (1:26). The judges refer to Moses and Aaron. The counselors refer to David and Solomon (*Pesikta de-Rab Kahana, Piska* 15.11 end).

God's commandments summarized. The Torah traditionally contains 613 commandments. The rabbis suggest that Isaiah reduces them to six principles: "[1] Those who walk righteously; [2] and speak uprightly; [3] who despise the gain of oppression; [4] who wave away a bribe instead of accepting it; [5] who stop their ears from hearing of bloodshed; [6] and shut their eyes from looking on evil, they will live on the heights" (33:15–16) (*Babylonian Talmud Makkot* 24a; see also the citation for Trito-Isaiah).

Second Isaiah

Second Isaiah in the synagogue lexionary.* Judaism's liturgical tradition includes regular readings from the Prophets. Following the reading from the Torah (Pentateuch), one reads a complementary set of verses from the Prophets. One quarter of these prophetical selections come from the collective Isaiahs. Ten out of fifteen come from Second Isaiah.

Many selections from Deuteronomy are linked with chapters from Isaiah.

Isaiah 49–55 is quoted, although none of the verses from the Servant Songs are. This is because of the "christological interpretation given to the chapter by Christians . . . the omission is deliberate and striking."[15] The reading of a weekly section from the Prophets is mentioned in the Mishnah* as a familiar practice. The Christian Scriptures support this when Jesus reads from Isaiah (61:1–2) during a synagogue service (*Mishnah Megillah* 4:10; Luke 4:16–21).

---

15. Loewe, in Montefiore and Loewe, *Rabbinic Anthology*, 544.

Other liturgical references. Words from the Second and Third Isaiah's have influenced synagogue liturgy in a major prayer of the morning service. In the *Yotzer*, which praises God as Creator of light and darkness, the first sentence is adapted from Isaiah 45:7 (see *Babylonian Talmud Berakhot* 11b). Likewise, in the Sabbath hymn *Lekha dodi*, a number of phrases are taken from both Second and Third Isaiah (52:1, 2; 51:9, 17; 60:1; 54:4; 49:19; 62:5; 54:3).

Isaiah's enthusiasm. Isaiah's eager acceptance of his commission matches his enthusiasm in offering comfort and cheer ("Comfort, O comfort my people; Awake, awake, put on strength; I, I am he who comforts you; Rouse yourself, rouse yourself!"; 40:1; 51:9, 12, 17) (*Midrash Leviticus Rabbah* 10.2, end; *Pesikta de-Rab Kahana, Piska* 16.4 end).

Abraham chooses captivity. Second Isaiah refers to Abraham and Sarah (51:1–2). Tradition links this to Genesis 15:17, when God shows Abraham a smoking oven and a flaming torch. God tells Abraham that the smoking oven is *Gehinnom* (hell) and the flaming torch is Torah. As long as your descendants study Torah and they offer sacrifices they will be saved from *Gehinnom*. When they fail in their duty, they will be punished. Then God gives Abraham a choice. Should their future punishment be *Gehinnom* or captivity? Abraham opts for captivity. Hence, even as the exiles are returning they should remember that as unpleasant as was their captivity, it is preferable to *Gehinnom*! (*Midrash Exodus Rabbah* 51.7).

Comforting Zion. When comforting Zion, God promises that the waste places will be turned into Eden-like freshness (51:3). This has not yet happened. The midrash explains that God will comfort Zion and turn the desert into a garden, but it will be part of the World to Come (*Midrash Genesis Rabbah* [New Version] 97 end; 100.13 end).

Like Job, Jerusalem will receive double compensation. Rabbi Joshua son of Nehemiah teaches that if Job who sinned was eventually given a double recompense [Job 42:10], so eventually Jerusalem will be given a double recompense of comfort, [as it is written] "Comfort, O comfort my people, says your God" (Isa 40:1) (*Pesikta de-Rab Kahana, Piska* 16.6 end).

Torah and deeds of kindness. Rabbi Joshua of Siknin says, in the name of Rabbi Levi, The words "I have put my words in your mouth, and hidden you in the shadow of my hand" (51:16) refer to words of Torah and deeds of kindness. Thus you are taught that when a person engages in Torah [Jewish studies] and deeds of kindness, he merits refuge under the shadow of the wings of the Holy One. As Scripture says, "How precious is your steadfast

Third Isaiah

Third Isaiah in the synagogue's lexionary. During the morning service liturgy on the Day of Atonement, Yom Kippur, the prophetical reading is Third Isaiah's message, which suggests certain parameters for righteous behavior. It explains that God is ever ready to hear the prayers of the repentant (57:14—58:14).

Hope and salvation. Part of the Text Study at this chapter's conclusion includes a section on 61:1–11, "Hope and Salvation." The early rabbis see a special message in these verses. They suggest that the words of 61:9 are to comfort those who are mourners for Zion. Do not understand the word to be "their descendants" (*za'rm*) but rather "their arm" (*z'roam*)—and who is their arm? The Holy One shall stand by them, as it says in 33:2, "Be our arm every morning, our salvation in the time of trouble" (*Pesikta Rabbati, Piska* 34.1).

Elsewhere, the rabbis address 61:10, "I will greatly rejoice in the LORD . . . for he has clothed me with the garments of salvation, he has covered me with the robe of righteousness." The "rejoicing" might refer to different matters: the days of the Messiah; or the Time to Come which will have no end; deliverance from punishment in Gehenna (*Gehinnom*); when the inclination to do evil will have been rooted out of Israel; or when the angel of death will no longer have power over Israel (*Pesikta Rabbati, Piska* 37.2).

Isaiah contradicts the words of Jeremiah. Jeremiah says, "I will banish from them the sound of mirth" (Jer 25:10). Isaiah says, "I will greatly rejoice in the LORD" (Isa 61:10) (*Pesikta de-Rab Kahana, Piska* S6.1 end).

God offers compassion and comfort to Israel. Rabbi Samuel teaches that it is the way of a father to have compassion: "As a father has compassion for his children, so the LORD has compassion for those who fear him" (Ps 103:13). It is the way of a mother to comfort: "As a mother comforts her child, so will I comfort you; you shall be comforted in Jerusalem" (Isa 66:13) (*Pesikta de-Rab Kahana, Piska* 19.3).

God's commandments further summarized. The Torah traditionally contains 613 commandments. The rabbis suggest that Isaiah reduces them to six principles (see the section above on First Isaiah in rabbinic literature), and then they suggest that Isaiah reduces these principles even further, to two suggestions: "[1] Maintain justice [2] and do what is right" (56:1) (*Babylonian Talmud Makkot* 24a).

Text Study

First Isaiah

Isaiah 6:1–8; Isaiah's Commission

This passage is best known by verse 3, "Holy, holy, holy is the LORD of hosts." It is incorporated into the liturgy of Judaism and many Christian churches. The whole scene suggests the prophet Isaiah's familiarity with the temple in Jerusalem, its precincts and rites. Isaiah may be a priest, or from a priestly family. The prophet does not claim to see God, only the hem of a garment and the Seraphim. Isaiah does have an awareness that he is in God's presence.

Verse 1. This reference to a specific time sets Isaiah's "call" in the year 742 BCE.

Verses 2–3. The Seraphim appear as extra-celestial beings who attend upon the deity. In a note to this verse, the Roman Catholic volume *The Jerusalem Bible* suggests that "feet" here are a "Euphemism for sexual organs." This would explain why they use their wings to cover them.

Verses 4–7. The smoke suggests incense, which is part of the temple cult (Lev 16:12ff.) An echo of it is found in special masses found in the Roman Catholic and Orthodox as well as the Episcopal Churches, where burning incense is part of the ritual.

Isaiah's recognition that he is but human, and therefore flawed, echoes Abraham's statement that he is but "dust and ashes" (Gen 18:27). That the Seraph touches Isaiah's *lips* is appropriate symbolic action. It is with his lips that Isaiah will give expression to God's words. Only after he is purified and sanctified does Isaiah become God's messenger.

Verse 8. Isaiah's willingness to act contrasts with the lack of enthusiasm of many prophets, including Moses, Jeremiah, and Jonah. The Hebrew literally translates, "Who will go for *us*?" This can be understood as either the magisterial plural or a recognition that Isaiah, like his forebear Micaiah (1 Kgs 22:19), has stood before the heavenly council.

Isaiah 5:1–8, 18–21; Social Justice

In the opening lines of chapter 5 Isaiah begins with the pastoral image of a wedding feast. The poet sings of a friend who has built a beautiful vineyard. There are choice vines. A winepress is hewn out. Yet instead of grapes, it yields wild grapes. God then asks rhetorically, what else could I have done? "When I expected it to yield grapes, why did it yield wild grapes?" (v. 4). Next God explains that the wall will be trampled. It will become desolation and a ruin. "For the vineyard of the LORD of hosts is the house of Israel. . . . [God] expected justice, but saw bloodshed; righteousness, but heard a cry!" In this instance, the NJPS/*TANAKH* translation comes closer to capturing the word play in the Hebrew. There verse 7 reads: "[God] hoped for justice, but behold injustice, for equity, but behold, iniquity." The Hebrew also reflects this wordplay: "[God] hoped for *mishpat* [justice] but there was *mispah* [injustice], for *tzedaqa* [equity], but there was *tze-'aqa* [iniquity]."

In verses 8 and 18–21 Isaiah lays out in stark detail the immorality, the rapaciousness, as well as the traders in malevolence and evil that stand before him. They are venomous and corrupt. They are irredeemable hypocrites. Piously they call for God to execute divine justice, as if they were innocent of any wrongdoing. They compound their guilt by calling evil good, and good evil; bitter as sweet, and sweet as bitter (v. 20).

The purpose of the vineyard had been to plant and produce righteousness and justice. Instead there has been violence and corruption. God is angry. Isaiah condemns the rampant injustice and speaks out for the poor and the unprotected. God's relationship with the people is damaged by the moral corruption of Israel's leadership.

In the Christian Scriptures, Jesus' denunciation "of some, not all, Pharisees" reflects a similar sevenfold cataloging of woes, again featuring hypocrisy as a major misdemeanor.[16]

Rabbi Akiva, who lived a generation after Matthew, during the Roman oppression of Judea in the first third of the second century CE, explains that at first sin is like a spider's web, but eventually becomes as thick as a ship's rope. His "prooftext" is from Isaiah 5:18, "Ah, you who . . . drag sin along as with cart ropes." (*Midrash Genesis Rabbah* 22.6).

Isaiah 7:1–9; Judah under Siege

Isaiah speaks to a contemporary audience. They immediately understand his references. Living three thousand years later, it is not surprising that this

---

16. See *NOAB*, note on Matt 23:13.

section is particularly difficult to comprehend. Without an explanation of who is involved, this remains a very confusing narrative.

The background to these verses is the Syro-Ephraimitic War of c. 735–32.

Verses 1–9 make sense once the major characters are delineated. The country of Judah is under siege from two adjoining nations, Israel/Ephraim and Aram/Syria. Isaiah says simply: ignore them; they are no real threat to you. They are bluffing. To use the prophet's image in verse 4, they are but smoking stumps of wood. Their smoke creates the illusion of fire, but it is only an illusion. Judah's enemies are made up of the list below:

- Pekah = son of Remaliah = King of Israel (see 2 Kgs 15:27-28, 37; 16:5)
- Israel = Ephraim
- Samaria = the capital city of Israel (Ephraim)
- Rezin = King of Aram (see 2 Kgs 15:37; 16:5)
- Aram = Syria
- Damascus = the capital city of Aram (Syria)
- Son of Tabeel = an otherwise unknown figure who was to be placed as a "puppet" ruler to succeed King Ahaz of Judah

Isaiah 7:10–17; The "Immanuel" Passage

Will King Ahaz of Judah be faithful to God? Will he remain neutral? Will he ally himself neither with his besiegers nor with the Assyrians? Isaiah counsels/prophesies neutrality. Ahaz disregards this advice. He allies himself with the Assyrians under Tiglath Pileser III (2 Kgs 16:5-9; 15:29).

Verses 10–12. On the face of it, King Ahaz is being respectful of both God and Isaiah. "I will not ask . . . I will not put the LORD to the test" (v. 12). Yet behind his refusal is not faith but faithlessness, not respect but disrespect. Four hundred years earlier, Judge Gideon had asked for a sign. He was given it without any censure (Judg 6:17ff.) "It is evident that Ahaz knew that the sign would be given, that it would point to a way of life already declared in verse 9, and therefore would condemn the policy, reliance upon Assyria, on which he was already determined."[17]

Verses 13–17. When Ahaz refuses to accept the sign, what Isaiah intends to be a matter of hope now becomes a note of coming disaster. In verse 13 Isaiah addresses the royal entourage as much as King Ahaz. The siege will not last,

17. Herbert, *Book of the Prophet Isaiah 1–39*, 64.

Isaiah explains (see 2 Kgs 16:5). He points to a young pregnant woman who is standing nearby. Isaiah explains that before her child will be eating solids, the blockade will be lifted. The child's name will be Immanuel, meaning "God is with us." You should have listened to God. God is with us and shall not forsake us. Yet, because you refuse to obey, disaster shall come (v. 17).

The word for "young woman" in the Hebrew of verse 14 is *almah*. An *almah* is a post-pubescent female, as distinguished from a *betulah*, which is the word for "virgin." The *New Oxford Annotated Bible* (p. 876), in a comment to Isaiah 7:14, explains: "*Young woman*, Hebrew 'almah,' feminine of 'elem,' young man (1 Sam 17.56; 20:22); the word appears in Gen 24.43; Ex 2.8; Ps 68.25 [68:26 H], and elsewhere, where it is translated 'young woman,' 'girl,' 'maiden.'"

It was through a *mistranslation* that the word "virgin" appears. When *almah* was translated into Greek, the word *parthenos*, meaning "virgin," was used. In the Gospels, Matthew (1:23) relies on this late tradition. "Against the ancient christological interpretation, it can be shown that the whole context demands an event which is shortly to come about, and that the Hebrew word 'alma, like its Ugaritic equivalent *glmt*, does not simply correspond to the word 'virgin' but signifies a young woman without regard to whether she is married or single. The messianic interpretation of the verse is refuted by v. 17, as well as by the whole context of the passage."[18]

It is vital to understand these verses *in their proper context*. Readers of this, as with other prophetic passages, want to bear in mind that the prophets are speaking to a *contemporary audience*. That audience readily comprehends their allusions and references. As mentioned in the Introduction, the prophets fully expect that God's role in shaping history will be realized in the near future. It will be a matter of months or years—perhaps as much as a decade if not even earlier. Punishment, and latterly repentance and salvation, are *near-time* events. They will happen shortly. Their prophecies apply to their own days. They do not envision that their remarks will address to a far-off future time. The prophets are concerned with the here-and-now. They do not predict something to be realized hundreds of years, much less thousands of years, in the future.

Does Isaiah suggest that Immanuel refers to the "good news" of Jesus? The answer is no. *In its context* the reference to Immanuel is in the nature of a threat. Is an unhappy prediction. There will be temporary relief from

---

18. Kaiser, *Isaiah 1–12*, 101–2. Kaiser also dismisses the claim that this boy who is to be born the following year refers to Hezekiah, for Hezekiah already "was sixteen or seventeen years old" at this time (102). See also Levine, "Matthew," 468.

the problems at hand (hence "God is with us," Immanuel), yet the wrath of Assyria will follow.

There is no indication that Jesus was "called Immanuel, except subsequently, and occasionally, in the language of devotion."[19]

Isaiah 9:2–7 [9:1–6 H]; 11:1–10; Two Possible Messianic Passages

To what extent is it even correct to refer to "possible messianic passages" in Isaiah? The biblical prophets have no intention of their words being construed as "Messiah-oriented." Nonetheless, certain passages are considered by *later* religious leaders to be messianic, to refer to a human "Savior." As mentioned in the Introduction, there "is no *personal* messiah in the [Hebrew] Bible. Rather, we detect in this notion *soteriology*, human messengers or mortal agents, who carry out God's will and pave the way for salvation. In the Bible, God *alone* is the king-redeemer."[20]

What led later religious leaders, both Jewish and Christian, to refer to a (or the) Messiah? In 9:6 [9:5 H] Isaiah says, "For a child has been born for us, a son given to us . . . named Wonderful Counselor, Mighty God, Everlasting Father, Prince of Peace [*sar shalom*]."

Christianity sees this as referring to Jesus. Christian theologians directly link Jesus to Isaiah 7:14, the Immanuel passage. Jewish commentators in the Talmud and Midrash are just as sure that Isaiah 9:6 [9:5 H] refers to Hezekiah (*Midrash Genesis Rabbah* 97 [NV]; *Babylonian Talmud Sanhedrin* 94a; cf. *Midrash Ruth Rabbah* 7.2), to the future Messiah (*Midrash Deuteronomy Rabbah* 1.20), or to the peace of the Davidic line (*Midrash Numbers Rabbah* 11.7 on Isa 9:7 [9:6 H]).

In the case of Isaiah 11:1–9, there are clear connections between these verses of psalm-like quality and Isaiah 9. These prophecies are of a Davidic line that shall be filled with "the spirit of wisdom and understanding, the spirit of counsel and might, the spirit of knowledge and the fear of the LORD" (11:2). They are meant to contrast with the shallow faith and lack of courage of King Ahaz.

The word "anointed" (*mashiaḥ*, messiah) does not actually appear in the text itself. Isaiah suggests a powerful image: peace in the world of humans, peace in the animal world, and peace between humans and beasts. The words "the earth will be full of the knowledge of the LORD as the waters cover the sea" (v. 9) is a wonderfully poetic reference. It is a counterpart to the days following Noah and the flood, where humans

---

19. North, "Immanuel," 687.
20. Rosenthal, "Messianism Reconsidered," 552, 553.

are given dominion over all the animals, fish, and fowl (Gen 9:1–2). In Isaiah's words, there will be a future time of true peace between *all* God's creatures; peace—not water—is to cover the earth.

Second Isaiah

Isaiah 42:1–9; 49:1–13; 50:4–11; 52:13—53:12; The Servant Songs

Some of the strangest, and certainly most provocative, lines of the Bible are found in Second Isaiah's Servant Songs. These passages are found in four sections of Isaiah. These poems reflect a unique thought. They suggest that the death of the "servant" enables the total community to live. The servant bears their guilt; hence, they become guiltless. "Such human 'vicarious atonement' appears only here in Jewish literature and tradition; it is, of course, central to Christianity."[21]

These four sets of verses are referred to variously as the Servant Songs or the Suffering Servant Songs. The word "song" does not relate to melody. Rather it is a synonym for poem. All of Second Isaiah is written as poetry. The Hebrew for "poem" is the same word as for "song." The Servant Songs are:

1. 42:1–4 with their response, 42:5–9
2. 49:1–6 with their response, 49:7–13
3. 50:4–9 with their response, 50:10–11
4. 52:13—53:12

These passages are difficult to understand. One can easily have an immediate sympathy with the Ethiopian eunuch who in the Christian Scriptures reads some of the lines from the Fourth Song and then asks the Apostle Philip, "About whom, may I ask you, does the prophet say this, about himself or about someone else?" (Acts 8:34, see also vv. 26ff.)

Who is the servant? A number of possible answers can be given. Philip suggests the answer is Jesus. That same interpretation is found in

---

21. Sandmel, *Hebrew Scriptures*, 190. Shalom Paul adds, what "makes this servant song sui generis is the idea of suffering for another. The servant bears the sin for the many, and because of his afflictions the multitude is forgiven—an idea that became axiomatic to Christianity, which interpreted these verses as referring to the death and resurrection of Jesus." Paul goes on to write, "The roots of this belief that one can be held culpable for the sin of another, however, appear in a number of places throughout the Hebrew Bible." Paul then mentions Exod 20:5; 34:7; Num 14:18; Deut 5:9; Num 25:4; Ezek 4:4–6; Lam 5:7; and Gen 22:13 among other verses. Paul, *Isaiah 40–66*, 398.

the Gospel of Matthew.[22] These are faith statements within the context of the Christian Scriptures.

What are the (other) possible identities of the servant? Put very briefly, they include a figure or figures of:

1. The past, present, or future;
2. An individual or a collective;
3. The real or mythical.

Among the many answers given have been are Moses, Jeremiah, King Hezekiah, Isaiah himself, collective Israel, the pious of Israel, an unknown prophet, a future Messiah, and as noted above, in traditional Christian thought, Jesus of Nazareth.

Scholarly analyses of these passages are found in many standard references that deal exclusively with Second Isaiah. A good summary of the Servant Songs is found in James King West's *Introduction to the Old Testament*. One of the best discussions is found in the Anchor Bible Series, the volume by John L. McKenzie on *Second Isaiah*, as well as McKenzie's notes and comments to the various Songs themselves.[23] Some of the salient points include the following thoughts. The title itself, a "servant of God," is an honorific. It means one who God specifically commissions. The title "servant" certainly is used elsewhere in the Bible. In Second Isaiah, the title is applies to the people of Israel. Yet, in "spite of the superficial attractiveness of the Servant-Israel theory, the theory raises more problems than it solves."

There are various "voices" in these passages. In the first Song (ch. 42) God is the speaker. In the second and third Songs (chs. 49 and 50) the servant is the speaker. In the final Song (chs. 52–53) the speaker is not identified. Clearly, it is not God. This final passage is the most controversial. It unambiguously presents the servant as vicariously atoning for the sins of others.

The servant, a figure of affliction, dies. "His death has brought an atoning value for 'the many,' with whom the speaker is identified. The Servant

---

22. "Matthew reads Jesus as Isaiah's 'servant of Yahweh' . . . [I]t is not hard to see how Matthew interprets Isaiah 42. . . . Matthew read the larger context. God's servant Israel failed in its mission (42:18–19), so God chose one person within Israel to restore the rest of his people (49:5–7); this one would bear the punishment (cf. 40:2) rightly due his people (52:13—53:12)." Keener, *Commentary on Matthew*, 360.

23. West, *Introduction*, 399–404; McKenzie, *Second Isaiah*, xxxviii–lv. While she agrees that scholars debate whether the "'servant' refers to all Israel, ideal Israel, or individual role models in Israel," Tull seems to argue against a theory of four separate servant songs, seeing this all as part of Second Isaiah's address to Israel-as-God's servant. Tull, "Isaiah," 263.

was regarded as guilty, but he will see his own vindication and the fruit of his atoning death."[24]

Isaiah 51:1-11; Abraham and Sarah

Verses 1-2. These lines suggest to the exiles that even if they have some lingering doubts, they should think of their ancestors Abraham and Sarah. God promised them a brilliant future. Initially they were doubtful, but God's promise was kept.

The reference to Abraham and Sarah has several levels of meaning. Like Isaiah's audience in Babylon, Abraham and Sarah also came from Mesopotamia. They too began anew. They too traversed the desert wilderness before they came to the Promised Land. In addition, Isaiah utilizes very powerful, evocative (and sexually provocative) imagery here: Abraham is the "rock," and Sarah is the "quarry" (v. 1) of the preceding verse.

Verse 3. The image of God comforting Zion, and the presence of joy and thanksgiving, are quintessential Second Isaiah. The verb for "comfort" (*n-ḥ-m*, *nun-ḥet-mem*) is the same verb as in 40:1: "Comfort, O comfort my people." Notice here that in 51:3 that same verb appears *twice* just as it does in 40:1.

The allusion to Eden-like lushness is a striking contrast to the waste places, ruins, and desert. It echoes a similar vision in Ezekiel 36:35; 47:1ff.

Verses 4-6. In these verses the prophet turns from Israel and addresses the *peoples*. This is another major concept in Second Isaiah (in addition to comfort/hope). God is to be understood in increasingly universalistic terms.

The phrase in verse 4 "a light to the peoples" (*l'or amim*) differs only slightly from the "light to the nations" (*l'or goyim*) that is so familiar in the Servant Songs that precede it (42:6; 49:6).

This paraphrases the First Servant Song. It is "a striking example of the way in which the servant songs lived on and were handed down. The post-exile community—or a section within it—took up the possibility of salvation for non-Israelites" mentioned in 42:1-4. In the servant's name they proclaimed to the heathens that God's "salvation was available for them, and that the light which they had been awaiting was now there."[25]

---

24. McKenzie, *Second Isaiah*, xliii, xxxix.

25. Westermann, *Isaiah 40-66*, 235. N.B.: In view of Harvey Falk's thesis in *Jesus the Pharisee*, this corresponds well with the notion that Jesus had at least some Pharisaic support to teach God's words to the heathens.

Verses 9–11. Now Isaiah addresses God. These verses end up on a triumphal note, similar to verse 3.

The "arm [*zeroʻa*] of the LORD" echoes the narrative of the exodus. The same word (*zeroʻa*) is used in Exodus 6:6, "I will redeem you with an outstretched arm," and in the Song of the Sea, "by the might of your arm, they became still as a stone" (Exod 15:16).

The exodus theme continues directly in verse 10. "Was it not you who dried up the sea . . . a way for the redeemed to cross over?"—a clear reference to Exodus 14:16, 22.

In addition there are references to God, who made short shrift of the legendary monsters of the deep. Featured here are four separate entities from Near Eastern mythology: *Rahab* ("sea monster," v. 9), *Tannin* (the "dragon," v. 9), *Yam* (the "sea," v. 10), and *Tehom Rabbah* (the "great deep," v. 10).[26] These references are particularly appropriate since the exiles are living in Babylon. They would be familiar with the Babylonian epic *Enuma Elish*, which features a defeat of similar monsters.

Third Isaiah

Isaiah 61:1–11; Hope and Salvation

Verses 1–3. These verses are part of Third Isaiah's message of hope and salvation found in chapters 60–62. The prophet is speaking to the depressed and dejected.

Verses 4, 7–11. Here again is a message of hope. The ancient cities shall be rebuilt. Since you suffered so much, you will inherit double portions. You shall be like brides and bridegrooms.

---

26. Westermann, *Isaiah 40–66*, 241; see Gaster, *Myth, Legend, and Custom*, 576.

7

Jeremiah

Introduction

JEREMIAH PROPHESIES OVER A period of four decades, c. 627–585 BCE, speaking his words in Jerusalem. He is one of the greatest of the Hebrew prophets. He is the second of the Major Prophets. His book follows Isaiah and precedes Ezekiel. In the Christian Bible, the book of Lamentations follows Jeremiah, and then comes Ezekiel. In the Jewish Bible, Lamentations is part of the third section, *Ketuvim*/Writings.

Jeremiah is the eighth book of the second section of the Hebrew Bible, the Prophets/*Neviim* (see Introduction: "The Order of the Books of the Bible").

Jeremiah demonstrates vision, stature, and leadership. He is burdened by the condition of his people. His inward reflections and confessions tell the story of a man filled with pain and gloom. Jeremiah dares to challenge those with temporal power. In this way, he follows the precedents of Samuel, Nathan, Elijah, and First Isaiah. Jeremiah suffers for his courage. Still, he refuses to shirk from his duty. Similar to his predecessors, Jeremiah knows that "the prophet was not a *primus inter pares*, first among his peers. By his very claim, his was the voice of supreme authority. He not only rivaled the decisions of the king and the counsel of the priest, he defied and even condemned their words and deeds."[1]

Jeremiah's rhetoric is commanding. His poetry is beautiful in its imagery. Yet, from a modern sensibility, there is a difficulty with some of Jeremiah's language. In Hebrew the words for cities and countries are feminine

---

1. Heschel, *Prophets*, 480 (page 280 in the 2-vol. ed.).

nouns. Jeremiah uses women, therefore, as symbolic of evil. "Female figures personify the nation and the city of Jerusalem. Women's suffering symbolizes the pain of the entire people." Consequently, on one hand this gendered language is harmful, for "it uses women as symbols of wickedness, blames them for the fall of the nation, and exploits their experiences by applying them to men." On the other hand, "the book of Jeremiah . . . contains poetic imagery that portrays . . . women in a positive light."[2]

Geo-Political Background

The geo-political background to Jeremiah's prophecy is the steady decline of Assyrian domination and the corresponding ascendancy of the Babylonian Empire.

Assyria becomes a world power by the latter part of the eighth century BCE. Assyria destroys the northern kingdom of Israel in 722/721. This is during the life of First Isaiah. Some refugees flee to Judah. Many others from Israel—which had been compromised of the ten northern tribes—are exiled to the lands between the Tigris and Euphrates Rivers. For the next hundred years Judah, the remaining kingdom, is a vassal state to the Assyrians. Yet by 627 Assyrian power declines severely. The death of their ruler Ashurbanipal (669–27) signals the imminent collapse of this era. The Neo-Babylonians (Chaldeans) under Nabopolassar (626–25) fills this vacuum.

In Judah, King Josiah (640–9) instigates changes. He attempts to declare independence from Assyria. In addition, he initiates important religious reforms. About 615, in an attempt to stem the increasing military successes of the Neo-Babylonians, Assyria allies itself with its former foe, Egypt. Egypt seeks to regain its previous control over the landmass just east of the Mediterranean. This includes Judah-Phoenicia-Syria. In 612 the Neo-Babylonians crush the Assyrians. They destroy their capital city, Nineveh. In 609 the Egyptians, under Pharaoh Neco, seek to rescue their ally, the Assyrians, from total defeat by their mutual enemy, the Neo-Babylonians. They move their forces northward. King Josiah tries to stop this force by engaging them at Megiddo. It is unknown if Josiah acts independently or in cooperation with Babylon. He certainly does not want to see an Egypto-Assyrian victory. Still, this action is futile, for Josiah is killed and his dead body is brought in his chariot to Jerusalem amid great lamentation (2 Kgs 23:29ff.; 2 Chr 35:20–25). Josiah's son Jehoahaz succeeds his father on the throne.

King Jehoahaz (609) rules but a few months. His brother Jehoiakim follows. Jehoiakim rules for eleven years. His son Jehoiachin briefly succeeds

---

2. O'Connor, "Jeremiah," 270, 272.

him. Over these years, Jehoiakim (and his son Jehoiachin) try to break away from Babylonian domination, but fail. The Babylonians lay siege to Jerusalem, and King Jehoiachin (who only rules for three months) concedes defeat in 597. The Babylonian ruler, Nebuchadnezzar, allows Judah to continue as a vassal state. He does, however, deport King Jehoiachin, the queen mother, the court officials, military leaders, as well as skilled artisans, bringing them to Babylon. He sets King Jehoiachin's uncle Zedekiah, another one of Josiah's sons, on the throne requiring vassalage to Babylon (2 Kgs 24:10–17).

Regrettably, Zedekiah's rule is a disaster for Judah. He is unable to stop a rebellious group from agitating for independence. Finally, the Babylonians decide to put an end to the matter. In 589 they invade, and by 587/586 the southern kingdom ceases to exist. The Babylonians burn to the ground the temple built by Solomon.

Religious Background: Josiah's Religious Reforms (c. 622 BCE)

The collapse of the Assyrian Empire and the rise of the Babylonian Empire are the dominant issues geo-politically in the Near East in Jeremiah's lifetime. Within Judah itself, beginning around 625 a religious revolution shakes the nation.

King Josiah's religious reforms often are mistakenly associated with the "discovery" of the Book of Deuteronomy (2 Kgs 22–23). This takes place in the eighteenth year of his reign, 622/621. Without doubt, Josiah welcomes this "find." The religious reformation begins several years earlier. The book of Kings reports that the full reform takes place in 622. Further, it suggests (2 Kgs 22:13; 23:3) that these reforms are based on "the book of the law," of which a copy is found during the repairs to the temple. That the temple is being repaired when the book is discovered strongly suggests that reforms are already in progress.

King Josiah actively roots out religious syncretism. He destroys Canaanite and probably Assyrian idol worship as well (2 Kgs 23:4–14; 23:15–20; 2 Chr 34:3–7). Josiah seeks to centralize political *and* religious power in Jerusalem. He invites religious leaders from the outlying areas to come to Jerusalem. He wants them to take their place among the Jerusalem priesthood and to function at the temple (2 Kgs 23:8).

A national fervor matches these reforms and changes. As Assyria goes into political decline, Judah flexes its political and religious muscles.

The long-term effects of the Josianic reforms are limited. The writer of Kings (2 Kgs 23:25) applauds his actions. Undoubtedly, there are some positive effects. Others, including the displaced priesthood, resent the reforms.

Nonetheless, whatever changes are instituted, they do not *sufficiently* change the national character of the citizens of Judah. Jeremiah himself criticizes the degree of the people's repentance (Jer 6:16–21). Many of the wealthy as well as the powerful barely acknowledge the covenantal relationship with God (Jer 7:1ff.). Immorality is rife.

Following Josiah's death in 609, religious reform ends (Jer 7:16–20, 30–31). In the mind of the Deuteronomistic historians, this results in the destruction of the temple and the fall of Judah.

The Temple's Destruction

The destruction of the temple by the Babylonians in 586 BCE is an incredible loss for the people of Judah. They are utterly dejected, depressed, and devastated. God's house had stood for nearly four hundred years. Now it is gone. The building symbolized God's presence. It represented God's care for the people and the nation. Now it has been destroyed. Razed, burnt, smoldering ruins, the Holy of Holies had been violated and obliterated! To comprehend the enormity of this event, compare this to the complete and utter destruction of the major historical buildings of the capitol of one's own country. For the United States, this would mean the complete destruction of major buildings in Washington, DC, including the White House, the Capitol building, and the Supreme Court building. In Canada this would mean the destruction of Ottawa's Parliament Hill, the Supreme Court building, and the Library and Archives building. In Great Britain, it would be equivalent to the destruction of London's Palace of Westminster, Buckingham Palace, and the National Gallery. For France, this might mean the destruction of Paris' Palais Bourbon, Palais du Luxembourg, Château de Versailles, the Sorbonne, and the Louvre. Judah's capital is destroyed. Its leadership exiled. It is a national disaster of unprecedented magnitude. Jeremiah's voice has prophesied this day, but the people have not believed.

The Book of Jeremiah

Divisions in the Book of Jeremiah

Jeremiah is a very difficult book to read. It is not in set down in chronological order. Rather, it is *a collection of collections* set down by the prophet's circle of supporters. In broad outline, it consists of the following units:

Jeremiah 1–25	Prophecies against Jerusalem and Judah
Jeremiah 1–6	Largely from the period of King Josiah
Jeremiah 7–20	Largely from the period of King Jehoiakim
Jeremiah 21–25	Largely from the period of King Zedekiah
Jeremiah 26–45	Biographical narratives (including the Book of Consolation, chs. 30–33)
Jeremiah 46–51	Prophecies against foreign nations
Jeremiah 52	Historical appendix (cf. 2 Kgs 24:18—25:30)[3]

Jeremiah 1–25; Prophecies against Jerusalem and Judah

As noted, the book of Jeremiah is a *collection of collections*. It is a group of books by and about the prophet Jeremiah. It contains poetry, preaching, narrative, history, biography, as well as prophecy. *A great difficulty in reading Jeremiah is that his prophecies are* not *set down in chronological order*. Even the prophecies associated with specific rulers are not in chronological order.

It is clear that Jeremiah dictates some of his utterances to a scribe, Baruch son of Neriah. At times, Jeremiah makes specific reference to a given ruler (Josiah, Jehoiakim, and Zedekiah). Sometimes his pronouncements are more generically directed toward Jerusalem or Judah.

In chapter 1, God warns Jeremiah that his will be a difficult task. God says, "Stand up and tell them everything that I command you. . . . They will fight against you; but they shall not prevail . . . for I am with you." (vv. 17, 19).

Jeremiah warns of a hot wind coming from the north. This is a reference to Assyria, and later Babylonia. He warns of disaster if Judah will not turn from their evil ways. God asks Jeremiah to "Run to and fro through the streets of Jerusalem. . . . Search its squares and see if you can find one person who acts justly and seeks the truth—so that I may pardon Jerusalem" (5:1). Jeremiah reports that he is unsuccessful. "They felt no anguish. . . . They have refused to take correction. They have made their faces harder than rock; they have refused to turn back" (5:3).

Chapter 7 portrays Jeremiah going to the temple in Jerusalem. He berates the people for their hypocrisy. He warns them not to oppress the alien, the orphan, and the widow. He tells them not to shed innocent blood. Do not worship other gods. Do they think that they can "steal, murder, commit adultery, swear falsely, make offerings to Baal . . . and then come and

---

3. West, *Introduction*, 361. See also Schreiber, *Man Who Knew God*, xiii–xvi.

stand before [God] . . . and say 'We are safe!'?" (7:9–10). (See the Text Study sections at the conclusion of this chapter, "The Temple Sermon" and "The Temple Sermon Continued.")

On another occasion, Jeremiah again speaks out at the temple. As earlier, he condemns the actions of the people. One of the priests overhears him and places him in stocks as a punishment (20:1–2).

Jeremiah knows that he is preaching an unpopular message. He struggles in his mission. He wonders at times, is this what God really wants? Should he stay still? Yet he cannot be quiet. The threat of a Babylonian attack is real to Jeremiah. Sadly, it is not self-evident to the populace around him. People scorn him. He feels "compelled to speak judgment. Vigorously he shouted out his warning . . . but people mocked him and asked him to prove it. Where was the terror he proclaimed?" At moments when he decides to refrain from speaking out, "the compelling power of God still ruled him and he was constantly gnawed by guilt and the knowledge that he had to cry out whatever words God gave him."[4]

Jeremiah rightly feels depressed and dejected. He is regarded as a fool and an alarmist. He seems unable to effect change. He gives vent to his frustration. He says, "Cursed be the day on which I was born! The day when my mother bore me, let it not be blessed! Cursed be the man who brought the news to my father, saying 'A child is born to you, a son,' making him very glad. . . . Why did I come forth from the womb to see toil and sorrow, and spend my days in shame?" (20:14–15, 18).

Jeremiah 26–45; Biographical Narratives

In chapter 27, Jeremiah urges King Zedekiah to submit to the will of Babylon. He urges Zedekiah not to listen to those advisors who counsel rebellion. Chapter 29 contains a letter that Jeremiah writes to his fellow compatriots who had already been exiled to Babylon (c. 597 BCE). He says to them, your banishment from Judah will be for an extended period. It will be decades in duration. Jeremiah declares there will be no sudden return to the holy land. "Thus says the LORD of hosts, the God of Israel, to all the exiles whom I have sent into exile from Jerusalem to Babylon: Build houses and live in them; plant gardens and eat what they produce. Take wives and have sons and daughters; take wives for your sons, and give your daughters in marriage . . . seek the welfare of the city where I have sent you in exile, and pray to the LORD on its behalf, for in its welfare you will find your welfare" (29:4–7)

---

4. Boadt, *Jeremiah 1–25*, 151; see also Brueggemann, *Commentary on Jeremiah*, 181–87; Schreiber, *Man Who Knew God*, 2–4.

Chapters 30–31 form the first part of the Book of Consolation. This is a subsection in its own right. It offers hope to those who had been sent into exile years earlier from the northern kingdom of Israel. It also offers hope to those from Judah who recently were banished from the land. At the heart of this small book are words that speak to a new covenant that God will establish. God will write it on the hearts of the people. Chapters 32–33 continue the Book of Consolation. These chapters are written as prose.

Chapter 36 contains prophecies from an earlier period. They are written during the reign of King Jehoiakim (609–598). These date to the years 605–4. Jeremiah dictates them to his scribe, Baruch son of Neriah (36:1–4). This chapter relates the dramatic—and symbolic—episode of the burnt scroll (see the Text Study section at the close of this chapter, "The Burnt Scroll.")

Jeremiah is imprisoned for what some consider his seditious remarks (chs. 37–38). Jerusalem's capture and the fall are detailed in the next chapters. Against his will, Jeremiah is taken to Egypt (ch. 43). Jeremiah prophesies that Egypt will know God's wrath.

Jeremiah 46–51; Prophecies against Foreign Nations

These chapters are prophecies against various nations: Egypt, Philistia, Moab, Ammon, other peoples, and then Babylon.

Jeremiah 52; Historical Appendix

Jeremiah concludes with a kind of historical appendix, largely duplicating material found in 2 Kings 24:18—25:30.

Jeremiah's Theology

Jeremiah's speaks of the need for morality. He explains that the people need to know God in a different manner. Trust God. Know God. Have a deeper faith. A term that appears again and again in Jeremiah is "heart." "The heart is devious above all else; it is perverse—who can understand it? I the LORD test the mind and search the heart, to give to all according to their ways" (17:9–10). If people change their ways, if they turn their thoughts to God, Jeremiah suggests that they will be like a tree planted by the water, rooted in the soil, unafraid of drought (17:8).

Trust in God! That is the way to achieve salvation! "Thus says the LORD: Do not let the wise boast in their wisdom, do not let the mighty boast in their might, do not let the wealthy boast in their wealth; but let those who boast boast in this, that they understand and know me." (9:23–24 [9:22–23 H]).

Jeremiah believes that the people need to be punished for their wrongdoing. Yet, he predicts that in a future time God will establish a new covenant with them. "I will make a new covenant with the house of Israel. . . . I will put my law within them and I will write it on their hearts" (31:31–33). (See the Text Study sections at the conclusion of this chapter, "The Book of Consolation" and "The New Covenant.")

Following defeat, like his younger contemporary Ezekiel, Jeremiah predicts a future of hope. It will be a different community. It will not be based on a political unit or a set geographical area.

Such a community does in fact emerge in the exile and after. That Jeremiah and Ezekiel stress—perhaps to a unique degree—the inward and personal nature of that relationship to God surely prepared for its formation. Jeremiah teaches the people that God wants their trust and obedience even more than their religious/ritual cult. God *does not need* the house in Jerusalem. This message gives comfort and hope in his day and immediately thereafter. It also proves comforting following the destruction of the second temple by the Romans in 70 CE.

Jeremiah in the Christian Scriptures

Jeremiah 31:31–34 is an important passage for Christianity. The "new covenant" of which Jeremiah speaks is understood as *the* "New Covenant" or "New Testament" with the "New Israel," that is, the followers of Jesus.

In the Gospel of Luke, Jesus directly refers to the "new covenant" (Luke 22:20). The image repeats in the 1 Corinthians description of the Last Supper (1 Cor 11:25). Further, in 2 Corinthians Paul speaks of "God, who has made us competent to be ministers of a new covenant, not of letter but of spirit; for the letter kills, but the Spirit gives life" (2 Cor 3:5–6). This is a faith statement that consciously and viciously disassociates Christianity from Judaism (cf. 2 Cor 3:7ff.).

In the Epistle to the Hebrews, a letter to former Jews who are now Christians, the words of Jeremiah 31:31–34 find full expression (Heb 8:7–12; 10:16–17).

Jeremiah denounces Jerusalem's citizens at the temple. This is the basis for the incident recorded in Mark 11:11–21 (cf. Matt 21:12ff.; Luke 19:45ff.; John 2:13ff.) Jesus remarks that the temple has become "a den of robbers." This is the same phrase as Jeremiah's "den of robbers" (Mark 11:17; Jer 7:11.)

Jesus curses the fig tree, which then dries up from the roots (Mark 11:12–14, 20–22). The Gospel writer understands this is as a symbolic statement about the changing times. It reflects Jeremiah's statements where he speaks of the person of faith being compared to a tree planted by water, and how it shall never fear its roots drying. The person who trusts in mortals, on the other hand, shall be barren (Jer 17:5–8.)

Jeremiah's rough handling by some priests and prophets, and being protected by the princes and the people (Jer 26), is echoed in Mark 11. The scribes and chief priests oppose Jesus. The people are in awe of Jesus. Pilate seems, like the princes in Jeremiah's day, to be sympathetic to the accused man (Mark 15:8–15, Luke 23:13ff.). The connection between Jesus and Jeremiah is further strengthened by the fact that at one point a number of people assume Jesus *is* Jeremiah redivivus (Matt 16:14).[5]

Jeremiah in Rabbinic Literature

An example of true prophecy. Jeremiah's Temple Sermon and the subsequent rough handling by some priests brings attention to the otherwise unknown prophet/martyr Uriah son of Shemaiah (26:20ff.) Uriah predicted the destruction of Jerusalem. This is heralded as true prophecy. It is linked to Zechariah's prophecy of a positive future. Just as the earlier prophet was correct (in Jer 26:18), so will Zechariah's prophecy also come about in time: "Old men and old women shall again sit in the streets of Jerusalem . . . the city shall be full of boys and girls playing" (Zech 8:4–5) (*Midrash Lamentations Rabbah* 5.18.1; see also *Babylonian Talmud Makkot* 24b end—although there seems to be some confusion between Uriah and Micah the prophet).

Preplanning. Jeremiah depicts Rachel weeping for her children (Jer 31:15–17). Jacob buried Rachel there purposefully. He knew—nearly a thousand years earlier! (see Gen 35:19 and 1 Sam 10:2)—that the exiles would pass by her grave and her voice would arise and plead their case (*Midrash Genesis Rabbah* 82.10 end; see also *Midrash Genesis Rabbah* 97 [MSV]). This is not a problem for the midrashic tradition. According to the rabbis, there is no such thing as linear time when it comes to the Torah. Past, present, and future time merge. They are all part of one undivided continuum. *Ayn muqdam um'uḥar baTorah*, "There is neither later nor previous time in the Torah" (*Babylonian Talmud Pesahim* 6b).

---

5. For a development of the connections between Jesus and Jeremiah, see Zucker, "Jesus and Jeremiah."

Never underestimate a woman's word. According to midrashic tradition, when the temple was destroyed Abraham himself was so upset that he came before God and lamented these events. Abraham asked God, How could you do this? The ministering angels likewise compose lamentations.

God, it is related, tersely replied that the people "transgressed the whole of the Torah." God then calls the Torah to come and testify against Israel. The Torah comes forward, but Abraham challenges the Torah. Abraham points out that each letter of the alphabet points to a word where Israel has been righteous. Abraham recalls to God that the deity was willing to call for the sacrifice of Isaac. Surely this should account for merit for Abraham's children, the people of Israel. Next Isaac and Jacob come before the heavenly throne. They argue on behalf of Israel. Moses presents a long case, but it is to no avail. Moses then calls upon Jeremiah, but he too is unsuccessful. Finally, Rachel breaks into speech and presents her case. She says that as she was not jealous of Leah, so likewise God, "a ruler who lives eternally and is merciful, should not be jealous of idolatry in which there is no reality" (a reference presumably to the idol worship of the Jerusalemites; see Jer 7:17ff., 8:19; 11:10 et al.)

God hears Rachel's plea and immediately capitulates. God says, "For your sake Rachel, I will restore Israel to their place." Further, Scripture explains, "Thus says the LORD: A voice is heard in Ramah, lamentation and bitter weeping. Rachel is weeping for her children; she refuses to be comforted for her children, because they are no more" (31:15). This is followed by, "Thus says the LORD: Keep your voice from weeping, and your eyes from tears; for there is a reward for your work, says the LORD: they shall come back from the land of the enemy" (31:16) (*Midrash Lamentations Rabbah*, Proem 24, end).

An everlasting love. God's love for Israel is to be "an everlasting love" (31:3). It does not say, "with abounding love," but "with eternal love." You might think the love with which God loves Israel was for three years or two years or a hundred years. Not so. God's love is everlasting and to all eternity (*Tanna Debe Eliyyahu*, ch. [6] 7, p. 31 [74]). This very line "with an everlasting love" (*Ahavat olam*) is incorporated into the Jewish evening service liturgy, the second paragraph following the "call to worship" (*Barkhu*).

The child who was ashamed to return. The child of a monarch took to evil ways. The ruler sent a tutor urging the child to repent and return. The child wished to return, but was ashamed. The monarch then sent the message, how can a child be ashamed to return to one's parent? In like manner, God (the Ruler of Rulers) sent Jeremiah (the tutor) with a message of repentance. Israel was ashamed (see 3:25) and so God said, are you not returning to your Parent? Hence the words "I have become a [parent] to Israel" (31:9) (*Midrash Deuteronomy Rabbah* 2.24 end; *Pesikta de-Rab Kahana*, Piska 24.16 end).

Offering comfort. While there is a tradition that prophets begin their books with words reciting Israel's guilt, they close them with words of comfort. The rabbis debate whether Jeremiah is the one exception to this rule (*Midrash on Psalms*, Ps 4:12).

When God commands, people follow. Although Jeremiah initially refused to prophesy, he was compelled to do so. "Do not say 'I am only a boy'; for you shall go to all to whom I shall send you, and you shall speak whatever I command you" (1:7) (*Midrash Exodus Rabbah* 4.3).

Jeremiah compared to Moses. There are several parallels between the life of Moses, and that of Jeremiah. Both prophesied for forty years. Both prophesied concerning Judah and Israel. Someone from his own tribe rose up against him. One was thrown into the river, one into a pit. One was saved by a maidservant, one by a manservant (Exod 2:5; Jer 38:10). Each came with words of reproof (*Pesikta de-Rab Kahana*, Piska 13.6).

The new covenant. The "new covenant" refers to the World to Come. Being but human, one learns here but forgets. It is different in the World to Come. At that time God will teach humans directly and it will be inscribed on their hearts (*Midrash Ecclesiastes Rabbah* 2.1; *Midrash Song of Songs Rabbah* 1.2, 4).

Praise of God continues in the World to Come. Although many ceremonial laws will cease in the World to Come, thanks to God will remain in force forever. This interpretation is based on the line, "Give thanks to the LORD of hosts, for the LORD is good, for his steadfast love endures forever" (33:11) (*Midrash Leviticus Rabbah* 9.7).

Text Study

Jeremiah 7:1–20, 30–31; The Temple Sermon

Verses 7:1–15 describe the "Temple Sermon." Jeremiah causes consternation in the opening period of the reign of King Jehoiakim (26:1ff.) The religious reforms enacted by King Josiah, Jehoiakim's father, were neglected.

Verses 1–2. Three times in the first two verses one finds the characteristic term *d'var*, the "Word" of the LORD.

Verses 3–4. Verse 3 has the familiar phrase, "Thus says the LORD." Then comes an abrupt message: Mend your ways and your actions; reform the whole pattern of your conduct! Do not assume that a mere building will save you! It is an illusion to cry, "The temple of the LORD, the temple of the LORD, the temple of the LORD." This threefold repetition is a powerful rhetorical device.

Verses 5–7. Jeremiah calls for true justice: protection for the stranger, the orphan, and the widow.

Verse 9. The crimes listed here violate many of the Ten Commandments, specifically the eighth, sixth, seventh, ninth, and second commandments.

Verses 16–18. In verse 16 there is an echo of the rejection of the people found in Isaiah 6:8–10. The reference to the queen of heaven and the dough cakes are probably for the Assyrian-Babylonian goddess Ishtar.

Verses 30–31. It appears from these verses that the abominable pagan rites featured in King Manasseh's day (2 Kgs 23:10), including child sacrifice (!), were reinstituted under the impression that God actually desires this! (cf. Mic 6:7).

Jeremiah 26:1–24; The Temple Sermon Continued

Verses 2–6 contain an abridged version of the Temple Sermon of chapter 7.

Verses 7–9 explain how Jeremiah is seized by some priests and prophets (possibly court prophets). They demand his execution for sedition.

Verses 10–19. The officials (princes) and the people contradict the priests and the prophets. They say, No this is not a crime. There is precedent in the days of King Hezekiah. They refer to the words of the earlier prophet Micah of Moresheth (cf. Mic 3:12). "One must say that the conduct of these princes certainly reflects credit upon them, and warns us against accepting Jeremiah's pessimistic evaluation of his people (e.g., v 1–5; ix 1–8) without qualification. There *were* good men in Judah!"[6]

Verses 20–23 contain a reference to another prophet, Uriah son of Shamaiah, who like Jeremiah prophesied against Jerusalem. Although he fled, he was brought back to Judah and executed. Speaking forthrightly could be dangerous. Yet, this was not a matter of heroes and villains. Elnathan son

---

6. Bright, *Jeremiah*, 172, emphasis original; see also Longman, *Jeremiah, Lamentations*, 181–83.

of Achbor, one of the princes in Judah, helps to bring Uriah back to Jerusalem. At another point, however, Elnathan tries to persuade the king not to burn the scroll that contains Jeremiah's criticisms (see Jer 36:25 and the Text Study below, "The Burnt Scroll").

The fact that many chapters separate the "original" temple sermon and its shortened version here is an indication of how the book of Jeremiah is an edited version of several different sources. The "patchwork quilt" nature of Jeremiah is also seen in the fact that chapters 26 and 27 are said to come in the reign of Jehoiakim, as are chapters 35 and 36. In the meantime chapters 29, 32, and 34 clearly come from the period of King Zedekiah.

Jeremiah 36:1–32; The Burnt Scroll

This chapter shows the lengths to which Jeremiah dares to go in order to speak God's word. He is in hiding. There is no doubt that he knows that his life is in danger. He speaks through his proxy, Baruch son of Neriah.

The message of the scroll is read three times. Baruch initially reads it twice. The first time is to the people at the temple. He reads it a second time, by their own request, to a group of court officials. The people's reaction is unrecorded. The officials are perturbed and worried. Are they fearful and upset because the prophecy details their wrongdoing and future calamity? Alternatively, are they concerned about such seditious talk? The latter view is probable. They tell Baruch to go into hiding with Jeremiah. An official takes the scroll and reads it a final time to the king and his closest advisors. King Jehoiakim and his entourage show neither fear nor dismay. They are contemptuous. Although the court officials beg him not to do so, after he listens to the prophecy Jehoiakim burns it in a brazier (36:20–25).

These events take place in 605, following the victorious battle of the Babylonians over the Egyptians at Carchemish. Soon the Babylonians will invade Judah.

Verse 4. Jeremiah literally dictates the prophecy to Baruch son of Neriah. Since it covers many years of prophecy, it requires several columns.

Verses 16ff. The officials are excited but fearful. They also want reassurance that this is really God's word and not something made up by Baruch himself. Note the reference to *scroll* and *ink*.

Verses 21–25. There is an eyewitness sense to this description of the scroll being read and the king then literally cutting it after three or four columns are read and tossing it into the brazier before him. The ruler and his advisors blatantly disregard the other court officials, who are horrified at the king's action.

Verses 27-32. For his contempt for God's word, God condemns Jehoiakim to death. His courtiers will know only disaster.

Jeremiah 31:1-3, 15-22, 29-30; The Book of Consolation

These verses contain some of the strongest messages of hope in Jeremiah. Although the present looks dismal, do not despair. Do not give in to your dejection. God cares. A bright future still awaits the people of Israel. The covenant is eternal and a time of renewal will yet come.

Verses 15-17. According to biblical tradition (1 Sam 10:2ff.) Rachel's tomb is near Ramah. Jeremiah evokes the spirit of Rachel, who is the mother of the Joseph (Ephraim) tribes, and therefore by extension, all of Israel. She mourns for her "children" who had been dispersed by the Assyrians over a hundred years earlier in 721. God promises that they shall return. Second Isaiah (Isa 62:10ff.) echoes these words.

Verse 18. "You disciplined me, and I took the discipline." This active/passive image is also seen in Jeremiah 17:14: "Heal me, O LORD, and I shall be healed; save me, and I shall be saved." This verse also refers to Ephraim. In the prophet's mind (as will be seen in Ezekiel 37:15ff.), there is the hope/expectation that the tribes will be reunited. It is possible, indeed probable, that the ten northern tribes have not "disappeared" but are living in scattered cities in Babylonia. When the southern kingdom was exiled to Babylonia, they may have integrated themselves and intermarried with their cousins. Through marriage they become one united people, if not a united kingdom.

Verse 22. "A woman encompasses a man" (NRSV); "a woman courts a man" (NJPS/*TANAKH*); "a female shall compass a man"[7]; "a woman will surround a man" (alternatively, "will go about seeking" or "will protect") (NIV*); "a woman protects a man" (RSV*); "a woman turned into a man" (NEB*). The Hebrew is difficult. In the note to his translation, Bright explains that there have been numerous emendations to this text, but that none commands confidence. He writes: *"female shall compass a man.* This is a literal translation, but the meaning is wholly obscure. . . . Quite possibly we have here

---

7. Bright, *Jeremiah*, 276.

a proverbial saying indicating something that is surprising and difficult to believe, the force of which escapes us."[8]

Verses 29-30. This phrase about parents, children, and guilt is paralleled in Deuteronomy 24:16 and Ezekiel 18:2ff.

Jeremiah 31:31-34, 35-37; The New Covenant

Verses 31-34 contain a unique and special message. It is a very moving passage, offering a vision of great hope for a future time, but as always with the prophets, this is a time that will be in living memory of at least some of those who hear his voice. This is not a description of a far-off event, centuries in the future.

Judaism and Christianity interpret and understand these verses differently (see the section above, "Jeremiah in the Christian Scriptures") Jeremiah's prophecy suggests a time will come when there will be an updated covenant. It is with the same partners, God and Israel. This is the plain meaning of these verses. Verse 34 concludes, for "I will forgive their iniquity, and remember their sin no more."

Verses 35-36. As there is a set order to the world of nature, so only if those laws were abrogated would "Israel would cease to be a nation" for God.

Verse 37. A similar thought is expressed.

---

8. Ibid., 282. Stulman suggests that Israel embraces or "encompasses" her God. Stulman, *Jeremiah*, 270.

8

Ezekiel

Introduction

EZEKIEL SON OF BUZI probably begins his career in Jerusalem. Nonetheless, he addresses most of his prophecies to the exiled community in Babylon. His pronouncements span from the years prior to the destruction of the temple in Jerusalem to some years thereafter (c. 593–71[563?] BCE).

> Ezekiel lived through the greatest crisis in ancient Israel's history: the final destruction of Judah and its capital, Jerusalem; the loss of independence in the promised land, exile of all the leading citizens to Babylonia; and the tearing down of the temple and removal of the House of David from kingship (2 Kings 25; Jeremiah 39–41, 52; Lamentations 1–5; 2 Chronicles 36). It was a double tragedy, for each of the losses just listed had both political and theological ramifications for the people, and not only were their physical lives disrupted but their faith was shaken as well.[1]

Ezekiel is the ninth book in the second section of the Hebrew Bible, the Prophets/*Neviim* (see Introduction: "The Order of the Books of the Bible").

Ezekiel is the third of the Major Prophets. His book follows Isaiah and Jeremiah, and it precedes Hosea. In the Christian Bible, the books of Daniel and then Hosea follow Ezekiel. Daniel is not considered a prophet in the Jewish Bible. The book of Daniel is part of the third section of the Hebrew Bible, *Ketuvim*/Writings.

---

1. Boadt, "Book of Ezekiel," 2:713; see also Block, *Book of Ezekiel*, 1–17.

Geo-Political Background

The historical background for the book of Ezekiel parallels that of his (probably older) contemporary, Jeremiah. King Nebuchadnezzar of Babylonia wreaks havoc in Judah. The best of the Judean/Jerusalem leadership, including craftsmen, warriors, various officials, and sections of the nobility, as well as the temple treasures, are taken to Babylonia in the year 598/597 BCE. The book of Kings describes the scene. "King Jehoiachin of Judah gave himself up to the king of Babylon, himself, his mother, his servants, his officers, and his palace officials. The king of Babylon took him prisoner. . . . [King Nebuchadnezzar] carried away all Jerusalem, all the officials, all the warriors, ten thousand captives, all the artisans and the smiths. . . . He carried away . . . the elite of the land" (2 Kgs 24:12, 14–15). Among those captives is the prophet Ezekiel.

Nebuchadnezzar appoints Jehoiachin's uncle in his place, changing his name to Zedekiah. In 594/593 King Zedekiah joined an anti-Babylonian coalition. This is about the time that Jeremiah fights with those whom he labels "false prophets." This is the group that predicts the imminent fall of Babylon and the return of the exiles (Jer 27–28).

About 589 Judah actually revolts against Babylonia. In 588 Nebuchadnezzar returns. He lays siege to Jerusalem. As is noted earlier in the chapter on Jeremiah, Jerusalem finally falls victim to the siege and famine. It is destroyed in 586.

The Book of Ezekiel

Ezekiel is unique among the Bible's prophets because he is the first one to speak his words to the people after the temple's destruction, as well as to a community outside of the Promised Land. He explains that God's presence also can be known outside of Israel, and that God is present even though what had been thought of as God's earthly abode has been demolished. This marks him as a link between the pre-exilic and the exilic periods.

Early on Ezekiel predicts the destruction of Jerusalem and Judah. He lives to know of the fall of the city and the destruction of the temple. In the remaining years of his prophecies he changes his message from doom to comfort, from devastation to consolation.

In the opening line of the book there is a reference to "the thirtieth year." It is unclear what this means. If it refers to the thirtieth year of his life, then he is born about the same time as the "discovery" of the Deuteronomy scroll during the reign of King Josiah. It may mean that he prophesied for thirty years. In any case, Ezekiel probably grows to maturity during the Josianic reform. He is familiar with the temple and its rituals (see chs. 40–48). He appears to be a priest, or at least from a priestly family (1:3).

Ezekiel is married, yet his wife dies during the siege of Jerusalem. She is called the "delight of [his] . . . eyes." Yet, God tells Ezekiel not to mourn for her. A greater mourning is to come: that for the city, the temple, and the people (24:15ff., 25–27).

Whether Ezekiel remains in Babylon or travels between Babylon and Jerusalem is unknown. It is likely he remains in captivity. Yet, emotionally, psychologically, and spiritually he also feels himself part of the Jerusalem community.

Ezekiel's image of the "valley of dry bones" (ch. 37) is well known. In a different prophecy (ch. 1) he speaks of a strange contraption that has "wheels within wheels."

> Passionateness and a fertile imagination tending to the baroque, shine through his writings. He is the master of the dramatic, representational action. . . . He was famous for his (often lurid) imagery [20:49 (21:5H)]. His actions and his images are more numerous and complex than those of any of his predecessors. As a visionary too he has no peer; indeed he innovated a genre: the transportation-and-tour vision, so common in later apocalypse. It is no wonder that people flocked to his "entertainments" [33:30ff.][2]

Yet the book of Ezekiel contains some of the most difficult chapters to translate that are found in the entire Bible. This applies to both the prose sections and the poetry.

Divisions in the Book of Ezekiel

The book of Ezekiel is

> one of the most highly structured among those of the prophets. It is clearly divided into three major sections that reflect different aspects of Ezekiel's ministry. Chaps. 1–24 contain oracles of judgment against Israel; chaps. 25–32 contain oracles delivered against foreign powers; and chaps. 33–48 contain oracles of salvation on behalf of Israel. In intention, the foreign oracles of 25–32 can be included with 33–48 as words of hope, thus creating two equal halves. While there may be individual units

---

2. Greenberg, "Ezekiel," 1092.

within each of these sections that more naturally belong to one of the other sections, the pattern has been organized for a definite purpose: to show that the prophet preached warning and judgment to the Judeans up until the final catastrophe of 586 B.C.E. when the city fell completely to the Babylonians; and that he preached hope and promise of restoration after that date.

... As it stands, the program of restoration in the second half dominates the order of the whole. The oracles of judgment help Israel understand why God let the city of Jerusalem fall and the old kingdom end for good; the oracles directed to pagan nations serve as a prelude to the establishment of a new kingdom of Israel by announcing punishment on all who oppress God's people; and the oracles of consolation focus on the new order that God will establish for Israel. This last section has two major movements: (1) a promise of a new exodus and conquest of the land in chaps. 33–39; and (2) a new division of the land and rebuilding of the holy city in chaps. 40–48.[3]

Alternatively, the book can be divided into 4 sections:

Ezekiel 1–24   Ezekiel's call; his early prophecies; judgments against Judah and Jerusalem; symbolic acts; leading up to the fall of Jerusalem (c. 593/592–87/586)

Ezekiel 25–32 Denunciation of foreign nations (Ammon, Moab, Edom, Philistia, Tyre, Sidon, and Egypt)

Ezekiel 33–39 The future restoration of Israel

Ezekiel 40–48 The restored temple in Jerusalem with an idealized priestly code

Ezekiel 1–24; Ezekiel's Call; His Early Prophecies; Judgments against Judah and Jerusalem; symbolic Acts; Leading Up to the Fall of Jerusalem

Ezekiel's prophecy is distinctive for several reasons. His use of symbolism is unparalleled. He draws diagrams on a brick to show how Jerusalem will be defeated (4:1ff.) He cuts his beard into three parts. He burns a third. He chops a third. He throws the last third to the wind. All these indicate what will happen to Jerusalem and its citizens: fire, destruction, and dispersal (5:1ff.) In chapter 12, God tells Ezekiel to mimic publically what it means to go into exile. He is to cut a wall in his own house. Then he is to take a

---

3. Boadt, "Book of Ezekiel," 2:711.

backpack of provisions, just as will be the fate of the Jerusalemites when Babylon destroys their capital.

His style of writing is unique among the prophets. He creates elaborate picture stories. Examples include "the allegory of the two eagles in chapter 17, the great mythical cedar tree in chapter 31, or his description of Egypt as the great sea monster Leviathan in chapters 29 and 32. He describes the city of Tyre as a great ship sinking with all its cargo, and compares the two kingdoms of Israel and Judah to two sisters who choose to live as prostitutes (chapters 16 and 23)."[4] In another instance, he depicts Judah as a useless vine. It is barely good for fuel as opposed to the image of a good vine elsewhere in the Bible (Ezek 15:1ff.; Jer 2:21; Hos 10:1; and Ps 80:8, 14 [80:9, 15 H]). Another characteristic of Ezekiel is the use of the term *ben adam*, which in the Christian Scriptures is often a synonym or appellation for Jesus as the "Christ" or Messiah. In the context of this book it is only a phrase meaning "mortal!" or "O Man!"[5]

The first half of the book of Ezekiel mentions his commission from God. It includes condemnations and warnings to the people of Jerusalem. They are living an immoral life. God shall withdraw divine presence from the temple. Ezekiel's symbolic acts and his colorful visions fill this section. The opening three chapters detail Ezekiel's appointment as a prophet. This features the throne chariot vision with fire flashing, the four-faced animals, and the famous whirring wheels within wheels (1:6, 15ff.) God tells Ezekiel that he is to prophesy to rebellious Israel. A scroll is set before him. He is to ingest it, to internalize its message. Its taste is as sweet as honey (3:1–3). Ezekiel performs symbolic actions. He lies on his side for many days. He writes on a brick. He cuts his beard. He acts out the part of a refugee. He berates those prophets who preach peace when there will be no peace (Ezek 13:10; cf. Jer 6:13–14).

Chapter 16 bitterly describes Jerusalem as a faithless wife. She turns to whoredom and lewdness. Ezekiel offers similar images in chapter 23. Ezekiel states clearly that the people have brought upon themselves their own misfortune. The text then suggests that God will punish the people, who are represented by this figure of the errant female. God then is characterized "as an active, rather than passive, perpetrator of gender-based violence." Not only is that true here, but in other sources as well. "Within these verses, God, characterized as male, is regularly threatening, in judgment, to rape, or otherwise sexually abuse, the cities of Israel, Judah, and their neighbors, all characterized as female. . . . Such texts are the ultimate in biblical texts of terror."[6]

---

4. Boadt, *Reading the Old Testament*, 341.
5. As explained in *NOAB* in a note on Ezek 2:1.
6. Magdalene, "Ancient Near Eastern Treaty-Curses," 327. Magdalene refers to

As one scholar rightly points out, "dangers . . . abound for the unsophisticated reader. An overly simplistic reading of the marital metaphor between God and Israel may lead to the conclusion that a proper husband-wife relationship is one of mastery and submission, or that God condones rape as a suitable punishment for female adultery. The text is not only dangerous . . . [but] profoundly disturbing because it sanctions domestic violence and misogyny."[7]

Chapter 18 makes the case that individuals are responsible for their own acts. (See the Text Study at the conclusion of this chapter, "Individual Responsibility.")

Ezekiel 25–32; Denunciation of Foreign Nations (Ammon, Moab, Edom, Philistia, Tyre, Sidon, and Egypt)

Beginning with chapter 25, there are eight chapters filled with a series of denunciations of the seven nations surrounding Judah. Ammon, Moab, Edom, Philistia, Tyre, Sidon, and Egypt all are condemned and denounced in the strongest terms. He predicts that the Babylonians will come to destroy them.

Ezekiel 33–39; The Future Restoration of Israel

These chapters feature an abrupt change of course. They generally center on Israel's restoration. Chapter 33, however, begins with the image of the sentinel whose role is to warn the people to turn from their evil ways. (See the Text Study at the close of this chapter, "The Sentinel.")

Ezekiel's voice of hope is characterized by these lines, "But you, O mountains of Israel, shall shoot out your branches, and yield your fruit to my people Israel; for they will soon come home . . . the towns shall be inhabited and the waste places rebuilt" (36:8, 10).

Chapter 37 divides evenly between the vision of the valley of dry bones and the oracle of the two sticks, envisioning the reunification of Israel and Judah.

Trible's *Texts of Terror*. The texts cited in this essay are Isa 3:17–26; 47:1–4; Jer 13:22–26; Ezek 16:35–39; 23:9–10, 26–29; Hos 2:2–3 (4–5 H), 9–10 (11–12 H); Nah 2:6–7 (7–8 H); 3:5, 13; and Zech 14:2.

7. Kamionkowski, "Gender Reversal in Ezekiel 16," 171. Lapsley echoes these concerns in her thoughtful and disturbing commentary on Ezekiel. She offers context as she analyses Ezekiel's "sexually violent imagery," pointing out that understanding Ezekiel within his time "may yet yield insights of significance to women, and men, of today." Lapsley, "Ezekiel," 283.

Ezekiel 40–48; The Restored Temple in Jerusalem with an Idealized Priestly Code

The final nine chapters of Ezekiel describe his vision of the restored land. They detail with great specificity what the temple and its attendant priesthood will look like.

Ezekiel's Theology

Ezekiel's theology addresses several points:

- God judges human wrongdoing.
- God's presence remains with the people, even in exile.
- God acts for God's own sake.
- Both individuals and the nation are obliged to respond to God.
- A Davidic ruler will arise.
- The temple will be rebuilt, with all its ritual.

God Judges Human Wrongdoing

Ezekiel details the wickedness of the people. He mentions prostitution, child sacrifice, and adultery (16:15–21, 32ff.; 23:11–21.) Jerusalem is called a city of bloodshed (7:23; 22:2–4). Fathers and mothers are humiliated. Orphans and widows are wronged. Sabbaths are profaned. Sexual immorality is rampant (22:6–11).

Ezekiel's concerns include ritual/religious cultic matters as well as moral issues.[8] He condemns idol worship and promises retribution (chs. 6–7). He describes abominations that are going on within the temple. Creeping things, beasts, and fetishes are depicted on an entire wall. Women are worshipping Tammuz, a Babylonian deity. Sun worship has succeeded the worship of God (8:9–10, 14–16). This syncretism starts (or is reintroduced) during the reign of Jehoiakim (609–598 BCE). In the city of Jerusalem degenerate prophets offer false messages.

God seeks someone to protest, to "repair the wall and stand in the breach." No one can be found. God promises that destruction will come. "I have consumed them with the fire of my wrath; I have returned their conduct upon their heads" (22:30–31).

---

8. Newsome, *Hebrew Prophets*, 134.

God's Presence Remains with the People, Even in Exile

Exiled to Babylonia, the refugees from Judah are depressed. Psalm 137 captures well their feelings. "By the rivers of Babylon—there we sat down and there we wept. . . . How could we sing the LORD's song in a foreign land?" (Ps 137:1, 4) Ezekiel responds. God is not limited. God acts through history. There is a future time of hope. The images of the good shepherd, the valley of dry bones resurrected (chs. 34, 37), and the life-giving stream issuing from the restored temple (47:1–12) all convey hope to the exiles.

Underscoring Ezekiel's message is the idea that *God is the God of history*. Jeremiah and Second Isaiah both express this theme. Ezekiel focuses on several nearby nations. He predicts what will happen to them (chs. 25–32). The fact that these prophecies did not come about exactly as Ezekiel suggests is less important than the notion that God is portrayed as the ruler of the entire world.

God Acts for God's Own Sake

God will return many of the exiles. God will do so not alone because of their repentance, but because God *consciously* has chosen to act in this way. Ezekiel explains, "It is not for your sake, O house of Israel, that I am about to act, but for the sake of my holy name . . . the nations shall know that I am the LORD . . . when through you I display my holiness before their eyes" (36:22–23).

Both Individuals and the Nation Are Obliged to Respond to God

Ezekiel's two great messages are "individual responsibility" and "God's desire for human repentance." Ezekiel is not the first prophet to discuss individual guilt. His older contemporary Jeremiah likewise rejects the concept of children and parents being responsible for each other's actions (Jer 31:29–30; cf. Deut 24:16). Nowhere in the Bible "is there as clear an exposition of individualism as that which appears in Ezekiel 18 and 33. . . . Ezekiel answers the implied question of how Yahve can continue His relationship with the Israel which forfeited His benign providence and underwent the terrible destruction at the hands of the Babylonians. The old covenant was collective; the new covenant is individual. . . . The emphatic assertion of individualism and the possibility of repentance" are how God and Israel continue their bond. Yet the notion of individualism should not be overstated. God is going to create a new nation from the exiles. Yet, it is in part because God in effect "declares that He cannot permit Israel to dissolve into nothingness."[9] God will choose among the people and create a new Israel. God uses the metaphor of a shepherd. God says, "I will save my flock. . . . I will judge between sheep and sheep" (Ezek 34:22).

God acts because it is part of the divine plan. God does not act solely because of Israel's merit. God explains that the people will be given a new heart (Ezek 11:17–20; 36:26; cf. Jer 31:31ff.) As the multitude of bones in the valley indicates, this is a *group* restoration, not one of individual acts (Ezek 37:1–14). For Ezekiel there is an important and creative tension between the individual and the nation.

A Davidic Ruler Will Arise

Unlike Second Isaiah, or even First Isaiah, Ezekiel is not a universalist. Ezekiel speaks of a ruler in the Davidic line (37:24ff.; cf. 34:23–24). He envisions a restoration of both parts of the monarchy of Israel-Judah. Ezekiel centers his message on his own people. He does not specifically deny a future for the other nations; he just is not particularly concerned with them. He does expect them to recognize that God is triumphant in the entire world. God is bringing Israel back to the land. This is not because of Israel's repentance, but in order to glorify God's own name and fame. When "I have brought them back from the peoples and gathered them from their enemies' lands, and through them have displayed my holiness in the sight of many nations. Then they shall know that I am the LORD their God because I sent them into exile among the nations, and then gathered them into their own land. I will leave none of them behind" (39:27–28).

The Temple Will Be Rebuilt, with All Its Ritual

The restoration of the Jerusalem temple and specific details about the temple, the cult, and its personnel form the major theme of the final nine chapters of Ezekiel (chs. 40–48).

Ezekiel in the Christian Scriptures

The image of the divine presence in Ezekiel provides much material for the writer of the book of Revelation.[10] He depicts different stones and

---

9. Sandmel, *Hebrew Scriptures*, 162, 163; see also Greenberg, *Ezekiel 21–37*, 677–80.

10. Boxall, "Exile, Prophet, Visionary"; see also Buitenwerf, "Gog and Magog Tradition," 166.

multi-faced, multi-winged animals (Rev 4:1–8; Ezek 1:4ff., 26–28.) Revelation describes Jerusalem and its dimensions, as is true in the book of Ezekiel (Rev 21:9ff.; Ezek 40:2ff.; 48:30–35).

Ezekiel describes Gog as a person, and Magog as a country. In Revelation Gog and Magog are two persons. In both instances, these figures face defeat by God (Rev 20:7–10; Ezek 38–39).

The breath of God's spirit and God's sprinkling clean water find echoes in the Gospel of John (John 3:1–8; Ezek 37; 36:25). There are connections between the vine image in John's Gospel and Ezekiel's use of that image (John 15; Ezek 19:10–14).

While the "Gospel of John and the Revelation are most directly akin to" Ezekiel, it is likewise clear that "Jesus was well acquainted with the book of Ezekiel, from which he drew expressions to frame the new picture of Christian faith."[11] Ezekiel's good shepherd is echoed by Matthew, Luke, and John (Matt 18:12–14; Luke 15:3–7; John 10:2–18; Ezek 34:11ff.)

Ezekiel criticizes the people's rebelliousness. He castigates those who "have eyes to see but do not see, who have ears to hear but do not hear." Jesus in Mark's Gospel asks, "Do you have eyes, and fail to see? Do you have ears, and fail to hear?" (Mark 8:18; Ezek 12:2; cf. Jer 5:21).

Mark describes the coming of the Son of Man. "But in those days, after that suffering, the sun will be darkened, and the moon will not give its light, and the stars will be falling from heaven, and the powers in the heaven will be shaken." This reflects Ezekiel's words, "I will cover the heavens, and make their stars dark; I will cover the sun with a cloud, and the moon shall not give its light. All the shining lights of the heavens I will darken above you, and put darkness on your land, says the Lord GOD" (Mark 13:24–25; Ezek 32:7–8).

Ezekiel in Rabbinic Literature

Ezekiel has had a mixed reaction within Jewish thought. Ezekiel's prophecies nearly fail to enter into the Jewish canon (the "officially recognized" scriptures). Ezekiel's description of the temple and its activities is at such variance with past tradition as described in the Torah that some ancient rabbis vote against its acceptance. According to the Talmud, only through the diligent efforts of Hananiah son of Hezekiah (c. 50 CE) are the contradictory passages reconciled. Medieval exegetes explain that Ezekiel's references are for a future messianic time. Furthermore, Ezekiel's descriptions are patently ignored when the second temple is built and functioning (*Babylonian Talmud Shabbat* 13b).

11. Howie, "Ezekiel," 212.

Ezekiel is not very sophisticated. Ezekiel and Isaiah both describe the heavenly throne (Ezek 1:4–28; Isa 6:1ff.) Ezekiel's description is far more elaborate. These discrepancies are dismissed by explaining that, compared to Isaiah, Ezekiel is unsophisticated. Therefore, he is that much more in awe than Isaiah, the urbane city dweller (*Babylonian Talmud Hagigah* 13b).

God's glory continues. God shows Ezekiel the divine chariot and the glory of God. This is to prove that even though Israel has been banished, God's own glory is not diminished. Even though the temple and temple ritual of praise no longer exist, the celestial beings continue to worship and praise God as before! (*Midrash Leviticus Rabbah* 2.8).

Ezekiel's mystical chariot. The "chariot" described in Ezekiel's first chapter becomes a code word for certain mystical studies (the *Ma'aseh Merkavah*) that are restricted by the rabbis (*Babylonian Talmud Hagigah* 11b).

Provides answers for Shadrach, Meshach, and Abednego. Hananiah, Mishael, and Azariah (Shadrach, Meshach, and Abednego) ask Daniel if they should bow before Nebuchadnezzar's fiery statue. Daniel refers them to Ezekiel for an answer (*Midrash Song of Songs Rabbah* 7.8.1).

Ezekiel and the revival of the dead. Ezekiel's great miracle of prophesying and bringing about the revival of the dead (ch. 37) takes place on a Sabbath that is also the Day of Atonement. The image built by Nebuchadnezzar is toppled by a divine wind (the Divine Spirit), which then enters the dry bones and gives them life (*Midrash Song of Songs Rabbah* 7.9.1).

Whose bones? King Nebuchadnezzar sees that the fire does not destroy the three young men. Then the Babylonian king turns to all those Jews who have bowed down. He berates them. Not only are you so corrupt as to destroy your own homeland, now you bring evil to my country. You do not believe in the might of your God. You are content to worship an idol. Consequently, Nebuchadnezzar orders the 600,000 exiles slain. Twenty years pass. Ezekiel comes to the place where they are buried. He witnesses the "miracle" of their resurrection (ch. 37). Ezekiel is chastised for his lack of full faith. The newly resurrected also have doubts about their return to Israel (*Pirke de Rabbi Eliezer*, ch. 33).

Ezekiel praised. Ezekiel receives credit for contradicting Moses' statement that God visits the sins of the parents onto the children. Ezekiel explains, "The person who sins shall die" (Exod 34:7; Ezek 18:4) (*Babylonian Talmud Makkot* 24a).

God encourages repentance, but not indefinitely. "See how lovely repentance (rt.: ShVB) is! The Holy One said (in Mal. 3:7): RETURN (rt.: ShVB) UNTO

ME AND I WILL RETURN (rt.: ShVB) UNTO YOU. For, if there are some sins on one's hand and that person returns to the Holy One, he credits him as if he had not sinned. Thus it is stated (in Ezek. 18:22) : <NOT> ANY OF HIS SINS WHICH HE COMMITTED <SHALL BE REMEMBERED AGAINST HIM>. . . . But, when the Holy One has warned him a first time, and a second and a third, without him repenting, he exacts punishments from him, as stated (in Job 33:29): BEHOLD, GOD DOES ALL THESE THINGS <TWO OR THREE TIMES TO A PERSON>" (*Midrash Tanhuma, Genesis*, vol. 1, *Wayyera* 4.16, Gen 19:24ff., part I[12]).

Text Study

Ezekiel 18:1–32 (cf. 33:1–20; 3:16–21); Individual Responsibility

Chapter 18 sets out Ezekiel's theology/teaching of individual responsibility. Ezekiel does not "invent" this concept. He is the prophet who takes it to its greatest development (see Jer 31:29–30; Deut 24:16).

Verses 1–3. The "sour grapes" proverb and its rejection.

Verse 4. Different translations suggest variant words: "life" (NRSV, NAB, NJPS/*TANAKH*) or "soul" (NEB, NIV, RSV), i.e., the living being, the actual person.

Verses 5–9. Laws of correct living. The fifteen laws described here have a close affinity to Pentateuchal law. They govern relationships between God and humans. They mention idolatry as well as laws that focus on human interaction, sexual morality, cleanliness (menstruation), business dealings, and matters of judgment. These laws reflect a sure knowledge of the Ten Commandments, the Holiness Code (Lev 17–26), and the Book of the Covenant (Exod 20:22—23:33 [20:19—23:33 H]).

Verses 10–19. Ezekiel considers three generations. A righteous person has a violent, wicked child. The violent, wicked child alone shall die. Next, this violent, wicked child has a righteous child (i.e., the grandchild of the righteous person). The violent, wicked parent shall die; the righteous child shall live. There are some variations on the sins, and they are not in the exact order as in verses 5–9.

Verse 20. "The person who sins shall die." This verse summarizes the aforementioned relational non-responsibilities.

---

12. See this title in the bibliography.

Verses 21-24. Ezekiel takes morality and responsibility a quantum leap forward. Righteousness spurned brings punishments, just as wickedness rejected brings reward.

Verses 25-29. Israel questions God's justice and God repeats the notions just enunciated.

Verse 30. God explains that there will be *individual* judgment. Repentance again is stressed.

Verses 31-32. Ezekiel calls for a new heart and new spirit (see a similar comment in Jer 31:31-34, and God's statement in Ezek 11:17-20 and 36:26). God *is* placing a new heart in the people. Note in verse 32 that God says explicitly, "I have no pleasure in the death of anyone. . . . Turn, then, and live!" (cf. v. 23).

Ezekiel 33:1-20 ; The Sentinel

Verses 7-9. This, as in 3:16-21, refers to the sentinel who at least needs to give warning. Once the warning is given, the guard's duty is discharged.

Verses 10-11. These verses may sound similar to 18:29-30, but there is a *radical* difference. Here (in 33:10) Israel admits it is wrong. It voices its desire to change. "Our transgressions and our sins weigh upon us . . . how then can we live?" Then God repeats the call for repentance that the people may live.

9

Hosea

Introduction

HOSEA PROPHESIES ABOUT 745–25 BCE. He directs his words to the northern kingdom of Israel. As with several other prophets, Hosea often uses a common alternative name for Israel, namely Ephraim. The southern kingdom of Judah also concerns Hosea. He often refers to it although he does not mention Jerusalem by name (5:12, 13, 14; 6:4). Hosea's prophecies occur at the same time that Isaiah and Micah address the southern kingdom of Judah.

Hosea is the tenth book of the "second section" of the Hebrew Bible, the Prophets/*Neviim* (see Introduction: "The Order of the Books of the Bible"). The book of Hosea follows Ezekiel, and precedes Joel. In Christian Bibles, Daniel, and then Hosea follow Ezekiel.

Hosea is the first of the twelve minor prophets. The term "minor" refers to the fact that there is less material collected and preserved in the Bible about these twelve prophets than the major prophets Isaiah, Jeremiah, and Ezekiel. In the ancient world, "the twelve" often were classified as one book.

Geo-Political Background

The background to Hosea's pronouncements is the deteriorating political condition of Israel. Hosea follows the time of Amos and he speaks before the final destruction of the northern kingdom by the Assyrians under Sargon II in 722/721. Jeroboam II (d. 746) rules for four decades. This time of relative peace and prosperity would not be seen soon again. A succession of kings and assassinations fills the period ahead. Pekah ascends to the throne through bloodshed. He rules for five years (737–32). He is the same Pekah son of Remaliah who allies with King Rezin of Aram against the kingdom of Judah. Isaiah mentions them in connection with the Syro-Ephraimitic War (c. 735–32) and the siege of Jerusalem at the time of King Ahaz (Isa 7:1ff., cf. 2 Kgs 15:25ff.; 2 Chr 28:1–8.) As noted in the chapter on Isaiah, King Ahaz of Judah defies Isaiah and calls on King Tiglath Pileser III of Assyria. It would be only a matter of time before the fall of the northern kingdom.

Hosea's Message

Hosea's pronouncements complement those of his older colleague Amos.[1] Some years earlier Amos prophesies and preaches in Israel/Ephraim. Amos lashes out at specific abuses in society. He is appalled at the wide chasm between the rich and the poor, the perversion of the justice system, sexual immorality, gluttony, and a corrupt priesthood, to name just some of his concerns. Yet Amos rarely deals with matters of ritual worship. By way of contrast, in Hosea Israel's widespread worship of the pagan god Baal is both a fact and a symbol of its disloyalty to God.

Hosea's message is that Israel is turning from fidelity to God to the false worship of Baal. In chapter 4 Hosea succinctly observes that in Israel many people "sacrifice on the tops of the mountains, and make offerings upon the hills, under oak, poplar, and terebinth, because their shade is good. Therefore your daughters play the whore, and your daughters-in-law commit adultery" (v. 13).

> For Hosea, "loyalty" [*hesed*] marked the covenant of mutuality. Both covenant partners were expected to demonstrate this quality. There was inequality. YHWH's reliability was likened to the predictability of dawn and the spring rain (6:1–3). Israel's loyalty, on the other hand, was as fleeting as the morning cloud and the dew that evaporates all too quickly (6:4). She must repent and sow righteousness in order to reap the fruits of [*hesed*] (10:12). The people must keep loyalty and justice (12:7) [English 12:6]. Israel will, indeed, be punished for the abandonment of

---

1. "The date of Hosea cannot be set with certainty, but the material in the book suggests at least the period from the end of Jeroboam's reign to the fall of Samaria, approximately 752–21 B.C.E. This makes Hosea a contemporary of Amos. . . . When Amos prophesied at Bethel, he was confronted by Amaziah, the royal priest at the national sanctuary (Amos 7:10-17). Since Hosea was a contemporary of Amos, [it is possible] . . . that Amaziah was the wicked priest against whom Hosea prophesied (4:4; cf. Amos 7:10–12)." Seow, "Book of Hosea," 3:293.

her covenant responsibilities. But beyond judgment there is hope. Eventually, God will take Israel back as bride in righteousness, justice, mercy, faithfulness, and loyalty, and Israel will truly know YHWH (2:21-22—[English 2:19-20]).[2]

Infidelity has brought about foreign entanglements, and with them foreign religious cults. No recourse exists but punishment. This means exile from the land. "They shall not remain in the land of the LORD; but Ephraim shall return to Egypt, and in Assyria they shall eat unclean food" (9:3). Chastisement will come, not for a lack of God's compassion, but because Israel deserves and needs this rebuke. "For they sow the wind, and they shall reap the whirlwind" (8:7). As a parent laments a wayward child, and as a spouse laments a faithless partner, so does God grieve over this turn of events (11:1ff.; 2:2ff. [2:4ff. H]).

Hosea nonetheless concludes with a message of optimism and hopefulness. Following punishment and exile, Israel will repent, and eventually achieve reconciliation (14:1ff. [14:2ff. H]). The restoration, however, will take on a new aspect. God will set the covenant in such a way that Israel will remain faithful forever.

In the book of Hosea, promiscuity and idolatry are interchangeable. As the term "prostitute" sometimes means an actual person, and sometimes it refers to political promiscuity, so Hosea shifts between domestic family failure and national failures in the public spheres of worship and political/foreign relations.

The Book of Hosea

Divisions in the Book of Hosea

Hosea 1-3	Biographical and autobiographical information
Hosea 4-13	Pronouncements and prophecies
Hosea 14	Call for repentance; a message of restoration

Hosea 1-3; Biographical and Autobiographical Information

Chapters 1-2 describe in the third person God's instructions to Hosea. Go marry a prostitute, Gomer daughter of Diblaim, and conceive children (1:2-3). It also lists their offspring and their symbolic names. Chapter 3,

---

2. Ibid., 3:296.

which is spoken in the first person, focuses on Hosea marrying a faithless wife. Are we to understand these chapters literally, or is this metaphoric or symbolic language? See sections below on "Metaphoric Language in Hosea" and "Hosea and Gomer."

Hosea 4–13; Pronouncements and Prophecies

These chapters contain a collection of Hosea's prophecies, spoken over several years. Later his words were set down and arranged in some kind of order. Chapters 4–13 detail Israel's perfidy, betrayal, and disloyalty to God and to one another. During the years of prosperity the people have become religiously and morally complacent. The people are insincere. God says to Israel, "Your love is like a morning cloud, like the dew that goes away early" (6:4). What God wants is righteousness, not empty rites (Hos 6:6; cf. Isa 1:13–14; Amos 5:21–24; Mic 6:6–8). (See the Text Study at the conclusion of this chapter, "Accusations.")

God has loved Israel from her youth. Yet, she continually rebels. Israel shall know deserved punishment. Yet, God will not, cannot forget the people. Often Hosea uses the language of a law court: contending, accusing, indicting. For example, he speaks of an "indictment" (or "lawsuit") against the people (4:1; 12:2 [12:3 H]). He uses words like "contend" and "accuse" (4:4), "judgment" (NJPS "right conduct," 5:1), and he warns of the "day of punishment" (5:9; 9:7).

Hosea addresses the people at large (4:12; 7:13ff.; 9:1ff.); without mentioning a specific ruler's name, he mentions the monarchy (7:5; 10:7, 15), priests (5:1; 6:9), and prophets (4:5). While Hosea's words are mainly directed at the northern kingdom of Israel (often termed Ephraim, or by its capital city, Samaria), he also has words of accusation against the southern kingdom of Judah, whose citizenry likewise are faithless in their devotion to God (5:14; 6:11; 12:2 [12:3 H]).

Hosea 14; Call for Repentance; a Message of Restoration

In chapter 14, Hosea concludes on a note of return, reconciliation, and repentance. (See the Text Study section at the conclusion of this chapter, "A Message of Hope.")

Metaphoric Language in Hosea

Hosea is a poet of extraordinary ability. He suggests a variety of images both for God and for Israel. The metaphor of God-as-husband dominates the book. Israel as wanton wife/adulteress/promiscuous spouse/prostitute fills the first three chapters. Following the biographical information about the name of the prophet and the period of his prophecy comes Hosea's "commission" to obtain a prostitute as a wife. Hosea's life serves as a personal parallel to what is going on in Israel, for the land itself has been unfaithful to God (1:2).

Chapter 2 continues the image of God/husband and Israel/faithless wife. In mid-chapter is the wonderful wordplay that at the future time of the eternal covenant Israel will call God "my husband" (*Ishi*) and no longer "my master" (*Baali*). The word *Baali* has a double meaning. It can translate as "my master," that is, the patron of the prostitute. At the same time it can mean "my [god is] Baal" (2:16 [2:18 H]). This image of adulterous/promiscuous Israel is found in later chapters as well (6:10; 7:4; 9:1 et al.) As mentioned earlier, in the book of Hosea the term "prostitute" refers on occasions to an actual person and on other occasions to political promiscuity. (See the Text Study at the conclusion of this chapter, "An Unfaithful Spouse.")

Hosea and Gomer's children, following a longstanding biblical tradition, have symbolic names. Their first child is a son, *Jezreel*. Next a daughter is born, *Lo-ruhamah*. Finally comes a third child, another son, *Lo-ammi*. Most literally, *Jezreel* refers specifically to the Valley of Jezreel in Israel. In this context, however, it means the whole of the northern kingdom. As the text explains, God is going to put an end to the Israelite monarchy. *Lo-ruhamah* means "not pitied," for God will no longer have pity on the house of Israel to forgive them. Finally, *Lo-ammi* means literally "not my people," for God says, no longer are you my people, and no longer am I your God (1:4–9).

Hosea uses many metaphoric or symbolic examples drawn from nature. One source is flora (grapes, fig trees, vines, thorns and thistles, lily, olive, cypress—9:10; 10:1; 10:8; 14:5–6, 8 [14:6–7, 9 H]). A second source is fauna (heifer, wild ass, a lion, birds, leopard and bear—4:16; 8:9; 11:10–11; 13:7–8). Hosea also uses examples drawn from natural occurrences (dawn, rain, cloud, and dew—6:3–4).

Hosea and Gomer

A central metaphor in Hosea is Israel-as-God's-faithless-spouse. The prophet's wife, Gomer, cuckolds him, just as Israel abandons God for idol worship and immorality. The received text of Hosea casts Israel as an errant wife.

Consequently, "Hosea will always be a disturbing text for feminist readers because of its patriarchal presumptions."³ Yet, these images and metaphors are not *an attack on women.*⁴ *Rather, Hosea condemns and censures the people of his time. Hosea criticizes men as much as he criticizes women. Hosea's concern is generic faithlessness.*⁵ *Hosea's hope is for a time of reconciliation. "Return, O Israel, to the LORD your God, for you have stumbled because of your iniquity. . . . I will heal their disloyalty; I will love them freely, for my anger has turned from them" (14:1, 4 [14:2, 5 H]).*

One of the mysteries of the book of Hosea surrounds the identity of Hosea's spouse. Is Gomer, Hosea's wife, who is mentioned in chapter 1, the same person as the prostitute in chapter 3? Chapters 1 and 2 are biographical accounts. Chapter 3 is autobiographical. Is chapter 3 authentic Hosea, and does it repeat material from chapter 1 or not? Clearly, the "prophet's marriage to a promiscuous woman becomes an act symbolizing that 'the land fornicates away from YHWH.'"⁶

Gomer is labeled as

> a "wife of harlotry," [RSV; "wife of whoredom" NRSV, NJPS/TANAKH; "an adulterous wife" NIV; "a harlot wife" NAB]; but not because she is a prostitute; she is never labeled a *zonah*, the technical term for a prostitute. Rather, she is a "woman/wife of harlotry" (*'eshet zenunim*) [Hos 1:2] because she is habitually promiscuous. Her adulterous acts are evaluated pejoratively as being "*like* a harlot," although she is not a prostitute by profession. Instead of "wife of harlotry," a more accurate translation would be "wife of promiscuity" (or "promiscuous wife"), which avoids identifying Gomer as a prostitute. Similarly to "play the harlot" is more correctly rendered "to be promiscuous."⁷

---

3. Keefe, "Female Body, the Body Politic," 71. Keefe makes a very good case for this misreading of the text where "male is to God as female is to sinful humanity."

4. The same attributes that "women are rebellious, unfaithful and liable to turn against their husbands . . . [later] are ascribed to a male Israel. Neither, as some assume, does the text give a husband permission to mistreat his wife under the guise of justifiably punishing her for misdemeanors." Morrell and Kroeger, "Hosea," 435.

5. Hosea's intent is to address generic religious unfaithfulness. Nonetheless, as Fontaine makes clear, "classical commentators . . . displayed an almost prurient interest in Hosea's marital partner . . . for many of the male interpreters of Hosea, Gomer's harlotry was a 'a done deal', despite the poor quality of the 'evidence'; no 'hermeneutics of suspicion' troubled the outlook of the traditional commentaries." Fontaine, "Response to 'Hosea,'" 61–62.

6. Yee, "Hosea," 304. Dearman regards the image as "metaphorical." Dearman, *Book of Hosea*, 85; see 80–100, 363–68.

7. Yee, "Hosea," 301; see also Setel, "Prophets and Pornography." "The woman is not described as a *zona*, although most commentators speak inaccurately of Hosea's marriage to a harlot." Bird, "To Play the Harlot," 80.

Hosea in the Christian Scriptures

At one point, Matthew explains that Joseph and Mary go to Egypt to avoid Herod (Matt 2:14–15). This reference to an Egyptian sojourn, found only in Matthew's Gospel, substantiates the prophetic words, "When Israel was a child . . . out of Egypt I called my son" (11:1).

Later Matthew's Jesus, in a dispute with the Pharisees, quotes the words that God desires "mercy, not sacrifice" (Matt 9:13; 12:7; cf. Hos 6:6).

At the conclusion of the Gospel of Luke, it states "that the Messiah is to suffer and to rise from the dead on the third day" (Luke 24:46; cf. 1 Cor 15:4). This idea is based on a line in Hosea: "After two days he will revive us; on the third day he will raise us up" (Hos 6:2; see the section "Hosea in Rabbinic Literature" below.)

Paul refers to Hosea by name when he speaks about the symbolic names of the prophet's children, *Lo-ammi*, "not my people," and *Lo-ruhamah*, "not beloved" (Rom 9:25–26; cf. Hos 1:6-8). The author of the Epistle 1 Peter likewise refers to Hosea's children (1 Pet 2:10).

Corinthians features the saying, "Where, O death, is your victory? Where, O death, is your sting?" This is based on Hosea's comment, "O Death, where are your plagues? O Sheol, where is your destruction?" (1 Cor 15:55; Hos 13:14).

Luke contains the words, "Then they will begin to say to the mountains, 'Fall on us'; and to the hills, 'Cover us'" (Luke 23:30). Although the images are reversed, they are based on Hosea 10:8.

Hosea in Rabbinic Literature

Momentary anger. God's anger with Israel is temporary. In human terms, a royal couple has an altercation. One makes a threat about divorce. Some time later that same person orders a present for their spouse. Patently, the anger was but momentary (*Midrash Numbers Rabbah* 2.15).

Whose children are they? Hosea is faulted for not debating with God, for not defending Israel. When God tells Hosea, "Your children have sinned," Hosea should have said, "They are *your children*, the descendants of Abraham, Isaac, and Jacob."

Hosea does not argue but rather says to God, "The whole world is yours, exchange them for someone else." Consequently, God decides to see what Hosea would do under similar circumstances. God says to Hosea "Marry a prostitute and have children." Then God tells Hosea to send them away. God reasons, "If he does so, then I shall send Israel away."

Hosea explains that he cannot bear to send them away. God then "teaches" Hosea, "If you cannot bear to send them away and you do not even know if they are your own, how could I bear to separate myself from Israel, the children of Abraham, Isaac, and Jacob?" Hosea then prays and asks for forgiveness. God replies, "Pray for Israel, seeing that because of you I have decreed three decrees against them." Hosea prays, and the three decrees are annulled (*Babylonian Talmud Pesahim* 87 a–b).

Canceling the three decrees. The medieval commentator Rashi explains that later verses in Hosea cancel out the negative decrees associated with the names of Hosea and Gomer's children.[8]

Jezreel is the firstborn child. The secondary meaning of Jezreel (*Zera-el*, lit. "God sows," but metaphorically God "scatters" seed) is canceled by the later line, "The people of Judah and the people of Israel shall be gathered together . . . they shall take possession of the land . . . great shall be the day of Jezreel" (1:11 [2:2 H]).

Lo-ruḥamah ("not pitied") is Hosea and Gomer's second child. The word "pity" (*riḥamti*) in the line "I will have pity on *Lo-ruḥamah*" cancels the negative quality of the earlier decree (2:23 [2:25 H]).

Lo-ammi ("You are not my people") is their third child. The statement "You are my people" (*ammi atah*) cancels out the negative statement made earlier (2:23 [2:25 H]).

Hosea in the synagogue calendar. In the synagogue's liturgical lectionary of readings, Hosea 14:1–9 (14:2–10 H) is quoted along with Micah 7:18–20 and Joel 2:15–17 on the Sabbath of Repentance, between Rosh Hashanah and Yom Kippur.

Hosea in the daily prayer services. The famous "betrothal" verses of Hosea 2:19–20 (2:21–22 H) are recited when putting on *tefillin* (phylacteries). These *tefillin*/phylacteries are mentioned in Deuteronomy 6:8 ("Bind them as a sign on your hand, fix them as an emblem on your forehead.").[9]

Prayer and repentance. Hosea is the first prophet to teach people how to pray and repent (*Pesikta Rabbati, Piska* 44.5; *Midrash Genesis Rabbah* 84.19).

Repentance is always possible. Repentance is likened to the sea. As the sea is always open to all, so the gates of repentance are always open to

---

8. Montefiore and Loewe, *Rabbinic Anthology*, 244 n. 1; Rashi to Hos 2:2, 24, 25 and similar thoughts in *Pesikta Rabbati, Piska*, 44.2.

9. Phylacteries are mentioned in Matt 23:5. See Wilson's statements in *Our Father Abraham*, 117.

all. ... Therefore Hosea, admonishing Israel, says to them, *Return O Israel* (14:1 [14:2 H]) (*Pesikta de-Rab Kahana, Piska* 24.2).[10]

Healing will take place in the World to Come. Even though God brings deserved punishment, healing will follow in the World to Come. "Come, let us return to the LORD ... he has struck down, and he will bind us up. After two days he will revive us; on the third day he will raise us up" (6:1–2). "The first of the days the verse refers to is life in this world; the second of the days is life in the time of the Messiah. ... The 'third day' [refers] to life in the world-to-come" (*Tanna Debe Eliyyahu*, ch. [5] 6, p. 29, [67]).

Study, good deeds, and charity continue forever. A person should not say, I have learned Torah and Mishnah today; tomorrow I need not learn that. Nor should one say, I have done good deeds today; I need not tomorrow. Likewise, charity is ongoing. Keep in mind that one does these deeds to honor God, as it is said, "Let us press on to know the LORD" (6:3) (*Tanna Debe Eliyyahu*, ch. 13 [*Eliyyahu Zuta*], p. 195 [416]).

Text Study

Hosea 2:2–6, 13–20 (2:4–8, 15–22 H); An Unfaithful Spouse

Verse 2 (4 H). "Plead with your mother." Other translations include "Rebuke your mother," "Argue with your mother," and "Accuse your mother." On the face of it, Hosea is addressing his children, yet on another level it is God who is speaking. The word for "plead/rebuke/argue/accuse" (Hebrew: *riv*) reflects an angry quarrel, such as in a law court.

"[S]he is not my wife, and I am not her husband." This statement will be reconciled at verse 16 [18 H], but here God rejects unfaithful Israel. The putting away from face and breasts refers to some kind of objects, marks, or emblems indicating harlotry (see Gen 38:15 with Tamar and Judah; Jer 4:30; Ezek 23:40).

Verses 4–5 (6–7 H). The children mentioned share the punishment, but the primary accusation is aimed at the wife.

Verse 6 (8 H]). To "hedge up her way" and "build a wall against her." It is difficult to know what these terms mean. Among the possibilities is that the husband is fencing her in so that she cannot go out to find her lovers, or that he is locking her out so that she cannot return.

---

10. The actual *Piska* is considerably more complex. It is condensed here it to show the direct connection to Hosea.

Israel is the adulterous wife, a figure even worse than the paid prostitute, for she seeks amorous affairs.

Verse 13 (15 H). "Baals" or "Baalim." Here for the first time Hosea specifically links up Baal worship with Israel.

Verses 14–15 (16–17 H). These verses echo the exodus ("I will . . . bring her into the wilderness, and speak tenderly to her") and specifically mentions Egypt. Hosea recalls the long covenantal relationship between God and Israel. I will "speak tenderly" (lit. "on her heart"). The "heart" (i.e., mind) is an important image in Hebrew thought. Jeremiah and Ezekiel both speak of new hearts/ relationships (Jer 31:33; Ezek 36:26).

Verse 16 (18 H). "My husband; My Baal"; *Ishi/Baali*; "husband"/"master." (see the section on "Metaphoric Language in Hosea" earlier in this chapter).

Verse 18 (20 H). The animals mentioned here are reminiscent of Genesis 1. This is a time of total peace in field, sky, and sea. This presumably is only in Israel, not the whole world. There are three animals and three aspects of conflict mentioned, which might connect to Hosea and Gomer's three children—*Jezreel*, *Lo-ruhamah*, and *Lo-ammi*. There is a balance between God's creations (the animals), humankind's destructive creations (weapons), and humankind's peaceful creations (children)—which will "lie down in safety." This likewise is a poetic "threefold" introduction to the three "espousals" in verses 19–20 921–22 H).

Verses 19–20 (2:21–22 H). These verses epitomize the special relationship that will exist between Israel and God. "I will take you for my wife forever; I will take you for my wife in righteousness and in justice, in steadfast love, and in mercy. I will take you for my wife in faithfulness; and you shall know the LORD."

This passage contains a cluster of concepts that describe the ideal bond between Israel-the-people and God. Take you for my wife/espouse (*erus*), righteousness (*tzedek*), justice (*mishpat*), steadfast love/goodness (*hesed*), mercy/compassion (*rahamim*), faithfulness (*emunah*), and knowledge of/ devotion to God (*da'at elohim*).[11]

The image of Israel ever being God's people in unbreakable relationship[12] is taken up by Jeremiah in the "new covenant" section (Jer 31:31–34) and by Ezekiel in his "heart" passages (Ezek 11:19–20; 36:26–28).

---

11. Newsome, *Hebrew Prophets*, 40–41.
12. Ginsberg, "Hosea," 1011; Mays, *Hosea*, 14f.

Hosea 4:1–3; Accusations

Verse 1. In this indictment, Hosea cites the lack of faithfulness, loyalty, and knowledge of God. Yet, these are some of the same qualities that God promises will be part of the eventual divine-human reconciliation (cf. 2:19-20 [2:21-22 H]).

Verse 2. In these verses, Hosea reflects directly the language of the Ten Commandments. Lying, murder, stealing, and adultery use the same verb forms as the Ten Commandments.

Hosea 14; A Message of Hope

Verses 1-2 (2-3 H). These verses invite Israel to return. On one level, there is a sense of Israel-the-promiscuous-wife (chs. 1-3) returning to her husband. The issue, however, is not gender-based. This is a statement to Israel-the-rebellious-child, calling upon Israel to return to God. In the opening words of chapter 11 God says, "When Israel was a child, I loved *him*, and out of Egypt I called him *my son*." In chapter 5 Hosea speaks about Israel/Ephraim using male pronouns. "Israel's pride testifies against *him*; Ephraim stumbles in *his* guilt" (5:5).

Verse 4 (5 H). God speaks of healing, as in an earlier chapter God speaks of healing Ephraim in his infancy (11:3).

Verses 5-7 (6-8 H). God promises a luxuriant and fruitful future. God will be like dew for Israel. Note the contrast to the earlier image of evaporating dew (6:4). Israel will blossom, its shoots shall spread out, and they shall flourish like a garden, blossom like a vine. Note the contrast to the earlier statement that Ephraim shall be a desolation (5:9; cf. 5:12).

Verse 9 (10 H). Hosea concludes on a note similar to Proverbs (cf. Prov 4:11-12) that the ways of God are right, and that the upright walk in them.

10

Joel

Introduction

OTHER THAN LISTING HIS father as Pethuel, nothing is known about Joel—as a prophet, as a man, where, or in which era he lived. Although some scholars suggest an even earlier date, many place him in the Persian period, somewhere between the closing decades of the sixth century and the end of the fifth, or even later (c. 520–c. 350 BCE.)

Joel is the eleventh book of the second section of the Hebrew Bible, the Prophets/*Neviim* (see Introduction: "The Order of the Books of the Bible").

Aside from the reference to Joel in the opening line, his name does not appear again in this book. Further, there are no references to this prophet, or his father, anywhere else in the Bible. Although he mentions generic elders and priests, Joel does not formally name any of his contemporaries, neither rulers nor prominent leaders. Consequently, aside from noting that the temple has been rebuilt, it is impossible to describe the geo-political background for this prophet.

Two of the major themes in Joel are the locust plague and the terrible coming of the Day of the LORD.

The Book of Joel

Divisions in the Book of Joel

Joel 1:1—2:27 (chs. 1-2 H)	The present: A swarm of locusts devours the land. They are accompanied by a devastating drought
Joel 2:28—3:21 (3:1—4:21 H)	The future: The Day of the LORD is coming. God's spirit is overwhelming. There is judgment but also great relief from the former calamities.

Given these divergent time frames, scholars question whether Joel is the writing of one person or two different authors, although most favor one person.

In the Hebrew Bible Joel has four chapters, as it does in the Roman Catholic Bible. The Protestant Bible conflate chapters 2 and 3 into one chapter.[1]

Joel's literary ability is remarkable. He uses vivid, concrete examples with similes and metaphors. (See the Text Study at the conclusion of this chapter, "Images and Metaphors.") Assuming a later-sixth/early-fifth-century date, Joel shows familiarity with his prophetic predecessors, Amos, Zephaniah, Ezekiel, Second Isaiah, and Obadiah. He mimics a phrase from the Hebrew of Obadiah 1:17 in 2:32 (3:5 H). Joel consciously intertwines many past prophetic images into his own oracles.[2]

Joel 1:1—2:27 (chs. 1-2 H); The Present: A Swarm of Locusts Devours the Land. They Are Accompanied by a Devastating Drought.

A relentless onslaught composed of ravaging armies of locusts and other insects dominates the opening verses. Chapter 1 explains that what little the first wave leaves untouched, the next group wipes clean. Its "teeth are lions' teeth, and it has the fangs of a lioness. It has laid waste my vines, and splintered my fig trees; it has stripped off their bark and thrown it down" (1:6-7). There is nothing left to harvest. The priests cry out that the "day of the LORD" is coming (1:15). In chapter 2, tension mounts as the locusts enter the cities. No place is safe. They climb the walls. They enter the windows like thieves. They dash about all over the city. The very sun and moon seem darkened by their plentiful presence (2:8-10). Only at this point does God intervene. "Return to me with all your heart, with fasting, with weeping, and

---

1. Joel 1 = Joel 1; Joel 2:1-32 [= Joel 2:1-27 H and 3:1-5 H]; Joel 3 [= Joel 4 H].
2. For a detailed description of parallels, see Thompson, "Joel," 731-32.

with mourning" (2:12). The people respond and repent, which is followed by God's promise of future reward.

Joel 2:28—3:21 (3:1—4:21 H); The Future: The Day of the LORD Is Coming. God's Spirit Is Overwhelming. There Is Judgment but also Great Relief from the Former Calamities.

This next section begins with a tremendous outburst of energy (2:28–29 [3:1–2 H]). God pours divine spirit onto the people, young and old, sons and daughters, whatever one's social position. Great changes are coming. God promises "blood and fire and columns of smoke. The sun shall be turned to darkness, and the moon to blood" (2:30–31 [3:3–4 H]). God will save those who call upon the divine name. God will punish the enemies all around Judah and Jerusalem: Tyre, Sidon, and Philistia. Likewise, the Greeks are mentioned. All of these areas are directly to the west of Judah, either northwest or southwest. This predominant westward view is unique among the prophets, for so many had focused eastward on Aram, Assyria, Babylonia, and Edom. The nations will march against Zion, but they will not succeed. God will stand in judgment; God will shelter the people. In the end, God shall dwell in Zion. In the closing verse, Joel mentions Egypt and Edom, two traditional enemies. He notes that they will be a desolate wasteland (3:19 [4:19 H]).

Although some would suggest that these sections reflect different authors or different periods, a great deal argues for a literary unity within the book. "The lament (1.4–20) parallels the promise (2.21–27), the announcement of a catastrophe (2.1–11) matches the promise of better days ([3:1–3, 9–17 (4:1–3, 9–17 H)], and the summons to repentance (2.12–17) is set over against the promise of the spirit [2:28ff. (3.1ff. H)]." Likewise, there are examples of parallel expressions; knowing God's being in Israel, knowing God dwelling in Zion (2:27 and 3:17 [4:17 H]).[3] In addition there is the imagery of sun and moon being darkened (2:10; 2:31 [3:4 H]; 3:15 [4:15 H]).

The Locusts

Are these real locusts or purely metaphoric? Joel might well be describing an actual phenomenon. Certainly, his language is vivid and powerful. The early church fathers favored an allegorical interpretation as powers of

---

3. Childs, *Introduction*, 389 (acknowledging the work of H. W. Wolff, *Die Botschaft des Joel*).

darkness that threaten the church. Other explanations include suggestions as to specific empires that had threatened Israel: Egypt, Assyria, Babylon, Persia, Greece, and Rome. Not content to find explanations in the human world, still more imaginative suggestions are that the locusts are apocalyptic "supernatural creatures" or "YHWH's eschatological army . . . mythological creatures that embody the destructive power of God."[4]

Most modern scholars suggest the simple straightforward explanation that these are real locusts. A horde of such insects can devastate an agricultural community.

If these are actual insects, as with all natural phenomena, in the prophet's mind this plague of locusts stems from God. Since God is bringing them, they must be part of God's punishment.

God's voice precedes their terrible and terrifying attack. "The LORD utters his voice at the head of his army; how vast his host!" (2:11). The onslaught is overwhelming. "What the cutting locust left, the swarming locust has eaten. What the swarming locust left, the hopping locust has eaten, and what the hopping locust left, the destroying locust has eaten" (1:4).

Steeped in the prophetic tradition of his people, Joel uses previous prophetic utterances to great effect. Joel may see these latest curses upon the land, locusts accompanied by a drought, as a latter-day linear descendent of the God-caused drought that only ended following the confrontation between Elijah and the priests of Baal—"the watercourses are dried up, and fire has devoured the pastures of the wilderness" (Joel 1:20; cf. 1 Kgs 18:1, 2, 5). In addition, Joel connects the locusts of his day with the locust plague that motivated the Pharaoh to act at the time of Moses in accordance with God's demands. One of the words that Joel uses for locust is *arbeh*, the same word used for locust in Exodus (Exod 10:4, 12–19; Joel 1:4). He strengthens this connection when Joel paraphrases God's self-description of the divine attributes to Moses on Mt. Sinai. Joel suggests that God may forgive, for God is "gracious and merciful, slow to anger, and abounding in steadfast love" (Exod 34:6; Joel 2:13).

Interpreting the locusts as a punishment does not tell us about the nature of the people's wrongdoing. Joel is mute on this point, or he just is not specific. Perhaps he detects a general malaise in the land. It is not that the people have committed explicit acts. Joel does not speak of profaning the sanctuary or of syncretism. He does not address the oppression of the poor, the orphan, or the widow. Joel's condemnation seems to be less definite, yet more diverse. The call to repentance involves all Israel, literally old, young,

---

4. The locusts: apocalyptic "supernatural creatures" (Thompson, "Joel," 733); "YHWH's eschatological army . . . mythological creatures" (Barton, *Joel and Obadiah*, 46; see also Pfeiffer, *Introduction*, 574).

and all in between, from babies nursing on the breast to the elders, to the bride and bridegroom at their home (2:16). The widespread need for repentance is the natural corollary to the widespread presence of the locusts.

Set against this broadly based need for repentance involving all sectors of society is the "reward" of the outpouring of God's spirit. It will touch male and female alike, young and old, free and slave (2:28–29 [3:1–2 H]).

Apocalyptic Writing

Apocalypticism is a kind of religious thought that has its roots in the Persian religion Zoroastrianism. It is dualistic in nature. It involves two cosmic forces, God and some kind of adversary. There are two discrete, divergent, and distinctive periods: the present, which is dominated by forces of evil that suppress the righteous, and an eschatological future, eternal time in which God rules and blessings flow abundantly.

In the latter part of his book, Joel introduces apocalyptic (or apocalyptic-like) prophecy. "This particular passage in Joel [2:28—3:21 (3:1—4:21 H)] . . . uses images on a cosmic scale, including a battle between God and the pagan nations in the valley of Jehoshaphat somewhere near Jerusalem. This is the language of apocalyptic literature,"[5] a whole new development out of and away from classical prophecy.

This battle contrasts with the earlier image of the locusts, which are a sign (or a punishment) from God. The locusts are neither a cosmic force of evil that opposes God, nor do the locusts suppress the righteous for an extended time.

Although these armies are allied against God, in Judaism God is always in control. Any force or forces in opposition to God and God's will are *inferior*. In Christianity, the Satan figure is a considerably powerful being, and is a tempter and oppressor of humans. The Satan (devil) is still not equal to God's power.

Joel's Outpouring of Spirit . . . Visions

Joel predicts that in a future time God will pour divine spirit on all, and that sons and daughters shall prophesy and young men shall see visions (2:28 [3:1 H]). This is not the first example of group prophecy. There is an earlier instance recorded in the Torah, the reference to Eldad and Medad (Num 11:26–27). There Moses says, "Would that all the LORD's people were

---

5. Boadt, *Reading the Old Testament*, 408.

prophets, and that the LORD would put his spirit on them!" (Num 11:29). In both Numbers and Joel, the roots of the words used for "spirit" (rua<u>h</u>), and "prophecy" (from the letters *n-b-'a*, *nun-bet-alef*) are the same.

Joel in the Christian Scriptures

Joel's vision of the "day of the LORD" uses harvest imagery. A heavenly host is involved in this enterprise. This is echoed in the Christian Scriptures (Matt 13:39-42; Rev 14:14-20; Joel 3:11ff. [4:11ff. H]).[6]

The authors of Acts and Romans know Joel's prophecies (Acts 2:17-21; Joel 2:28-32 [3:1-5 H]; Rom 10:13; Joel 2:32 [3:5 H]).

Joel's words also influence the book of Revelation, sometimes termed the Apocalypse.

Joel's images take on a new and more powerful message in this final book of the Christian Scriptures. There the author mentions locusts, described "like horses equipped for battle . . . and their teeth [are] like lions' teeth" (Rev 9:7-8; Joel 1:4, 6; 2:4). On the terrible "day of the LORD," Joel asks rhetorically, how can one endure it? A similar question is asked in Revelation (Rev 6:17; Joel 2:11). Joel's descriptions of the sun eclipsed and the moon blood red are the bases for the same images in Revelation (Rev 6:12; Joel 2:31 [3:4 H]). Joel's sickle is repeated (Rev 14:15, 17-19; see Mark 4:29; Joel 3:13 [4:13 H]). Finally both books feature the life-giving water issuing from the temple (Rev 22:1; Joel 3:18 [4:18 H]).

Joel's description of the outpouring of spirit is the basis for an image in the book of Acts. Acts 2 refers to an event in the life of the early church. The late spring Jewish festival of *Shavuot*/Weeks/Pentecost commemorates God's gift of the Torah to Moses on Mt. Sinai. In Luke's description, the twelve apostles are in Jerusalem. Suddenly during the morning, they are "filled with the Holy Spirit." They speak in a variety of foreign tongues. Those who see them are amazed. Peter comes forward and explains that this is what Joel speaks about when he says, "I will pour out my Spirit." Peter then paraphrases Joel's words (Acts 2:4, 16ff.; Joel 2:28-32 [3:1-5 H]).

Paul draws upon Joel to emphasize his notion that salvation is a matter of faith. "For one believes with the heart and so is justified, and one confesses with the mouth and so is saved. . . . For there is no distinction between Jew and Greek; the same Lord is Lord of all and is generous to all who call on him." Paul follows up this teaching with Joel's statement that anyone who invokes God's name shall be saved (Rom 10:10, 12, 13; Joel 2:32 [3:5 H]).

6. Kodell, *Lamentations . . .* , 150.

Paul amplifies Joel's words. He suggests that Joel had only been addressing the Jews, and now the new teaching is for all humans. Joel's statement is very general and does not single out any faith or ethnic group. In reply to those who suggest that Judaism is particularistic and Christianity is universalistic, a "more prudent judgment is that Judaism and Christianity are both marked by motifs of universalism and particularism."[7]

Joel in Rabbinical Literature

God's spirit in the World to Come. Joel's image that God would "pour spirit" onto old and young alike refers to the World to Come. In this world, there are slanderers. People are motivated by the Evil Inclination (the *Yetzer hara*). Consequently, God withdraws the divine presence from among the people. This will be different in the next world. Having given the people a new heart (Ezek 36:26) God will restore the divine presence among the people. "Then afterward I will pour out my spirit on all flesh" (Joel 2:28 [3:1 H]). This homily then closes with the words: "All your children shall be taught by the LORD, and great shall be the prosperity of your children" (Isa 54:13) (*Midrash Deuteronomy Rabbah* 6.14).

All Israel will prophesy. In this world, only a few people have prophesied. In the World to Come, "all Israel will be made prophets" (and then comes the line from Joel 2:28 [3:1 H]): "Then afterward I will pour" (*Midrash Numbers Rabbah* 15.25 end).

A reward for remaining distinct. Joel 3:18 (4:18 H) says that, in the eschatological "day of the LORD," when Israel is dwelling safely in Zion, "the mountains shall drip sweet wine, the hills shall flow with milk." This is Israel's reward for maintaining its relationship with God by preserving its ethnicity. Israel performed the will of God when in exile, for it refused to mix with the nations and so kept the covenant with God (*Midrash Numbers Rabbah* 13.2).

Comforting Jerusalem. God said to the prophets, "Go comfort Jerusalem," [and it turned out that the words of comfort were contradictory. For example,] Joel came to offer comfort to Jerusalem. He said, God sent me to comfort you. Jerusalem asked, What comfort do you bring me? Joel replied, "[The Holy One said through me,] In that day the mountains shall drip sweet wine, the hills shall flow with milk, and . . . a fountain shall come forth from the house of the LORD" (Joel 3:18 [4:18 H]). Jerusalem answered, Yesterday you said to me, "Wake up, you drunkards, and weep; and wail, all

---

7. Sandmel, *Hebrew Scriptures*, 221.

you wine-drinkers, over the sweet wine for it is cut off from your mouth" (Joel 1:5); and now you say, "The mountains shall drip sweet wine." Which words shall I believe, yesterday's or today's? . . . [Several other prophets also unsuccessfully offer comfort.] Thereupon the Prophets came before the Holy One, saying to Him: Master of the universes, Jerusalem refuses to be comforted by us. The Holy One replied: Then you and I together shall go to her and comfort her: "Comfort, O comfort with me [*immi*] . . . says your God" (Isa 40:1) (*Pesikta de-Rab Kahana, Piska* 16.8). The rabbis take the Hebrew words from the literal text in Isaiah, "Comfort, O comfort *my people*" [*ammi*] and change the vowels to read "with me"—*immi*—so that God says to the Prophets, come and offer comfort "with me."

God speaks to the righteous on Yom Kippur, the Day of Atonement. "The LORD utters his voice at the head of his army; how vast is his host! Numberless are those who obey his command. Truly the day of the LORD is great" (Joel 2:11). The words "The LORD utters his voice at the head of his army" apply to [the blowing of the *shofar* (ram's horn) on] New Year's Day [Rosh Hashanah]; the words that follow, "how vast is his host!" apply to Israel. The words "Numberless are those who obey his command" mean that God increases the strength of the righteous who carry out his word. The words "Truly the day of the LORD is great" refer to the Day of Atonement [Yom Kippur], (which in the Land of Israel was called the Great Day) (*Pesikta de-Rab Kahana, Piska* 24.3).

Text Study

Joel 2:1–14; Images and Metaphors

These fourteen verses provide strikingly strong images, whether or not these marauders are a continuation of the first chapter.

Verse 1. The "day of the LORD is coming, it is near." Other prophets have used this phrase, or words very close to it (Ezek 30:3; Amos 5:18, 20; Zeph 1:7, 14), and Joel himself uses the words "day of the LORD" again and again (1:15; 2:1, 11, 31 [3:4 H]; 3:14 [4:14 H].

Verse 2. The darkness/gloom/cloud imagery reflects similar words in Zephaniah 1:15. Joel both echoes and answers a thought first expressed in chapter 1: "Has such a thing happened in your days, or in the days of your ancestors?" He replies, "Their like has never been from of old, nor will be again after them in ages to come." (Joel 1:2; 2:2).

Verse 3. The locusts front and rear appear as *fire* and *flame*, which shall be quenched in the eastern sea (Salt Sea) and the western sea (Mediterranean Sea), respectively, in verse 20. Prior to these marauders, the land is like the garden of Eden; following them it is desolate. Joel purposely reverses the positive image enunciated by Ezekiel (36:35) and Isaiah (51:3) where Eden-like lushness follows desolation. Joel also reverses the positive image of swords/plowshares and spears/pruning hooks described in Isaiah and Micah. He turns farm implements into weapons of war (Isa 2:4; Mic 4:3; Joel 3:10 [4:10 H]).

Verses 4–5. The attackers bring horses/war horses; they charge/leap; they rumble as chariots; they create a noise. They are a powerful army, underscoring that same phrase ("powerful army") in verse 2 (in Hebrew, *am rav v'atzum*; *k'am atzum*, vv. 2, 5).

Verses 7–9. Military metaphors and similes spill over; they build up, one on another. They are akin to the way that the attackers spill over and build up their assault upon the city, one on another. In these three verses Joel portrays the marauders as chargers/warriors/soldiers. They are charging/scaling/keeping their course/not swerving/not jostling/running/climbing/leaping/entering. The object of their attack is also described: the city/the walls/the houses/the windows.

Verse 10. The earth physically quakes or shakes with their onslaught. The heavens above metaphorically tremble. The dust stirred up by their pounding literally obscures sun, moon, and stars. Not since Zephaniah's day of trouble and distress (*Dies irae, dies illa*, Zeph 1:14–16), with its repetition of the word "day," has there been such a powerful example of images piled on images.

Verse 13. Rending heart, not clothing. This powerful inward image of repentance reflects the biblical custom of rending one's garment as a sign of mourning or great distress (see Gen 37:29, 34). A torn garment (*qeriya*) continues today as a sign of Jewish mourning.

Joel's image of the heart as indicative of the whole person is a familiar concept in biblical thought (see Deut 6:5; Jer 31:33; Ezek 36:26; Ps 16:9; Lam 2:19 et al.). *Midrash Ecclesiastes Rabbah* 1.16.1 lists numerous references to the heart.

11

Amos

Introduction

AMOS PROPHESIES DURING THE middle of the eighth century, c. 750 BCE. His words are spoken to the northern kingdom of Israel/Ephraim. Amos pioneers the way for his fellow prophets. He provides patterns found throughout the prophetic literature in the Hebrew Scriptures. The "practice of collecting and preserving the oracles of a prophet in a separate book came to begin with Amos. It was to have far-reaching results, first in the raising of the prophetic office to a consistently high level, which it was to hold for two centuries, then in the consolidation and crystallization of Israel's faith in a series of prophetic books."[1]

Amos is the twelfth book of the second section of the Hebrew Bible, the Prophets/*Neviim* (see Introduction: "The Order of the Books of the Bible").

The book of Amos contains four different kinds of material. (1) He prophesies against the nations. (2) He prophesies concerning Israel, as well as Judah. (3) There are stories about the prophet. (4) Finally, the book concludes with a prophecy of comfort for Israel. "The remaining prophetic books of the Bible are built on the same four categories, but they are not necessarily arranged in the same order and not every one has left prophecies in all four categories."[2]

Amos is the first *literary* prophet, not the first biblical prophet. His words continue a tradition that reaches back for two hundred years. Yet, it

---

1. Smart, "Amos," 117.
2. Haran, "Amos," 881.

is important to recall that while the book is named for Amos, he himself did not write down his own words. As mentioned in the Introduction, a prophet speaks; he is a preacher. It is only later that the prophet's words are set down and collected.

There is no written record in the Bible to explain why, how, or who wrote down Amos's addresses and prophecies. Unlike the book of Jeremiah, in Amos there is no mention of a disciple collecting the prophet's words. Perhaps Amos spoke extemporaneously, and then after a time, someone remembered and preserved his speeches. It is probable that Amos (as his successors) made many more pronouncements than are preserved in the Bible. Some statements may have been noted down but lost.

Amos explains about his commission. That information provides some details about this mid-eighth century figure. Including these items gives incentive to Hosea, Isaiah, Jeremiah, Ezekiel, and Micah (or to their disciples or editors) to do likewise.

Amos is the first prophet to suggest that a consequence of Israel's sins will mean exile.

Geo-Political Background

Unlike the geo-political tumult that forms the background for First Isaiah, Jeremiah, and Ezekiel, in the book of Amos the two nations of Israel and Judah are outwardly peaceful and prosperous. At the time of Amos's prophecies (c. 750 BCE), King Uzziah of the southern kingdom of Judah is well into his forty-one-year reign (783–42). His colleague to the north, Jeroboam II of Israel, likewise rules for a long time (786–46). There is political stability. Jeroboam II's successful rule in Israel receives scant notice in the Bible (2 Kgs 14:23–29). The great grandson of Jehu, who had overthrown the Omride dynasty, Jeroboam II and his father Jehoash both recover land that has been lost to the Syrians in former times. Assyria, the major powerbroker of that time, is concerned with internal political problems. This permits opportunity for some expansion.

Israel and Judah enjoy cordial relations. Business and trade prosper. "This was therefore a period of great prosperity for Israel. The stability of the region allowed for the safe conduct of caravans down the King's Highway, which was in Israelite hands. Trading with Egypt and Arabia in the [south] and Byblos and Syria in the [north] greatly increased the wealth of Israel and Judah. Amos describes this wealth, which is also evidenced in the archaeological remains of the time."[3]

3. Willoughby, "Book of Amos," 1:205.

A leisure class develops. Amos refers to well-built winter and summer residences, luxuriously decorated (3:15; 5:11). Bethel and Gilgal are active as religious cult-shrines (4:4–5; 5:21–25). These religious activities screen deeper ills in society. Judges take bribes. The powerless and the needy are without advocates. Injustice rules the land. Sexual immorality is widespread (5:12; 2:6–7). Women and men are profane and profligate (4:1; 2:7).

> The Israelites were a religious people. Pilgrimages to Bethel, Gilgal, and Beer-sheba, the sacred precincts of Israel, were commonplace (4:4; 5:5). Freewill and thanksgiving offerings and tithes were performed regularly (4:4), and there were many religious assemblies and festivals (5:21–23). By all criteria, then, the Israelites assumed that they were performing the cultic and ritual requirements necessary to appease Yahweh. Furthermore, they considered their wealth and security as evidence that Yahweh was pleased. They assumed that their steadfast devotion to cultic ritual exempted them from the requirements of righteousness and social justice and from the consequences of wrongdoing. Through sacrifice they could guarantee divine favor and their own survival. The peace and prosperity the nation enjoyed must have, to many Israelites, validated their lives, values, and assumptions as the chosen people of God.
>
> Yet the people had turned the official view around and were reasoning in reverse: their prosperity proved that they were righteous. The distinction, while a fine one, is nevertheless important: the obligation of the covenant was to pursue righteousness and justice; prosperity would follow as a by-product of God's pleasure. The pursuit of wealth rather than righteousness was an unacceptable short cut, and wholly abhorrent to Yahweh, according to the prophet.[4]

The Book of Amos

Amos preaches his prophecies at Bethel, which is the royal sanctuary of the northern kingdom (7:10ff.) Amos explains that he is an agriculturalist and a herdsman. Little is known about his origins and his life (7:14–15). Scholars speculate about Amos's formal education and his town of origin. No evidence exists about Amos's education or lack thereof. Many a country person has a wonderful command of language. Incisive words and insight are not the sole preserve of the city-dweller. To be unlettered is not to be ill spoken

---

4. Ibid., 1:206.

(see the Text Study sections at the conclusion of this chapter, "Amos's Imagery and Message" and "Powerful Rhetoric.")

Amos claims to come from Tekoa. There is a town in Judah by that name, in the general vicinity of Jerusalem and Bethlehem. Perhaps Amos is indifferent to regional borders. He may have traveled to and prophesied in the northern kingdom of Israel because he has concern about his coreligionists. Alternatively, Tekoa may be a village situated in the north, and simply is not recorded elsewhere in the biblical period. America has numerous cities and towns named Springfield, Portland, and Aurora. Why could there not be more than one Tekoa? The biblical text lends support for Tekoa's placement in the northern kingdom. Amos confronts Amaziah, the priest at Bethel in Israel. Amaziah then urges the prophet to *go* to the land of Judah and prophesy there. Amaziah tells Amos to "go." He does not say "return" to Judah (*lekh b'rah l'kha el eretz yehudah*, "go, flee away," 7:12).

Amos acts alone. He does not claim to be part of a prophetic guild. It is the priest Amaziah who suggests that Amos is a "professional prophet." Not so!, Amos retorts. God has sent me on this specific mission! (7:14–15.) It is likely that there are guilds of professional prophets supported by the monarchy, often foretelling what the rulers want to hear (see 1 Kgs 22). Amos explains that he is independent of these connections. He speaks only for God.

Divisions in the Book of Amos

Amos 1:2—2:3	A prophecy against the nations
Amos 2:4—6:14	A prophecy against Israel and Judah
Amos 7:1—9:6	Stories about the prophet
Amos 9:7–15	A prophecy of comfort, a kind of epilogue

Amos 1:2—2:3; A Prophecy Against the Nations

The book of Amos does not begin with Amos's words at Bethel, the royal sanctuary and capital of the northern kingdom. The opening line identifies the period when Amos is prophesying, during the reigns of Kings Uzziah and Jeroboam. Amos turns his immediate attention to Israel's neighbors, Damascus, Philistia [Gaza, Ashdod, Ashkelon, Ekron], Tyre, Edom, Ammon, and Moab. He employs powerful language. He repeats phrases for dramatic effect. Amos thunders, "Thus says the LORD: For three transgressions of

Damascus and for four, I will not revoke the punishment; because they . . ." ("For three transgressions of Gaza and for four; because they . . ."; "For three transgressions of Tyre and for four; I will not revoke the punishment; because they . . .") Then he lists their particular crimes (1:3, 6, 9, 11, 13; 2:1).

Amos 2:4—6:14; A Prophecy Against Israel and Judah

Next Amos focuses on his fellow compatriots. Initially he uses this selfsame powerful formula, "Thus says the LORD: For three transgressions . . . and for four, I will not revoke the punishment; because they . . ." The object of God's anger is first Judah and then Israel itself (2:4, 6).

Amos's condemnation is brutal and wide reaching. Moral corruption pervades the land. The righteous and the needy are treated as expendable. People regularly visit pagan cult prostitutes. Nazirites, who have pledged themselves to follow a life of abstinence from liquor, are forced to drink wine. Prophets are silenced (2:6–7, 12). A small minority of people live in great comfort. They have a "winter house as well as [a] summer house . . . houses of ivory . . . [and] great houses" (3:15). Amos denounces the upper classes. Wives are as guilty as their husbands are. He holds women as responsible as men. Amos terms these women the "cows of Bashan" (4:1). This is not a misogynistic remark by Amos. "It was common to apply animal metaphors to human beings; whether this was positive or negative depended completely on the context."[5] For example, in the Song of Songs a woman is positively likened to a mare, and a man to a gazelle.

Amos rails at those people who, thinking only of themselves, "oppress the poor, who crush the needy" (4:1). God will hold them responsible for their misdeeds. Amos thunders about the immoral life in Judah as well as in Israel. "Alas for those who are at ease in Zion, and for those who feel secure on Mount Samaria." He then describes their life of luxury. He predicts their punishment. "Alas for those who lie on beds of ivory, and lounge on their couches, and eat lambs from the flock, and calves from the stall, who sing idle songs to the sound of the harp, . . . who drink wine from bowls and anoint themselves with the finest oils . . . they shall now be the first to go into exile" (6:1, 4–7).

Amos 7:1—9:6; Stories About the Prophet

Verses 7:10–17 detail Amos's confrontation with Amaziah, the priest at Bethel.

---

5. Sanderson, "Amos," 208.

7:1—9:6 also contains several visions of God's judgment upon the people. Among Amos's metaphors are locusts, a shower of fire, and a basket of summer fruit (7:1, 4; 8:1). No matter where the people hide, God will find them and punish them. Even though they dig down to Sheol, or climb to the heavens, or hide on top of Carmel, or at the bottom of the sea, God will pursue them (9:1–3).

Amos 9:7–15; A Prophecy of Comfort, a Kind of Epilogue

Amos concludes on a note of hope. God will punish the wicked; God will not destroy the house of Jacob. The fortunes of Israel eventually will be restored (9:8, 11, 14.)

Amos's Theology

Central to Amos's thinking are three interconnected points:

- God rules over the universe.
- God has a special relationship with Israel.
- God holds Israel responsible for breaking the covenant.

Amos teaches that God cares about all nations. Judah-Israel's pagan neighbors act immorally. Consequently, God will punish those countries—Damascus, Philistia, Tyre, etc. Yet, God has a particular concern with Israel and Judah. God demands more of them, for "You only have I known of all the families of the earth" (3:2). (See the Text Study at the conclusion of this chapter, "A Special Relationship.") God is disappointed with Israel. Israel spurns the covenant. It rejects God.

Amos's promises of doom are based on social and moral corruption. God demands justice, not merely outward signs of the cult (i.e., ritual/religious practices). "Seek good and not evil, that you may live . . . establish justice in the gate." "Let justice roll down like waters, and righteousness like an ever-flowing stream" (5:14–15, 24).

Amos in the Christian Scriptures

In Acts, Stephen paraphrases Amos to suggest that the Jews have been idolaters from long ago (Acts 7:42–43; Amos 5:25–27). At the Jerusalem conference, James quotes from Amos (Acts 15:16–18; Amos 9:11–12).

Amos's caution to keep silent because it is an evil time finds reflection in a similar admonition in Ephesians. "Be careful then how you live, not as unwise people but as wise . . . because the days are evil" (Eph 5:15–16; Amos 5:13).

Paul's exhortation to "hate what is evil, hold fast to what is good" shows his familiarity with Amos's admonition to "Hate evil and love good" (Rom 12:9; Amos 5:15).

Amos observes, "They abhor the one who speaks the truth," a concept Paul puts as a question when he asks, "Have I now become your enemy by telling you the truth?" (Amos 5:10; Gal 4:16).

When the Synoptics speak about the crucifixion, they explain that darkness befell the day. "It was now about noon, and darkness came over the whole land until three in the afternoon, while the sun's light failed." This echoes Amos's warning, "On that day, says the Lord GOD, I will make the sun go down at noon, and darken the earth in broad daylight" (Luke 23:44–45; cf. Matt 27:45; Mark 15:33; Amos 8:9).

In Matthew and Luke, Jesus berates the populace in several communities around the Sea of Galilee (Chorazin, Bethsaida, and Capernaum) in a manner based on Amos's denunciation of Judah (Matt 11:21–23; Luke 10:13–15; Amos 2:4–5).

Amos in Rabbinic Literature

A concise commandment. Amos receives praise for reducing the essential commandments of God to one line: "Seek me and live!" (5:4) (*Babylonian Talmud Makkot* 24a).

Part of a select committee. A midrash explains that when the Messiah comes there will be a committee of advisors made up of fifteen notables (including the Messiah). Among these—Abraham, Adam, David, Elijah, Hezekiah, Jacob, Jesse, [the Messiah,] Moses, Methuselah, Samuel, Saul, Seth, and Zephaniah—will be Amos! (*Midrash Song of Songs Rabbah* 8.9.3 end). An alternative list exchanges Zedekiah for Hezekiah (*Babylonian Talmud Sukkah* 52b). This midrash has echoes in the Christian Scriptures, which also speak of a future committee that will sit in judgment (Matt 19:28; 1 Cor 6:2).

God's great power. The image of God as a lion (3:8) is quoted by the midrash that proclaims, "God is not merely like one lion, but like all the lions in the world!" (*Avot de Rabbi Natan*, ch. 2).

Prophets get only a glimpse of the future. While prophets may not have seen the totality of the future, they were able to see some of it, "As [one peeps] through a crack in the door." This is based on the line, "Surely the Lord GOD does nothing, without revealing his secrets to his servants the prophets" (3:7) (*Midrash Ecclesiastes Rabbah* 1.8.6).

God holds Israel to a higher standard. God holds the people Israel to a higher standard because they have been in an unbreakable covenant relationship since Sinai. "You only have I known of all the families of the earth; therefore I will punish you for all your iniquities" (3:2) (*Tanna Debe Eliyyahu*, ch. [15] 16, p. 76 [170–71]; *Babylonian Talmud Avodah Zarah* 4a).

Difficult days. In the years leading to the coming of the Messiah, there will be periods of difficulty. In the first year, some places will not receive rain in its proper season. This is a speculation based on "I would send rain on one city, and send no rain on another city" (4:7) (*Pesikta de-Rab Kahana, Piska* 5.9).

A call to repentance. During the period of the High Holy Days, the *shofar* (ram's horn) is sounded. It is a call to repentance. Amos's words, "Is a trumpet [*shofar*] blown in a city, and the people are not afraid?" are linked to his statement, "For thus says the LORD to the house of Israel: Seek me and live" (3:6; 5:4) (*Pesikta de-Rab Kahana, Piska* 24.1.)

Text Study

Amos 3:1–2; A Special Relationship

Verse 1. The reference to the Exodus is double-edged. God reminds the people of the exodus, which led to Sinai. Yet, by their action, the people reject the covenant. Furthermore, as they were exiled in Egypt as slaves, so they will be exiled again.

Verse 2. God demands more of Israel. God brought them out of Egypt for a special purpose: to be a priestly people and a holy nation. "You only have I known of all the families of the earth; therefore I will punish you for all your iniquities."

Amos 3:3–8; Amos's Imagery and Message

Verses 3ff. These lines repeat the idea of "cause and effect." The examples are primarily of a pastoral nature: lion/forest; young lion/den; bird/snare; prey/trap; lion's roar/fear. They underscore Amos's rural background.

Verse 7. God reveals the divine purpose to the prophets.

Amos 1:3ff.; 6ff.; 9ff.; 11ff.; 13ff.; 2:1ff. 4ff.; 6ff.; Powerful Rhetoric

In all of these verses Amos applies the same powerful rhetoric: "Thus says the LORD: For three transgressions of _____, and for four, I will not revoke the punishment; because they. . . . So I will. . . ." Amos indicts in turn Damascus, Gaza, Tyre, Edom, Ammon, and Moab. Then God turns divine wrath on Judah and Israel. The repetition of these accusations, starting with Israel's neighbors and then turning to his fellow Israelites, builds to a powerful climax. The numbers three and four, and their combination, seven, all are special numbers in the biblical world. The number seven, additionally, is a "sacred" number (seven days of the week, the seventh day being Sabbath/Shabbat; seven days for Passover/*Pesach*; the seven-branched candelabra [*menorah*] and so on).

12

Obadiah

Introduction

OBADIAH IS THE SHORTEST book in the Bible. It consists of one chapter, a mere twenty-one verses in length. Dating for the book varies between shortly after the temple's destruction (586 BCE) and c. 400 BCE. Thematically, there is a connection between Obadiah and the lament of Psalm 137, a poem ascribed to those exiled to Babylon. Pain and anger are evident in both compositions.

Obadiah is the thirteenth book of the second section of the Hebrew Bible, the Prophets/*Neviim* (see Introduction: "The Order of the Books of the Bible").

Geo-Political Background

In 586 BCE, the Babylonians capture Jerusalem, first looting the temple treasury, then burning the temple to the ground. They take many captives back with them northeast to Babylon, including the leadership of Judah and the artisan class. They leave behind "some of the poorest people of the land to be vinedressers and tillers of the soil" (2 Kgs 25:12). Other refugees flee to Egypt.

The Edomites, located to the south/southeast of Judah (ancient Edom is present-day southwestern Jordan/southeastern Israel) probably join with the Babylonians in attacking Jerusalem. "The book of Obadiah . . . constitutes a response to the trauma the Judean community experienced, the angry desire for revenge serving . . . the community's shock and rage at seeing

Jerusalem go up in flames and foreigners casting lots for Jerusalem (v. 11)."[1] In the years following Judah's defeat, the Edomites move northwest and settle in and around the area of Hebron, south of Jerusalem. The Edomites are considered the descendants of Esau. Tensions with Edom are ongoing for centuries. In the late biblical and then in the Roman period, Edom is termed Idumea (note the similarity in names: Edom/Idumea).

Many prophets condemn Edom. Ezekiel addresses their longstanding mutual hatred. Mt. Seir is associated with Edom. "Because you cherished an ancient enmity, and gave over the people of Israel to the power of the sword at the time of their calamity . . . therefore, as I live, says the Lord GOD, . . . I will make you a perpetual desolation" (Ezek 35:5–6, 9; cf. Lam 4:21f.; cf. Isa 63:1–6; Mal 1:1–5).

The Book of Obadiah

Divisions in the Book of Obadiah

Verses 1–9   The coming destruction of Edom

Verses 10–14   Edom's crimes against Israel, and a broader statement directed at the nations

Verses 15–21   Israel will be restored at the expense of other nations. (This last section is framed within a prophecy about the Day of the LORD.)

Verses 1–9; The Coming Destruction of Edom

Obadiah speaks with great anger. The flavor of the book is a firsthand account of recent grievances held against Judah's neighbor. In the first two verses Obadiah explains that "the Lord GOD [has spoken] concerning Edom [saying] I will surely make you least among the nations." Further, God says, "I will destroy the wise out of Edom, and understanding out of Mount Esau" (v. 8; Esau is associated with Edom).

---

1. Claassens, "Obadiah," 320; see also Barton, *Joel and Obadiah*, 120–23. According to biblical tradition, the conflict with Edom stemmed back to the time of the Jacob-Esau controversy (see Gen 27:41; 36:1ff.; Num 20:14–21; 2 Sam 8:13–14; 1 Kgs 11:14–17); Jenson, *Obadiah, Jonah, Micah*, 3.

Verses 10–14; Edom's Crimes against Israel, and a Broader Statement Directed at the Nations

A bitter list of particulars is read out against Edom. The phrase "you should not have" repeats with dramatic effect. "You should not have boasted on the day of distress. You should not have entered the gate of my people on the day of their calamity; you should not have joined in the gloating over Judah's disaster . . . you should not have stood at the crossings to cut off his fugitives; you should not have handed over his survivors on the day of distress" (vv. 12–14). (See the Text Study section at the conclusion of this chapter, "Cruel Edom; Judgment; Eschatological Verses.")

Obadiah's fury closely parallels words from his older (contemporary?) colleague, the prophet Jeremiah (cf. vv. 1–6 with Jer 49:14–16; 9–10).

Verses 15–21; Israel Will Be Restored at the Expense of Other Nations

This third section draws on earlier words of the prophets. This section "is very rich in references to earlier prophetic images. The nations drink poison (verse 16; cf. Jer. 25:15–16 and elsewhere); [verse 17] a remnant of Judah's citizens remain on Mt. Zion (Isa. 37:32); and [verse 18] Israel is a destructive fire (Isa. 10:12–19)."[2] The Day of the LORD, articulated years earlier by Amos, is also a phrase used by Obadiah (v. 15).

Obadiah in the Christian Scriptures

Obadiah is not quoted specifically in the Christian Scriptures. Parallels between verse 21 and Revelation 11:15 are possible. Likewise, the inference that as Israel drank a cup of bitterness on God's holy mountain, so will the nations drink a cup of bitterness, has connections with Jesus' use of a cup in the Gethsemane narratives. In both narratives, "'drinking the same cup' clearly means 'sharing the same fate.' The cup can denote suffering, even martyrdom."[3]

---

2. Brettler, "Book of Obadiah," 717.
3. Wright, *Jesus and the Victory of God*, 573.

Obadiah in Rabbinic Literature

Obadiah is the least important prophet. Isaiah is spoken of as the greatest of the prophets, while Obadiah is the least important (*Aggadat Bereshit* 14.32).[4]

Obadiah was a proselyte. Obadiah was an Edomite proselyte, hence the proverb, "From the forest comes [the handle of the] axe [that fells it.]" (*Babylonian Talmud Sanhedrin* 39b).

Obadiah identified. Some rabbis suggests that the prophet Obadiah is the same person who is mentioned as a chief servant for King Ahab (1 Kgs 18:3ff.) (*Babylonian Talmud Sanhedrin* 39b).

Edom a code name for Rome. Obadiah's anti-Edomite prophecies appeal to the Talmudic rabbis. The word Edom is connected to the Hebrew word 'adom ('a-d-m, alef-dalet-mem), which means "red" or "ruddy." The color of Rome's flag is red. To speak openly against Rome or the Roman occupation and cruelty is seditious. Consequently, the rabbis speak against Edom (i.e., "red") instead, and used this as code language. In this way, they predict the eventual fall of Rome.

Eventually Edom (Rome) will fall. In his dream Jacob sees a ladder and angels ascending it. These angels represent the nations of the world. Jacob sees "the prince of Edom [Rome] climbing and climbing.... At the sight of Edom's climbing our father Jacob grew afraid and said: 'Is one to suppose that this prince will have no come-down?' [God then reassures Jacob that Edom's (Rome's) fall is explained in Scripture.] 'Thus says the Lord GOD concerning Edom:... Though you soar aloft like the eagle, though your nest is set among the stars, from there I will bring you down, says the LORD'" (1:1, 4) (*Pesikta de-Rab Kahana, Piska* 23.2 beginning). This reference is particularly appropriate, because the eagle is another symbol for Rome.

Edom (Rome) will be destroyed by Israel. Rome sometimes is designated by the code word Edom, sometimes by Esau ("These are the descendants of Esau (that is, Edom)," Gen 36:1, cf. 43). Rome shall be destroyed by fire, and Israel will be the agent of that destruction. Rome "will be judged by fire, as stated (in Dan 7:11): <I LOOKED ON THEN BECAUSE OF THE SOUND OF THE ARROGANT WORDS WHICH THE HORN UTTERED.> I LOOKED ON UNTIL THE BEAST WAS SLAIN AND ITS BODY DESTROYED, GIVEN OVER FOR BURNING IN THE FIRE. The Holy One said (in Obadiah 18): THE HOUSE OF JACOB SHALL BE A FIRE, AND THE HOUSE OF JOSEPH A FLAME, <AND THE HOUSE

---

4. Quoted in Ginzberg, *Legends of the Jews,* 5:195 n. 72.

OF ESAU [i.e., Rome] SHALL BE STRAW; THEY SHALL BURN AND CONSUME IT> . . . , FOR {THE MOUTH OF} THE LORD HAS SPOKEN IT . . . Then after that <Scripture says> [in Obadiah 21]: THEN SAVIORS SHALL COME UP ON MOUNT ZION TO JUDGE THE MOUNTAIN OF ESAU [i.e. Rome], AND THE KINGDOM SHALL BELONG TO THE LORD" (*Midrash Tanhuma, Leviticus, Tsaw* 2.4 Lev 6:1ff. (8ff.), part IV[5]).

Other examples of anti-Roman sentiment. Anti-Roman sentiment "disguised" as criticism of Edom is found in numerous midrashim (*Midrash Leviticus Rabbah* 29.2; *Pirke de Rabbi Eliezer*, ch. 37 end). See also *Midrash Tanhuma, Exodus, Bo* 3.6 Exod 10:21ff., part VI, where the plagues brought upon Egypt God will bring to Edom, i.e., Rome.

Text Study

Obadiah 12-14; 15-21; Cruel Edom; Judgment; Eschatological Verses

Verses 12-14. These verses conclude the anti-Edomite opening section. They are strongly worded descriptions that outline the cruelty of the Edomites who show no compassion for the Judean refugees.

Verse 15. This verse serves as a crucial link between the specificity of the opening verses and the broader terms of "all the nations" in the rest of the chapter. The "Day of the LORD" is specifically mentioned. This is a day of judgment and destruction. This verse serves as a literary balance point between the second and third sections.

Verses 16-18. "Whereas 2-15 begins with Edom and ends with an eschatological judgment on all the nations, 16-18 begins with the nations and ends with the utter destruction of Edom. Thus, Edom and the nations are not to be separated into different prophetic oracles, but represent different aspects of the same event within the divine judgment."[6]

Verses 17-21. There is a strong eschatological sense to these verses. The day of God will result in the redemption of Israel. God will triumph, and a remnant shall once again possess the land. There are some general parallels between the thinking and prophecies of Obadiah and those of Joel and Zephaniah.

---

5. See this title in the bibliography.
6. Childs, *Introduction*, 414-15.

13

Jonah

Introduction

JONAH'S PROPHECY ADDRESSES NINEVEH, the capital city of Assyria, which suggests that it is written earlier than 612 BCE, when Nineveh is destroyed. Yet, the book of Jonah does not offer references to historical events or to personages. Aside from its size and population, Jonah mentions little else about Nineveh. It is likely, therefore, that the book of Jonah is composed several hundred years *after* the seventh century, and then located back in that earlier time.

Jonah is the fourteenth book of the second section of the Hebrew Bible, the Prophets/*Neviim* (see Introduction: "The Order of the Books of the Bible").

Commissioned by God, Jonah runs away. Told to travel northeast, he journeys southwest. Commanded to travel overland to Nineveh, he heads toward the sea to go by ship to Tarshish. Jonah is the Bible's most reluctant prophet.

Jonah's desire to escape God's call is pointless. Aboard the ship, he is caught in the midst of God's power. On the Mediterranean Sea, a violent storm tosses about Jonah's vessel. Thrown overboard and imprisoned within the belly of a great fish, Jonah ponders his fate. (Please note, the biblical text quite clearly indicates a fish, not a whale!) Finally, Jonah offers up a prayer. After three days, he is spewed out upon a distant shore. Commissioned a second time, Jonah sets out for the country of Nineveh. Once there, a chastened Jonah speaks. Yet he delivers his prophetic message sparingly. His entire prophetic output is one half-sentence long. When Nineveh repents, Jonah is nothing short of furious. He openly displays his anger. His insolence toward God is shocking.

Geo-Political Background

In terms of historical context, for three hundred years, c. 900–600 BCE, the dominant force in the ancient Near East is Assyria. In modern terms, it is the "superpower" of the day. Assyria is centered in northern Mesopotamia. It has major cities along the Tigris River. The Assyrians are fierce conquerors. They use intentional cruelty in warfare as a means to subdue their enemies.

Years earlier, a man by the same name, Jonah son of Amittai, from Gath-hepher, had prophesied correctly that Jeroboam II (c. 785 BCE) would expand his territory (2 Kgs 14:25). *The prophet of the book of Jonah is a different person.*

The Book of Jonah

Divisions in the Book of Jonah

Jonah divides neatly into its four chapters.[1]

Jonah 1	Jonah's commission and the prophet's immediate departure
Jonah 2	Jonah prays for deliverance
Jonah 3	Jonah's second commission
Jonah 4	Jonah displeased and disbelieving

Jonah 1; Jonah's Commission and the Prophet's Immediate Departure

Jonah begins with the prophet's commission and his immediate departure in the opposite direction. "Prophetic reluctance is a common motif in the Hebrew Bible (cf. Moses, Elijah, and Jeremiah), but Jonah's abrupt flight in the opposite direction (1:3) is more than resistance; it is a bizarre response to a strange request. His attempt to run from God's presence parodies Ps. 139:7–10, which states the impossibility of such escape."[2]

---

1. "In very general terms chapters 1 and 3 put Jonah in the context of the outer 'pagan' world. In both cases the leader of the pagans (the captain, the king) acknowledges that there is a single divine power to whom they turn . . . Chapters 2 and 4 contain the inner discussion between Jonah and God represented in the language of prayer, of divine responses in words and actions, and some physical activity directed against Jonah's body." The two parts of the book of Jonah are compared and contrasted in this article. Magonet, "Book of Jonah," 3:937.

2. White, "Jonah," 212.

Jonah attempts to flee by sea to the furthest place westward to which someone could sail. God causes a great storm to waylay the prophet. When confronted by his shipmates, Jonah confesses that he is the cause of the storm. Reluctantly, but at Jonah's insistence, the sailors throw Jonah overboard. A large fish swallows Jonah.

Verses 4–16 contains an acrostic of movement where what begins in one direction moves toward its opposite end. (See the Text Study section at the conclusion of this chapter, "An Acrostic of Movement.")

Jonah 2; Jonah Prays for Deliverance

Jonah seeks deliverance from his watery grave. This reads like a psalm of thanksgiving. God hears Jonah's plea and orders the fish to spew Jonah out on dry land.

Jonah 3; Jonah's Second Commission

Jonah is given a second chance to serve as God's prophet. He reluctantly utters his half-sentence proclamation of prophecy (v. 4b). Miraculously the citizens believe God. The ruler rises from his throne, dons sackcloth and ashes, and requires the same of humans and beasts. God sees their repentance and forgives them.

Jonah 4; Jonah Displeased and Disbelieving

Jonah cannot believe that God has forgiven the Ninevites. He goes to the east of the city to see what will happen. Overnight God first creates and then takes away a plant that offers shade for Jonah. Meanwhile, the city apparently remains repentant. Jonah is infuriated. He speaks of his frustration. At the book's conclusion, God asks Jonah rhetorically, should I not have compassion on the many citizens of Nineveh?

Jonah is a book of intrigue, anger, humor, and fantasy. It is a kind of parable. It is a didactic narrative[3] (see the Text Study section at the conclusion of this chapter, "The Numbers 3 and 4.")

3. Limburg, *Jonah*, 22–28. The "Book of Jonah serves as a subversive sequel to the story of Noah. The Jonah narrative adopts much of the Noah story's language and many of its themes in order to invite comparison." Klitsner, *Subversive Sequels in the Bible*, 2.

Although seeming to criticize the book for being "the ultimate patriarchal book in which women never appear," Harper explains that this story "transcends gender and implicitly attacks racism, sexism, ageism, and any -ism that questions God's full

The formulaic "word of the LORD" appears twice in the book. It initiates the first section of the book, and the second section as well (1:1; 3:1). The words "Israel" and "prophet" do not appear at all. The recipients of Jonah's prophecy are a people living *outside* of the land of Israel. They are Israel's enemies. Nineveh is Assyria's capital, which is the cruelest nation of the ancient Near East.

The historicity of Jonah presents great problems. Is there really a storm that rages so severely, and the next moment abates as Jonah is thrown overboard? Is there a plant that grows overnight to such proportions, and then withers as quickly? Is Nineveh thirty miles across (a figure based on a person walking ten miles in one day, for it is recorded that Nineveh is "three days' walk across," 3:3)? The book proposes that Nineveh's 120,000-person population repents overnight. Would this not be recorded elsewhere? Aside from Jonah, there is neither biblical nor extra-biblical confirmation of this strange occurrence.

Jonah is probably set down somewhere between 400 and 200 BCE. Is this a book stressing universalism, or particularism? On the universalism side, there are concepts found in (Second/Third) Isaiah 40–66 that Israel will be a "light to the nations," and that God might yet have compassion through Israel's ministry. Jonah does go and preach to a foreign nation. At the same time, there is a sense of particularism. Jonah clearly is reluctant to go to Nineveh. He is displeased when God repents of the decision to destroy the foreign city. These sentiments suggest a time when the exclusiveness engendered by Ezra (latter half of the fifth century) has long been at work in the community.

There are a number of words and technical phrases that indicate late Hebrew language structure, and the influence of Aramaic. These point to a composition date for Jonah in the fifth century or later.

Jonah reflects qualities of some of his predecessors. Like the primarily action-oriented lives of and narratives about Samuel, Elijah, and Elisha, there is considerably more narrative and movement, and less dialogue, in this book than in any of the other literary prophets.

Jonah sits under a plant and complains, as does Elijah (Jon 4:6–9; 1 Kgs 19:4). The book of Jonah speaks of God changing a decision. A similar prophecy is found in Jeremiah (Jon 3:8–10; Jer 18:7–10). The Ninevites remark that perhaps God will take note of their repentance. Joel raises a similar question (Jon 3:9; Joel 2:14). In addition, both Jonah and Joel echo descriptions of God's attributes that first appear in the Torah: gracious,

---

acceptance of all human beings." Harper, "Jonah," 458.

compassionate, slow to anger, abounding in kindness, renouncing punishment (Jon 4:2; Joel 2:13; Exod 34:6–7.)

There are several major concepts taught in Jonah:

- God is omnipresent; the God of Israel and of the nations as well.
- God is omnipotent.
- Repentance is possible.
- Knowledge brings responsibility.[4]

Jonah in the Christian Scriptures

The most prominent use of the book of Jonah comes in Matthew (12:40), where Jesus likens his own coming entombment for three days to the days that Jonah spends in the midst of the "belly of the sea monster" (NRSV); "sea-monster's belly" (NEB); "belly of a huge fish" (NIV); "belly of the whale" (NAB).

Luke mentions that as Jonah was a sign for the Ninevites, so likewise will the Son of Man be a sign for the present, evil generation (Matt 12:39–41; Luke 11:29–30).

Jonah in Rabbinic Literature[5]

Jonah is angry with God. Earlier in his life, Jonah predicts the destruction of Jerusalem. When this does not come about, he is labeled as a "false prophet." This is particularly galling since his patronymic, Amittai, can mean "truthful one" (from the Hebrew word *Emet*, "truth") (*Pirke de Rabbi Eliezer*, ch. 10).

Jonah wants to protect Israel's reputation. When God sends Jonah to Nineveh, the prophet rejects this role for two reasons. On one level, he has a presentiment that the Ninevites will in fact repent. As a loyal Israelite, he does not want to see this. Then, he has concerns with what God will do to Israel if God sees a pagan nation readily repent while Israel remains stubborn (*Mekilta de Rabbi Ishmael, Pisha* 1.79ff[6]; cf. *Midrash Lamentations Rabbah*, Proem 31, where God takes up that very point[7]).

Jonah condemned. The rabbis strongly condemn Jonah for his suppression of God's prophecy. He purposely withholds honor due to God. For this

---

4. For a more detailed analysis of these points, see Zucker, *Israel's Prophets*, 188–91.
5. Zucker, "Marvels of Midrash," 5–6; idem, "Jonah's Journey." See also idem, *Israel's Prophets*, 191–93.
6. See this title in the bibliography.
7. See Ginzberg, *Legends of the Jews*, 6:349 n. 27.

transgression, God limits Jonah's prophetic message (*Sifre, Deuteronomy, Piska* 177; *Mishnah Sanhedrin* 11.5; *Babylonian Talmud Sanhedrin* 89a end; *Mekilta, Pisha* 1.100–103).

Jonah's worries. Jonah is concerned, on a more personal level, that if/when the Ninevites repent, he will once again be labeled a false prophet (*Pirke de Rabbi Eliezer*, ch. 10).

The third day. Jonah languishes in the belly of the great fish for three days before he is "saved." This three-day period has many biblical precedents. Isaac is rescued on the third day of their journey (Gen 22:4). There are similar salvific events after three days (Gen 42:17–18; [Exod 19:16ff.; Josh 2:16; Esther 5:1]), most notably in Hosea where it says, "After two days [God] will revive us; on the third day [God] will raise us up" (Hos 6:2) (*Midrash Esther Rabbah* 9.2). The rabbis see this as a statement about physical bodily resurrection—something very far from the Jonah passage, but it supports their contention of the importance of the third day.

Text Study

Jonah 1; An Acrostic of Movement

Jonah 1:4–16 contains an acrostic of movement where what begins in one direction moves toward its opposite end. This amazing outline reads:

A   Verses 4–5; The sailors fear the sea, which is angry.
  B   5; The sailors cry to their gods.
    C   5–6; They attempt to save the ship and fail.
      D   6; Jonah is called on to get help from God.
        E   7; The sailors seek the reason for storm.
          F   7; Jonah's guilt is discovered.
            G   8; Jonah is asked to explain why.
              H   9–10; *Jonah fears Yahweh, who created the sea.*
            G   10; Jonah is asked to explain why.
          F   10; They know that Jonah is guilty.
        E   11; The sailors ask Jonah to save them.
      D   12; Jonah tells them what will help.
    C   13; They attempt to save the ship and fail.
  B   14; The sailors now cry to Yahweh as God.
A   15–16; The ship calms and the sailors fear Yahweh.[8]

8. Boadt, *Reading the Old Testament*, 410.

The Numbers 3 and 4

The numbers three and four, or lists of three or four items or events, or combinations of threes and fours appear prominently in Jonah. This tightly structured writing suggests that this book is a consciously written parable, whether or not based on historical events.

i. God's name appears thirty-nine times in Jonah (3 x 13). Four different terms are used for God: *Yahweh, Elohim, El,* and *Yahweh Elohim*.

ii. Jonah is within the fish three days and three nights. Nineveh is three days' walk across (1:17 [2:1 H]; 3:3).

iii. The word "lots" (dice) appears three times, all in one verse (1:7).

iv. The word Tarshish is used three times in one verse (1:3). It also appears once more (4:2), and therefore is also an instance of four.

v. The "fish" appears three times in a row (1:17; 2:1 [2:1–2 H]). As with the word Tarshish, "fish" appears once again at the end of that particular episode (2:10 [2:11 H]).

vi. Following the Ninevites' repentance, in one verse God has three reactions: God sees what they do, renounces the punishment, and does not do it (3:10).

vii. God "provides" three items: a plant, a worm, an east wind (4:6, 7, 8).

viii. In the final chapter Jonah and God "dialogue" three times: first in 4:2–3, 4; then in 4:8, 9; and lastly in 4:9, 10–11. Significantly, God has the last word.

ix. Dry land is mentioned three times (1:9, 13; 2:10 [2:11 H]).

x. Nineveh is mentioned nine (3 x 3) times (1:2; 3:2, 3, 3, 4, 5, 6, 7; 4:11).

xi. In Nineveh, depending on one's interpretation, there are three or four designations: great, small, king (and nobles) (3:5, 6, 7). There are also four designations: human, animal, herd, flock (3:7).

xii. The ship is mentioned four times (1:3, 4, 5, 5). The first three times the word is *oniyah*; the fourth time the word is *sefinah*, translated as "ship" in the NRSV, and as "vessel," a synonym for ship, in the NJPS/TANAKH.

xiii. In Hebrew, the word "sea" is mentioned twelve times (3 x 4) (1:4, 4, 5, 9, 11, 11, 12, 12, 13, 15, 15; 2:3 [2:4 H]). In the NJPS/TANAKH, *yam* is twice translated as "overboard," and in 2:4 it is in a plural form, *yamim*).

xiv. There are 120,000 inhabitants in Nineveh (3 x 4 x 10,000) (4:11).

xv. Jonah's three narrative chapters plus the psalm chapter total four.

xvi. In the Hebrew text, Jonah is mentioned eighteen times ([3 x 3] + [3 x 3]) (1:1, 3, 5, 7, 15; 1:17, 17 [2:1, 1 H]; 2:1 [2:2 H]; 2:10 [2:11 H]; 3:1, 3, 4; 4:1, 5, 6, 6, 8, 9).

xvii. In Jonah, there are forty-eight verses (3 x 4 x 4).

xviii. The city will be overthrown in forty days (4 x 10) (3:4).

14

Micah

Introduction

MICAH PROPHESIES IN JERUSALEM during the last decades of the eighth century, c. 740–700 BCE. He is concerned with social justice. It is at the center of his thinking. Micah's signature line is "He has told you, O mortal, what is good; and what does the LORD require of you but to do justice, and to love kindness, and to walk humbly with your God?" (Mic 6:8). Micah foretells doom for Samaria, which is the capital of the northern kingdom of Israel. Micah likewise foretells doom for Jerusalem and for the towns of Judah. Guilt abounds among those in authority: judges, prophets, priests, and the leading citizens.[1] Although Micah mentions the names of Omri and Ahab (Mic 6:16), he lives over a century later; their names are meant as representatives of ungodly behavior.

Micah is the fifteenth book of the second section of the Hebrew Bible, the Prophets/*Neviim* (see Introduction: "The Order of the Books of the Bible").

Geo-Political Background

The dominant political power in the wider region of the Near East is Assyria. Their furious and frightening might hovers at the edge of Micah's prophecies. As part of its foreign and military policy, Assyria consciously uses its practices of cruel, inhuman torture toward those who oppose it.

---

1. Wolff, *Micah: A Commentary*, 14.

"Assyria's imperial strength, its military might, its practices of enslaving the vanquished, and its policy of calculated cruelty which included such atrocities as ripping up pregnant women to destroy the recalcitrants' unborn next generation . . . [produced an] unprecedented fear."[2] Those who hear Micah certainly are well aware of these facts.

Micah's Theology and Social Concerns

Religion and morality are a seamless phenomenon for Micah. God demands the highest morality; God also makes cultic (ritual-religious) demands. An unjust society is as reprehensible to this prophet as perverting established religious rituals. The men and women who cheat the poor and deny justice are more than merely immoral in a secular sense. Their crimes have a societal dimension to be sure. Micah, however, does not divide his life into aspects of religion and aspects of government. Judges who judge for a fee, judges who capitulate to the rich merely because of their wealth, are at total variance with God's laws as enunciated in the Torah. "You shall not render an unjust judgment; you shall not be partial to the poor or defer to the great: with justice you shall judge your neighbor" (Lev 19:15; cf. Mic 7:3). These laws that address magistrates are just as binding as other laws in that section in Leviticus, which deals with robbery, illicit carnal relations, and the prohibition against divination.

Micah focuses his concerns on the poor and the exploited. Like Amos before him, Micah denounces misuse of power. "Alas for those who devise wickedness and evil deeds on their beds! When the morning dawns, they perform it, because it is in their power. They covet fields, and seize them; houses, and take them away; they oppress householder and house, people and their inheritance" (Mic 2:1–2; cf. Amos 4:1; 8:4). Micah's words form a biblical version of the current criticism of globalization, where multinational conglomerates misuse power to swallow up the innocent or unwary, such as offering cheap loans and foreclosing at the first opportunity. Micah attacks the pervasive amorality of his compatriots. Justice is perverted. It is sold to the highest bidder. "The faithful have disappeared from the land, and there is no one left who is upright; they all lie in wait for blood, and they hunt each other with nets. Their hands are skilled to do evil; the official and the judge ask for a bribe, and the powerful dictate what they desire; thus they pervert justice" (Mic 7:2–3).

---

2. Wolff, *Micah the Prophet*, 3. See also Waltke, *Commentary on Micah*, 3–8.

Micah, Isaiah, and Hosea

Micah, First Isaiah, and Hosea prophesy in a similar time and place. Micah, however, is a younger contemporary of his prophetic colleagues. He condemns Samaria, the capital of Israel. By Samaria, he means the whole northern kingdom of Israel. Micah likewise focuses his wrath on Judah, and then on Jerusalem. Whereas Isaiah centers primarily on Jerusalem, Micah's major concern is the countryside. He comes from Moresheth (or Moresheth-Gath) located in the sloping hill country southwest of Jerusalem. Micah comes from a rural community. He has great sensitivity for impoverished country people, accompanied by a distrust of those who dwell in large cities. He views these capitals of Samaria and Jerusalem as representative of the corruption that is found in Israel and Judah (Mic 1:5).

At some point, however, Micah comes to Jerusalem and prophesies its future destruction. "Hear this, you rulers of the house of Jacob . . . who abhor justice and pervert all equity, who build Zion with blood and Jerusalem with wrong! . . . because of you Zion shall be plowed as a field; Jerusalem shall become a heap of ruins" (Mic 3:9–10, 12). Micah is the first prophet to suggest this. A century later, during the time of the prophet Jeremiah, people still recall his words. "Micah of Moresheth, who prophesied during the days of King Hezekiah of Judah, said to all the people of Judah: 'Thus says the LORD of hosts, Zion shall be plowed as a field; Jerusalem shall become a heap of ruins'" (Jer 26:18).

Micah suggests a similar fate for Samaria (Mic 1:6).

Micah and Isaiah share similar concepts. Each is concerned with the rich and powerful oppressing the poor (Mic 3:1–3, 8–9; Isa 5:8–12). God will bring conquering armies through the countryside to Jerusalem (Mic 1:10–16; Isa 10:27ff.) They use similar images, from soothsaying to horses and chariots (Mic 5:10ff. [5:9ff. H]; Isa 2:6ff.) Both speak of false prophecy (Mic 2:6; Isa 30:10). Going up to God's mountain, to the house of the God of Jacob, as well as turning swords into plowshares are other shared images (Mic 4:1–3; Isa 2:2–4).

Like Hosea, Micah explains that God demands justice, not merely empty ritual acts (Mic 6:6–8; Hos 6:6.) They both use the language of the law court (Mic 6:1ff.; Hos 4:1–3).

The Book of Micah

Divisions in the Book of Micah

The book of Micah can be divided into four sections:

Micah 1:1—3:12	Prophecies of judgment concerning Samaria (Israel) and Judah
Micah 4:1—5:15 (5:14 H)	Prophecies of hope and restoration
Micah 6:1—7:7	Laments, denunciation, and promise of punishment
Micah 7:8–20	Restoration and God's victory; defeat of Israel's enemies

Micah 1:1—3:12; Prophecies of Judgment Concerning Samaria (Israel) and Judah

Micah begins with a description of the time and concerns of his prophecy. Although he also addresses the northern kingdom, in this superscription he mentions only the Judean rulers Jotham, Ahaz, and Hezekiah (1:1).

Micah stands with God and the powerless common people. They are opposed by three powerful sources in the society: the ruler, civil servants/magistrates, and other prophets.

These groups covet what belongs to others. They pervert justice. Their religiosity is hypocritical. The ruler/civil servants/magistrates crave other people's property. They seize fields, houses, and homes. They hold the reins of power. They wickedly trample justice. They figuratively devour the flesh of the people and break their bones. These magistrates "abhor justice and pervert all equity . . . build Zion with blood . . . give judgment for a bribe" (3:9–11; cf. 2:2; 3:1–3). Their actions will bring retribution. Their covetousness, rapacity, and lawlessness will result in their overturn. They will sow but reap nothing. They will plant but harvest naught. They will become an object of horror and mockery (3:12; 6:15–16).

The prophets of Micah's day fare no better. They mislead the people. As long as their stomachs are full, they speak words of comfort. Furthermore, they "declare war against those who put nothing into their mouths." They say that God is with them and that no calamity will befall them. All that the prophets do is "give oracles for money" (3:5, 11). Micah rebukes his fellow prophets. Those who do not listen to God's real word will be in the dark. God will not respond to them (3:6–7).

1:2—3:12 features prophecies and punishments against Samaria and Judah. Micah denounces in strong terms the rapaciousness of his audience. They are tireless in their greed. They lust for control. They work from early dawn to add to their own power and property. They oppress women. They force children into servitude (2:2, 9). (See the Text Study at the conclusion of this chapter, "Micah Dialogues with Those Accused of Moral and Social Abuse.")

The false prophets will be silenced; "they shall all cover their lips, for there is no answer from God" (3:7).

Micah 4:1—5:15 (5:14 H); Prophecies of Hope and Restoration

In contrast to the previous section, chapter 4 begins with the promise of a glorious future. "In days to come the mountain of the LORD's house shall be established as the highest of the mountains . . . many nations shall come and say, 'Come, let us go up to the mountain of the LORD . . . that he may teach us his ways . . . out of Zion shall go forth instruction, and the word of the LORD from Jerusalem'" (4:1-2). Zion is portrayed as a woman through whose birthpangs a new and better world will come. In that future time, explains chapter 5, Israel will live at peace, and idolatry will vanish (4:3-4, 9-10; 5:3, 10ff. [5:2, 9ff. H])[3] (see the Text Study section at the conclusion of this chapter "An Idyllic Future.")

Micah 6:1—7:7; Laments, Denunciation, and Promise of Punishment

Chapter 6 and much of chapter 7 returns to a series of pronouncements and prophecies of punishment against the people. They had great leaders in the past in Moses, Aaron, and Miriam (6:4). Do they really think that God wants ritual above righteousness? God makes it clear what is desirable and what is not. "He has told you, O mortal, what is good; and what does the LORD require of you but to do justice, and to love kindness, and to walk humbly with your God?" (6:8). God will desolate the land. Judah shall be the scorn of others (6:16).

---

3. "It is Zion pictured as a woman in leadership who will bring good government over the land . . . in this chapter [chapter 4] daughter Zion becomes a positive image. . . . In the new ideal, the land of God's promise (portrayed as a woman) has power, strength and sovereignty." Harper, "Micah," 469-70.

Micah 7:8–20; Restoration and God's Victory; Defeat of Israel's Enemies

The latter part of chapter 7 returns to a prophecy of hope for the future. Verse 8 (and, some suggest, v. 7) explains that God's vindication will come. Walls will be rebuilt. Boundaries shall be extended. God will pardon iniquity and take delight in clemency (7:9, 11, 18).

These latter *salvation* sections promising divine forgiveness and the hope for future restoration are an editor's later addition to Micah. They probably are added during the post-exilic period, late in the sixth century BCE or after.

Micah in the Christian Scriptures

The early church community sees Micah's statement of the new ruler coming from Bethlehem "as an oracle concerning Christ, Matthew 2:6 quoting most of [Micah chapter 5] verse 2 [1 H] as evidence that it was to be in Bethlehem that the Christ child would be born" (Mic 5:2–4 [5:1–3 H]).[4] The Gospel of John also refers to Bethlehem as connected with the Messiah (John 7:42)

The familial unrest and discord is echoed in the Synoptic Gospels (Mic 7:6; Matt 10:21, 35–36; Mark 13:12; Luke 12:53).

The image of a woman in labor is featured in both Micah and Revelation (Mic 4:10; Rev 12:2).

In Matthew's Gospel, Jesus paraphrases Micah's call for social justice, "to do justice, and to love kindness, and to walk humbly with your God" (Matt 23:23; Mic 6:8).

Micah's idyllic future set out in 4:1–5 is often compared to the "city on a hill" imagery in Jesus' Sermon on the Mount (Matt 5:14).

John suggests that there is a saying, "One sows and another reaps." This image is suggested earlier, although in a different context, in Micah (John 4:37; Mic 6:15).

Micah's closing words that God will "show faithfulness to Jacob and unswerving loyalty to Abraham, as you have sworn to our ancestors from the days of old," finds echoes in the Magnificat (Mic 7:20; Luke 1:54–55; cf. Gen 12:1ff.; 17:7; Rom 15:8).

---

4. Newsome, *Hebrew Prophets*, 50.

Micah in Rabbinic Literature

Micah summarizes all of God's commands. Micah's signature statement is, "He has told you, O mortal, what is good; and what does the LORD require of you but to do justice, and to love kindness, and to walk humbly with your God?" This is regarded as a sterling example of summarizing God's demands for a correct covenantal relationship, both in terms of rite and in terms of right (6:8) (*Babylonian Talmud Makkot* 24a).

Other nations deserve their punishment. Before Israel other nations are offered the Ten Commandments. They reject them. Consequently, God will discipline them for their rejection. "In anger and wrath I will execute vengeance on the nations that did not obey" (5:15 [14 H]) (*Pesikta de-Rab Kahana*, Piska S.1.15).

God urges Moses to ignore the people's anger. In Exodus Moses calls out to God and seeks help, for the people are so angry they want to kill him. "Go on ahead of the people," explains God (Exod 17:5). In Hebrew, the term for "go on" could also translate as "bypass" or "pass over/before." God says to Moses, act as I do, and cites Micah 7:18, "Who is a God like you, pardoning iniquity and *passing over* the transgression?" (*Midrash Exodus Rabbah* 26.2). In short, God says to Moses, forget their complaints, overlook their sins.

Honor God by honoring one another. You show your love for God when you love one another, when you honor each other, and when you respect one another. You show your love for God when there is no [sexual] immorality, no dishonesty, no unseemly conduct, so that you will not be disqualified from bearing witness to God. The support for these ideas are Micah's words, "to do justice, and to love kindness, and to walk humbly with your God" (6:8). An additional meaning is suggested for the final phrase about walking with God. When people act in this proper way, God will descend and will walk humbly with them (*Tanna Debe Eliyyahu: The Lore of the School of Elijah*, ch. [28] 26, p. 143 [311–12]).

Rewards will come later in life. Although the righteous experience discord early in their lives, later they will know concord. A prooftext for this is from Micah. "I must bear the indignation of the LORD . . . until he takes my side. . . . I shall see his vindication" (7:9) (*Tanna Debe Eliyyahu*, ch. 11 [*Eliyyahu Zuta*], p. 192 [409–10]).

Text Study

Micah 2:6–11; Micah Dialogues with Those Accused of Moral and Social Abuse

This passage offer a glimpse of the heated reaction that Micah finds when he preaches prophecies against the rulers/civil servants/magistrates and his fellow prophets. Verses 6–10 are a dialogue, or the reporting of a dialogue. Then the last line is Micah's aside to himself, or perhaps it is the prophet's remark to a disciple.

Verse 6. In the opening verses of this chapter, Micah indicts those in power. Now they respond to him. "Do not preach," they say. They do not like his words and they tell him so!

Verse 7. Micah replies to them, "Do not my words do good to one who walks uprightly?" This leads naturally into the accusation of verses 8f.

Verses 8–9. Micah calls the rulers/wealthy civil servants/magistrates "enemies" of the common people. They literally and figuratively strip the poor of their clothes. They drive women out of their homes. They deprive the coming generation of their rights.

Verse 10. This could be the civil servants and others telling Micah he is not to physically stop and to rest. Rather, he is to move along and preach elsewhere (or preferably not to speak at all). Alternatively, it could be that the "Arise and go" is Micah telling his audience that they are polluting the land with their speech and actions.

Verse 11. This may be an aside or a comment to a disciple. Micah suggests that a prophet prophesying platitudes and the easy life is just what they would like to hear. It could be the prophet's sarcastic and bitter concluding remark to his audience.

Micah 4:1–5; An Idyllic Future

This is probably one of the most widely read passages in the Bible. It is lovely poetry with a series of internal parallels.

Verse 1. God's house shall be established in the mountains/raised above the hills.

Verses 1–2. Peoples shall stream to it/nations shall come.

Verse 2. Mountain of God; house of the God of Jacob; instruction from Zion; word of God from Jerusalem.

Verse 3. These joyous images of swords/spears and plowshares/pruning hooks are the counterpart to the terrible and terrifying prophecies and condemnations of chapters 2 and 3.

At the end of the previous chapter, Zion was to be plowed up and Jerusalem become a heap of ruins (3:12). Here we see Zion/Jerusalem flourishing. Likewise, in chapter 2 fields and homes were taken away. In this chapter people sit under vine and fig tree with none to disturb them (2:2, 9; 4:4).

15

Nahum

Introduction

NAHUM'S SOLE SUBJECT IS his rejoicing over the imminent collapse and destruction of Nineveh, the capital of the Assyrian Empire. The Neo-Babylonians lay siege to and destroy Nineveh in 612 BCE. Nahum refers to the destruction of the Egyptian city of Thebes, which the Assyrians themselves capture in 663. Therefore, the probable dates for Nahum's prophecy are c. 650–10.[1] There are only three chapters in the book.

Nahum is a contemporary of Jeremiah, Zechariah, and probably Habakkuk as well. None of these prophets, however, mentions their counterparts in their books. There is no satisfactory explanation for the fact that one prophet does not refer to another, much less to all of his prophetic contemporaries. Perhaps when these books are edited, the editor assumes that this is common knowledge.

Nahum explains that with Nineveh's downfall, the festivals again can be celebrated in Judah (1:15 [2:1 H]). Even though he does not claim this, it is possible that Nahum is a prophet and a priest.

Nahum is the sixteenth book of the second section of the Hebrew Bible, the Prophets/*Neviim* (see Introduction: "The Order of the Books of the Bible").

---

1. Roberts, *Nahum, Habakkuk, and Zephaniah*, 38–39. In Hebrew, Thebes is called *No Amon* (Nah 3:8). Amon was the tutelary deity of the city of No.

Geo-Political Background

As noted in previous chapters, the Assyrians purposely and effectively use terror and torture as part of their foreign and military policy. "Assyria's reputation for ruthless aggression was unsurpassed among the conquering empires of the ancient world. The Assyrian annals themselves are replete with examples of the infamous scorched-earth tactics, displacements of conquered peoples, and brutal reprisals administered against rebellious vassals. It was inevitable, therefore, that events heralding the empire's collapse should have brought a malevolent satisfaction to many of its long-suffering victims."[2] Nahum's words reflect that sentiment. Those who for so long brutally oppress others are now themselves conquered and destroyed. They will experience the horror they afflict on their victims.

The Book of Nahum

Divisions in the Book of Nahum

The Book of Nahum can be divided into two sections:

Nahum 1:1–14	The power of an angry God. These opening verses praise God as being slow to anger, but great in power.
Nahum 1:15—3:19 (2:1—3:19 H)	The fall, pillage, and destruction of Nineveh. The viewpoint is from within the city.

Nahum 1:1–14; The Power of an Angry God

The literal opening word of Nahum's prophecy is the Hebrew term for "oracle." This is a formulaic word, *Massa* (*m-s-'a*, *mem-sin-alef*), meaning "an oracle," "a pronouncement," or possibly "a burden." It is the same term found in Zechariah 9:1 and 12:1, the opening word of the prophecies of Second and Third Zechariah. Habakkuk and Malachi also begin with the word "oracle." The word is found elsewhere in the Bible, most frequently in First Isaiah (Isa 13:1; 15:1; 17:1, 19:1; etc.).

God is jealous and avenging, taking vengeance on enemy forces. The context for Nahum's prophecy is the (imminent?) destruction of Nineveh, the capital city, and therefore a symbol of the cruel Assyrian Empire. While God is "slow to anger but great in power . . . the LORD will by no means

---

2. West, *Introduction the Old Testament*, 351.

clear the guilty" (Nah 1:3). This verse echoes some of God's attributes depicted in Exodus 34.

Nature quakes before God. God "rebukes the sea . . . dries up all the rivers . . . mountains quake . . . and the hills melt" (1:4–5). Here Nahum shows familiarity with images in Psalm 114. None can stand before God. God will make an end of those who oppose the divine will. Although not named specifically in this verse, Nahum addresses Nineveh (which is mentioned in v. 1, "An oracle concerning Nineveh") saying, "Your name shall be perpetuated no longer. . . . I will make your grave" (1:14).

These verses can be read as an acrostic psalm/poem based on the Hebrew alphabet. (See the Text Study section at the conclusion of this chapter, "An Alphabetic Acrostic.")

Nahum 1:15—3:19 (2:1—3:19 H); The Fall, Pillage, and Destruction of Nineveh

Chapters 2 and 3 contain powerfully descriptive language. "Confusion and fear reign . . . soldiers rush everywhere . . . pandemonium becomes defeat, hope utterly collapses . . . the enemy destroys all that the city held precious. Then . . . the scene shifts . . . to a reflection on what we have just witnessed. . . . Assyria . . . has become the prey for others."[3]

"The shields of his warriors are red; his soldiers are clothed in crimson. . . . The chariots race madly through the streets, they rush to and fro through the squares; their appearance is like torches, they dart like lightning" (2:3–4 [4–5 H]).

The English words "devastation, desolation, and destruction!" capture well the Hebrew alliteration which reads, *Bukah, um'vukah um'vulakah* (2:10 [11 H]). (See also the Text Study section at the conclusion of this chapter, "Intense Battle.")

Nahum depicts Nineveh as a debauched prostitute, who is "gracefully alluring, [a] mistress of sorcery, who enslaves nations through her debaucheries" (3:4). In very strongly worded, consciously female-demeaning language, the prophet describes what will happen to Nineveh when the invaders conquer the city. (See the Text Study section at the conclusion of this chapter, "Misplaced Anger at Women.")

---

3. Boadt, *Jeremiah 26–52, Habakkuk, Zephaniah, Nahum*, 250; see also Han, "Nahum," 27–30.

Nahum in the Christian Scriptures

While Nahum is not quoted directly in the Christian Scriptures, several passages suggest familiarity with the book.

In Luke, Jesus grieves over the fate of Jerusalem. He says, "Indeed, the days will come upon you, when your enemies will set up ramparts around you and surround you, and hem you in on every side. They will crush you to the ground, you and your children within you, and they will not leave within you one stone upon another" (Luke 19:43f.) This reflects Nahum's sentiments about Nineveh. "Yet she became an exile, she went into captivity; even her infants were dashed in pieces at the head of every street. . . . All your fortresses are like fig trees . . . shaken they fall. . . . The gates of your land are wide open to your foes; fire has devoured the bars of your gates" (Nah 3:10, 12–13; cf. Hos 10:14).

Following the Lamb's opening of the sixth seal in the book of Revelation, and the subsequent cosmic upheavals, all classes of society cry out, "the great day of their wrath has come, and who is able to stand?" This sounds like Nahum's question, "Who can stand before his indignation? Who can endure the heat of his anger? His wrath is poured out like fire, and by him the rocks are broken in pieces" (Rev 6:17; Nah 1:6). The notion that God will destroy human evil is certainly a theme in the Christian Scriptures (Rev 18–19), but that idea is not exclusive to Nahum's prophecy.

In Romans, Paul reports that Scripture says, "How beautiful are the feet of those who bring good news!" This indicates his familiarity with Nahum's statement, "Look! On the mountains the feet of one who brings good tidings, who proclaims peace!" (Rom 10:15; Nah 1:15 [2:1 H]; cf. Isa 40:9; 52:7).

Nahum in Rabbinic Literature

God protects individuals. A human ruler sends armed forces against an area. It kills good and bad alike, regardless of any personal loyalty among the citizenry. God is different. Even if an entire generation is wicked and rebellious, if there is even one righteous person, God saves that person. The prooftext from Nahum reads, "THE LORD IS GOOD, A STRONGHOLD IN THE DAY OF TROUBLE; AND HE KNOWS THOSE SEEKING REFUGE IN HIM" (1:7) (*Midrash Tanhuma, Genesis, Noah*, 2.10, Gen 8:1ff., part IV).

Humans ruled by emotion; not so God. Humans succumb to anger and jealousy. By contrast, God rules over divine emotions, choosing at times to exercise anger and wrath, and sometimes not to do so. The Hebrew says

Baal ḥeimah, literally, God is "Master of/over wrath" although in its context it probably means "wrathful" (1:2) (*Midrash Genesis Rabbah* 49.8).

Offering comfort. The rabbis suggest that God does not smite a country and then leave her desolate. God offers comfort by pointing out comparable disasters. After bringing disaster to Assyria, God said, are you not like Egypt, "Are you better than Thebes that sat by the Nile?" (3:8) (*Pesikta de-Rab Kahana, Piska* 16.7).

An attack on Israel is an attack on God. The rabbis refer to the line, "From you one has gone out who plots evil against the LORD" (1:11). They say that King Sennacherib literally wants to wipe away the name of Jerusalem (cf. 2 Kgs 18–19). He instructs his soldiers each to bring him a handful of the earth of Jerusalem, so that its very name and place will disappear. An attack on Israel is regarded as an attack on God. Sennacherib is defeated. God says to Sennacherib, "Would I permit my children to be destroyed? Would I permit my people to be destroyed? Would I permit my inheritance to be destroyed?" The prooftext comes from Nahum, "Why do you plot against the LORD? He will make an end" (1:9) (*Tanna Debe Eliyyahu*, ch. [7] 8, p. 44 [103]).

Text Study

Nahum 1:2–4; An Alphabetic Acrostic

Verses 1:2–4. In the opening verses of chapter 1, it is possible to see an incomplete alphabetical acrostic, from *alef* through *tzadeh* (1:1–14).[4] It is likely that the rest of the alphabet psalm/poem was lost. Taking but the first seven letters in the Hebrew alphabet, *alef, bet, gimel, [dalet], hey, vav, zayin* . . . :

1:2a	alef	a*yl kano* . . . , "A jealous and avenging God"
1:3b	bet	b'*sufah* . . . , "His way is in whirlwind and storm . . ."
1:4a	gimel	*go-ayr* . . . , "He rebukes the sea . . ."
	dalet	
1:5a	hey	h*arim* . . . , "The mountains quake before him"
1:5b	vav	*va-tisa* . . . , "the earth heaves . . ."
1:6a	zayin	*za'mo* . . . , "Who can stand before his indignation?"

4. *Biblia Hebraica*, 7th ed.

Nahum 3:1–3; Intense Battle

The vivid imagery of the opening lines of chapter 3 are as intense as any description of a fiercely fought battle, replete with flashing swords, chariots and horsemen, hand-to-hand combat, and heaps of mutilated and dying corpses and carnage nearly beyond description. There is a vivid sense of detail that rivals a painting by Goya.

Nahum 3:4–6; Misplaced Anger at Women

Nineveh is personified as a woman. She is a debauched prostitute and a witch. She is "gracefully alluring." She uses her wiles as a "mistress of sorcery" to enslave "nations through her debaucheries and peoples through her sorcery" (3:4.) Nahum describes what will happen to Nineveh when the invaders conquer the city. This is strongly worded, consciously female-demeaning language.

The victors will humiliate Nineveh. The conquering army's anger, however, is described specifically in terms of debasing women. In this passage, God is depicted as acting for the armies, for these verses are written in the voice of the first person. "I am against you, says the LORD of hosts, and will lift up your skirts over your face; and I will let nations look at your nakedness and kingdoms on your shame. I will throw filth at you and treat you with contempt" (3:5–6).[5]

Given Nineveh's conscious foreign policy of using violence and terror to subdue her enemies and vassals, this brutal description of demeaning her citizens is not commendable, yet it is at least understandable as an emotion.[6] This is a time for vengeance.

Regrettably, then as now, rape and pillage often are instruments of war. Women often are the victims of misplaced anger and violence (see the section "Women in Lamentations" in the chapter on Lamentations in the companion volume *The Bible's WRITINGS*). There a writer notes that the

---

5. "To read Nahum ... [illustrates] how easily the description of a woman (whether literal or metaphoric) as a seductive but dangerous whore can be used to justify contempt and even violence against her." Galambush, "Nahum," 332. Similar language—but directed at Jerusalem (!)—is used by Nahum's contemporary, Jeremiah (Jer 13:22, 26–27).

6. Consider Habakkuk's words, probably directed at Assyria, when that prophet writes: "Alas for you who make your neighbors drink, pouring out your wrath until they are drunk, in order to gaze on their nakedness!" (Hab 2:15). While this could be taken literally, it is likely that Habakkuk means this metaphorically. The Assyrians poured out their wrathful terror and then humiliated their defeated foes, stripping them of clothes.

book "evokes the pain of women who have lost their children, who know sexual abuse, who are victims of war and famine."[7]

Nahum's description of Nineveh's humiliation is not without some ironies. "Nineveh was dedicated to Ishtar (whose two chief characteristics, incidentally, were her erotic and warlike nature). . . . Nahum presumably missed the special irony of his personification of Nineveh as a woman. Assyria was profoundly hated because of its brutality in conquest, which was planned and executed by men. When women were involved at all, far from being perpetrators of the bloodshed, they were part of the booty (3:1), suffering the special treatment reserved for women captives, rape."[8]

---

7. O'Connor, "Lamentations," 282.

8. Sanderson, "Nahum," 219; see also O'Brien, *Nahum*, 80–99; Lanner, "Who Will Lament Her?"

16

Habakkuk

Introduction

THERE ARE NO BIOGRAPHIC details to provide a date for Habakkuk's prophecy.[1] Habakkuk refers to the Chaldeans as a "fierce and impetuous nation, who march through the breadth of the earth, to seize dwellings not their own" (1:6). In this context, "Chaldeans" is synonymous with the Neo-Babylonians that defeat Assyria. This use as a synonym is similar to how "America" is used as a synonym for the United States.

Habakkuk probably speaks during the final decade of the seventh century BCE. His prophecy may also reflect the near-universal lament over the untimely death of popular King Josiah at Megiddo, as the monarch fought in battle against Pharaoh Neco (609.)

"In its three short chapters Habakkuk contains the word 'violence' six times (1:2, 3, 9; 2:8, 17a, b) which is 10 percent of all the occurrences in the Bible. More than that, almost every verse gives a picture of violence even when the word is not being used."[2]

---

1. Most "contemporary scholars maintain that Habakkuk lived during the rise of the Neo-Babylonian Empire in the latter part of the 7th century, from the latter years of Josiah (640–9) to the reign of Jehoiakim (609–598) or perhaps Jehoiachin (598) . . . It should be kept in mind, however, that decisions concerning Habakkuk's dates and the relation of his message to the historical events of his time are dependent on a literary assessment of the book and the identification of several key references including the 'righteous' (1:4, 13; 2:4), the 'wicked' (1:4, 13; 3:13), the subject of the 'woe' oracles (2:6–20), and the Chaldeans (1:6)." Sweeney, "Book of Habakkuk," 3:2.

2. Sanderson, "Habakkuk," 222–23.

habakkuk

Habakkuk is the seventeenth book of the second section of the Hebrew Bible, the Prophets/*Neviim* (see Introduction: "The Order of the Books of the Bible").

Geo-Political Background

The Neo-Babylonian armies shatter the might of the Assyrian empire in 612 with the defeat and destruction of Nineveh, Assyria's capital city. Many people throughout the Near East celebrate the news of the Assyrian defeat. In terms of the Hebrew Bible, Nineveh's impending doom inspires Nahum to speak his passionate words about God's (eventual) destruction of the wicked (see chapter above on Nahum). A somber mood follows the shouting and celebration at the fall of this hated enemy.

Why in the first place do the righteous suffer?

Where does one assess blame?

Habakkuk, a younger contemporary of Nahum, provides an answer.

The Book of Habakkuk

Divisions in the Book of Habakkuk

Habakkuk 1:1	A superscription identifying Habakkuk
Habakkuk 1:2–4; 1:5–11; 1:12–17; 2:1–5	A cycle of complaints spoken by the prophet; God's responses. (See the Text Study sections at the conclusion of this chapter, "Dialogue with God, the Prophet's Concern," and "Dialogue with God, God's Response.")
Habakkuk 2:6–19	A series of "alas" or "woe" oracles
Habakkuk 2:20—3:19	A hymn or a psalm beginning with a condemnation of the evil city (presumably Jerusalem); God pouring divine wrath upon various nations. The chapter concludes with the city (Jerusalem?) joyfully restored to glory.

Habakkuk 1:1; A Superscription Identifying Habakkuk

Habakkuk is mentioned by name twice in his book: in the first verse, and at the beginning of chapter 3. His name appears nowhere else in the Hebrew Bible. In the opening verse, as with Nahum (with whom there are certain affinities; see the section below, "Habakkuk and Nahum"), the very first word is the term "oracle."

Habakkuk 1:2–4; 1:5–11; 1:12–17; 2:1–5; A Cycle of Complaints Spoken by the Prophet; God's Responses

Habakkuk is unique among the prophetic books for featuring a direct dialogue with God. Like his contemporary Jeremiah, Habakkuk wants to know why it is that the wicked prosper (cf. Jer 12:1–2). Later, the book of Job will raise this issue of evil's success (cf. Job 21:7). Only in Habakkuk is there such a direct response to the question.

Habakkuk offers several answers to the problem of evil in the world:

- History has meaning when viewed from a long perspective, with the filter of faith.
- Individuals and nations need to be righteous.
- The righteous live by their faith.
- Wealth is temporary and ruthlessness is eventually punished.
- God can overturn an evil nation.
- Evil shall fail; not might but right.
- Trust in God, rejoice in your faith and your communication with God.[3]

Habakkuk 2:6–19; A Series of "Alas" or "Woe" Oracles

Beginning with 2:6 and continuing through 2:19, Habakkuk presents a series of five "woes." It is likely that the object of his anger is Assyria. Each woe begins with the word "alas"[4] (Hab 2:6, 9, 12, 15, 19).

Representative of this section are these words: "Alas for you . . . have plundered many nations, all that survive of the peoples shall plunder you. . . . Alas for you who build a town by bloodshed, and found a city on iniquity!" (2:6, 8, 12).

---

3. Developed from Leslie, "Habakkuk." Roberts, 88–116.

4. Or "ah" in NJPS/*TANAKH*. The Hebrew is *hoy*. Cf. *oy* in Isa 3:9, 11; 6:5; Jer 4:13, 31, 6:4, Ezek 16:23, etc.

Habakkuk 2:20—3:19; A Hymn or a Psalm

Chapter 3 is a hymn, or psalm, sometimes titled Habakkuk's Prayer. It may include the last verse from the previous chapter. The theme celebrates God's power and victory. As with the earlier chapters, Habakkuk portrays God as a powerful and potent force that will bring salvation to the innocent. "In fury you trod the earth, in anger you trampled nations. You came forth to save your people, to save your anointed." "I will rejoice in the LORD; I will exult in the God of my salvation" (3:12–13, 18). (See the Text Study at the conclusion of this chapter, "Habakkuk's Psalm.")

Habakkuk and Nahum

Habakkuk follows Nahum in the Bible. The two books complement each other. This may mean that a later editor's hand molded and possibly rearranged these books.

Each book contains a psalm. In Nahum, the psalm introduces the rest of the material. In Habakkuk, it serves as a conclusion.

The psalm serves as a way to refocus the other chapters. In Nahum, the psalm is theocentric, i.e., God-centered, and then secondarily derives the meaning of human events from the divine purpose. "In Habakkuk the order is reversed. The reader begins with the problems of human history and only subsequently are they resolved in the light of a divine oracle." In Nahum, the very specific and particular destruction of Nineveh is used to illustrate God's plan. "In Habakkuk the historical sequence is replaced by a new theological pattern of redemptive history" which is consciously much vaguer and blurs any real historical connection.[5]

Habakkuk in the Christian Scriptures

In Romans Paul illustrates his central theme of the *justification by faith, and faith alone*. Paul's words, although based on Habakkuk, nonetheless subtly change biblical Habakkuk's meaning. This is clear when comparing the relevant verses (Rom 1:16–17; Hab 2:4; cf. Gal 3:11; Phil 3:9; Heb 10:38).

Different Bible translations handle this in various ways. Below are examples from four standard Christian texts.

---

5. Childs, *Introduction*, 454.

New Revised Standard Version (NRSV)

"Look at the proud! Their spirit is not right in them, but the righteous live by their faith." (Hab 2:4)

"For I am not ashamed of the gospel; it is the power of God for salvation to everyone who has faith, to the Jew first and also to the Greek. For in it the righteousness of God is revealed through faith for faith; as it is written, 'The one who is righteous will live by faith' [alternatively, 'The one who is righteous through faith will live']." (Rom 1:16–17)

New English Bible (NEB)

"The reckless will be unsure of himself, while the righteous man will live by being faithful [alternatively, 'by his faithfulness']." (Hab 2:4)

"For I am not ashamed of the Gospel. It is the saving power of God for everyone who has faith—the Jew first, but the Greek also—because here is revealed God's way of righting wrong, a way that starts from faith and ends in faith [alternatively, "... wrong. It is based on faith and addressed to faith"]; as Scripture says, 'he shall gain life who is justified through faith.'" (Rom 1:16–17).

New International Version (NIV)

"See, he is puffed up; his desires are not upright—but the righteous will live by his faith [alternatively, 'faithfulness']." (Hab 2:4)

"I am not ashamed of the gospel, because it is the power of God for the salvation of everyone who believes; first for the Jew, then for the Gentile. For in the gospel a righteousness from God is revealed, a righteousness that is by faith from first to last [alternatively, 'is from faith to faith'], just as it is written: 'The righteous will live by faith.'" (Rom 1:16–17).

New American Bible (NAB)

"The rash man has no integrity; but the just man, because of his faith, shall live." (Hab 2:4)

"I am not ashamed of the gospel. It is the power of God leading everyone who believes in it to salvation, the Jew first, then the Greek. For in the gospel is revealed the justice of God which begins and ends with faith; as Scripture says, 'The just man shall live by faith.'" (Rom 1:16–17)

Paul significantly changes Habakkuk's prophecy. Paul begins with trust in God. He suggests that this leads to righteousness. Paul says *if* you trust in God, *then* you shall attain righteousness *and* life.

Habakkuk begins with the righteous person. That person *lives by being faithful*. The person therefore trusts in God. Habakkuk begins with the faithful life. For Paul faithfulness is the means to an end.

In terms of the centrality of faith,

> Paul's explanation . . . is that . . . the power of faith . . . replaces the Law.
>
> Paul begins first with the assertion that the Gospel which he preaches is a living power of God to bring man to salvation. One receives this salvation through believing in it; faith, indeed, is the only way to righteousness and salvation. Gentile and Jew alike have pursued the wrong way, the Gentile pursuing 'wisdom,' and the Jew the Law of Moses.
>
> . . . Salvation comes apart from the Law, in the gift of the Christ. And man, whether Jew or Gentile, believing in the Christ, attains salvation.[6]

Habakkuk offers a negative image of the "fisher of innocent people." In the Christian Scriptures the image refers to the disciples, who will be called ones who "fish for people," in a positive way (Hab 1:15; Matt 4:19, Mark 1:17; Luke 5:10; cf. Jer 16:16).

A phrase in Acts reflects knowledge of Habakkuk (Acts 13:41, Hab 1:5).

Habakkuk's hymn (in ch. 3) forms part of the liturgy of many Christian churches.

Habakkuk in Rabbinic Literature

God's laws summarized. All of God's laws can be condensed into a single dictum. They are either Amos' statement "Seek me and live" (Amos 5:4) or Habakkuk's "The righteous live by their faith" (Hab 2:4) (*Babylonian Talmud Makkot* 24a).

Without governmental laws chaos would reign. Habakkuk likens humans to the fish of the sea created by God. They are without proper governance (1:14). If governments do not set down laws and statutes and enforce them fairly, like the fish of the sea, might not right will rule. "Pray for the welfare of the government, for were it not for fear of the government, human beings

---

6. Sandmel, *Jewish Understanding*, 91–92.

would swallow up their neighbors alive" (*Babylonian Talmud Avodah Zarah* 4a; *Mishnah Avot* 3.2).

A latter-day Habakkuk. As Habakkuk challenges God for an answer (2:1), so the rabbinic figure Honi (Onias) the Circle-Drawer (first century BCE) draws the figure of a circle, steps in it, and refuses to move until God answers him (*Midrash on Psalms*, Ps 77.1; cf. *Babylonian Talmud Taanit* 23a–b).

Habakkuk in rabbinic legends. Habakkuk appears in rabbinic legend in a number of instances. He joins his contemporaries Isaiah, Micah, and Joel in escaping Jerusalem during the villainous days of King Manasseh (*Seder Olam* 20).[7]

According to the Apocrypha, he also is there to feed Daniel while he is in the lions' den. Habakkuk has been residing in Jerusalem. Then an angel of God orders Habakkuk to go to feed Daniel. Habakkuk demurs, saying he has never been to Babylon. Further, he does not know where the lion pit is located. Such excuses never work. An angel takes him, carries the prophet by his hair, and flies him to Babylon where he feeds Daniel. Habakkuk then returns to Jerusalem by the same method.[8]

Habakkuk in the synagogue's liturgy. Habakkuk chapter 3 is the prophetical reading for the second day of the festival of late spring, *Shavuot*/Weeks/Pentecost.

Text Study

This section, which is part of the second dialogue cycle, features two divisions: the complaint of the prophet, and then God's reply (1:12–17; 2:1; and 2:2–5).

Habakkuk 1:12–17; Dialogue with God, the Prophet's Concern

Verses 12–13. The section begins with the prophet praising God. Habakkuk acknowledges God's eternity. Yet this praise is barbed. God designated an unspecified group—"them"—for judgment and punishment. God nonetheless is too pure to look upon evil. Consequently, Habakkuk asks, why do you look upon treachery, and then remain silent when the innocent suffer? Habakkuk says this disparity in power is God's doing! Habakkuk is asking what is it about God's nature that allows this to happen.

---

7. Quoted in Ginzberg, *Legends of the Jews*, 4:278; cf. 6:373 n. 100.

8. *Bel and the Dragon* 33ff.; cf. Jossipon 3.8b–8c, quoted in Ginzberg, *Legends of the Jews*, 4:348; cf. 6:435 n. 13.

Verses 14–17. Habakkuk gives the image of the powerful exploiting the powerless. He offers the metaphor of someone fishing who draws in his or her catch.

Habakkuk 2:1–5; Dialogue with God, God's Response

Verse 1. This opening verse provides a bridge between 1:12–17 and 2:2–5. Perhaps time passes and, in frustration, Habakkuk takes this "stand." Habakkuk indicates that he will wait for God's response. Is this a physical rampart? The same Hebrew verb root for "watch" (*tz-f-h, tzadeh-fey-hey*) in "I will keep watch [I will wait]" in Habakkuk is used in Ezekiel for "sentinel" ("watchman," NJPS/*TANAKH*), for people in his day (Hab 2:1; Ezek 3:17; 33:7).

Verses 2–3. God tells Habakkuk to inscribe the reply on tablets so that they can be read clearly. In the book of Exodus, the same word for "tablets" (*luhot*) is used for the tablets on which Moses inscribed the Ten Commandments. Is this coincidental? Alternatively, does Habakkuk purposely use this term to underscore the importance of this teaching?

The response may not come as quickly as Habakkuk would like. God tells him to be patient. Even if "it seems to tarry, wait for it; it will surely come, it will not delay" (2:3).

Verse 4. This "is an answer, again not in terms of thought, but in terms of existence. Prophetic faith is trust in Him, in Whose presence stillness is a form of understanding"[9] (see above in the section, "Habakkuk in the Christian Scriptures" for another discussion about the message).

Verse 5. This verse is a difficult to translate. The sense is that in contrast to the righteous man who lives by his fidelity/faith/faithfulness, the arrogant/proud/wicked person (of 2:4a and 2:5) will be punished. In this context, the word *yayin* does not translate as "wine"; rather it is "arrogant," "defiant," or "wicked."[10]

---

9. Heschel, *Prophets*, 143.

10. Goldingay and Scalise, *Minor Prophets II*, 68–69. Regarding *yayin* see the NJPS/*TANAKH* note on this verse.

Habakkuk 2:20—3:19; Habakkuk's Psalm

Verse 2:20, even though it closes out chapter 2, it seems to fit more properly in chapter 3. It addresses God as being "in his holy temple" and admonishes all people to "keep silence" before God.

Taken by itself, chapter 3 divides into several sections. "It has a simple but elegant structure in four parts, arranged in a chiastic pattern of A:B : B:A."[11] The A verses serve as praises of God (vv. 2, 16-19). They are spoken in the form of the first person ("I have heard of your renown, and I stand in awe"; "I hear, and I tremble within . . . yet I will rejoice in the LORD," 3:2, 16, 18). The internal B verses, 3-7 and 8-15, may refer to the desert experience during the time of Moses, and then to God as a powerful God of history. These verses are stated in the second person: "You brandished your naked bow. . . . You trampled the sea with your horses"(3:9, 15.)

Verse 3:1. The chapter begins with a statement that this is "A prayer of the prophet Habakkuk according to the Shigionoth." This may be some kind of musical instrument, or a direction as to how the psalm was to be enunciated. There are similar "directions" in verses 3, 9, 13, and 19.

Verses 3:3-7. Habakkuk mentions a number of place names in these verses: Teman, Mount Paran, the tents of Cushan, and the land of Midian. Broadly, this might reflect the movement of the Israelites toward the Promised Land, with God leading the people along the "ancient pathways" (v. 6).

Verses 3:8-15. These verses describe God in mythic language, raging and fighting against unnamed enemies. "Many of the same phrases and metaphors can be found in other hymns of praise of God's victory in battle (Exod 15; Jgs 5; Deut 33; Pss 18 and 68). These stem from very ancient liturgical traditions that bring together the forces of nature—the lightning, storms, volcanic fire, thunder, wind, flooding torrents—and the personal intervention of divine beings who use these frightful manifestations of natural power as their weapons."[12]

An alternative interpretation of this psalm is that it is a petition to deliver the land from some unnamed invaders, who are mentioned in verse 16: "I wait quietly for the day of calamity to come upon the people who attack us." In this view, the author seeks God's help in verse 2: "I stand in awe, O LORD, of your work. In our own time revive it."

Verses 16-19 express "the psalmist's confidence that God will answer the petition. These sections bracket a description of a theophany in vv 3-15,

---

11. Boadt, *Jeremiah 26-52*, 189, see Kodell p. 147.
12. Boadt, *Jeremiah 26-52*, 195.

which consists of two parts. . . . Verses 3–6 describe the deity's approach, and verses 7–15 depict God's victory over the enemy in mythological terms. The theophany expresses the psalmist's confidence that God will deliver the land (v 13), demonstrating the steadfast faith of the righteous in 2:4."[13]

---

13. Sweeny, "Book of Habakkuk," 3:4.

17

Zephaniah

Introduction

FIFTY YEARS OF PROPHETIC inactivity, or prophetic silence, ends with Zephaniah's pronouncements. God's word has not been heard since the time of Isaiah and Micah. It is likely that Zephaniah prophesied in Jerusalem, prior to the seminal date of 622/621 BCE, the time of the "discovery" of the scroll of the teaching (Deuteronomy). He is a contemporary of, or perhaps even a bit older than, Jeremiah. Zephaniah explains that he lives during the reign of King Josiah (640–9). He claims to be a descendant of (King?) Hezekiah. Zephaniah is the eighteenth book of the second section of the Hebrew Bible, the Prophets/*Neviim* (see Introduction: "The Order of the Books of the Bible").

This book follows familiar prophetic patterns of oracles of disaster and judgment, which in turn are followed by oracles of salvation. Zephaniah commences with an apocalyptic picture of universal world judgment. This judgment begins in Judah/Jerusalem, but reaches out to the nations. In the final chapter, there is a further divine judgment on Jerusalem, and on the nations. The book ends with promises of redemption for the nations, and then for Zion.

Although there are no extant books of prophecy and prophets since about the time of King Hezekiah, it is clear that the words of Isaiah of Jerusalem and Micah of Moresheth are remembered and revered. To some extent, Zephaniah is influenced by his prophetic forebears. For example, there are parallels between his words and those of the prophets of the 8th century, such as Isaiah (cf. Zeph 3:1–3; and Isa 1:21–23) and Micah (cf. Zeph 3:3–5; Mic 3:1–12) . . . [likewise] Zephaniah's theme of the exaltation of Zion (3:14–18), to which the nations will bring tribute (3:10), reminds one of Isa 2:2–4 (= Mic 4:1–4). Zephaniah also shares features and concerns with his contemporary Jeremiah and with the 6th-century prophets Ezekiel and Deutero-Isaiah; among these shared features is apocalyptic eschatology (1:2–3, 7–8, 14–18), a development of late preexilic prophecy that flourished in the prophetic writings of the Exile.[1]

Apparently Zephaniah "shows no interest whatsoever in women as distinct from the society as a whole. His book never alludes to any women, named or unnamed, individually or as a group, in any context, positive or negative."[2]

Geo-Political Background

King Josiah reigns during the closing decades of the seventh century BCE. Assyria, which has dominated so much of this period, is in military decline. This means there is less outside pressure on Judah. This allows Josiah to make some of his religious reforms, including the elimination of many foreign places of worship or shrines. He also centralizes worship in Jerusalem. To understand better the historical context for the prophecies of Zephaniah, read the appropriate sections dealing with the monarchy of Josiah in this volume, in the chapter on the book of Kings (see also the relevant material in the chapter on Chronicles in the companion volume *The Bible's WRITINGS*).

The Book of Zephaniah

Divisions in the Book of Zephaniah

Zephaniah 1:1   Zephaniah's ancestry and time of prophecy

Zephaniah 1:2—2:3   The devastating results of the Day of the LORD

---

1. Kselman, "Book of Zephaniah," 6:1077–78.
2. Sanderson, "Zephaniah," 226. Nonetheless, Heffelfinger argues, "Zephaniah presents several issues for feminist interpretation" which include "domination and power relationships" as well as "Zephaniah's rhetorical aim of producing shame and humility." Heffelfinger, "Zephaniah," 340.

Zephaniah 2:4–15	The nations all about will know God's wrath; Philistia, Moab, Ammon, Ethiopia, and Assyria are specifically named
Zephaniah 3:1–8	Judgment on Jerusalem and the nations
Zephaniah 3:9–20	A message of hope and salvation for the nations and Jerusalem

Zephaniah 1:1; Zephaniah's Ancestry and Time of Prophecy

As noted, Zephaniah explains that he lives during the reign of King Josiah (640–9), and claims as his literal ancestor, Hezekiah.

Zephaniah 1:2—2:3; The Devastating Results of the Day of the LORD

The corruption Zephaniah sees in the society around him horrifies him. King Manasseh's long reign (687–42), which has recently ended, brought an abundance of pagan worship. Manasseh repudiated God's laws for a moral life. The narrative in Kings (2 Kgs 21:1–11; 2 Chr 33:1–10) spells out the full depravity of this king's rule. Among his crimes are child sacrifice, divination, various kinds of pagan worship, and the death of the innocent. Manasseh typifies an evil king. It is time for someone to cry aloud for justice and righteousness.

Zephaniah calls for a complete rejection of these idolatrous practices and all that they imply. God threatens the complete destruction of Jerusalem and Judah. "I will stretch out my hand against Judah, and against all the inhabitants of Jerusalem; and I will cut off from this place every remnant of Baal" (1:4). God is offended at the depravity of the citizenry. Zephaniah projects his own personal anger as well. Zephaniah is zealous. He is filled with righteous rhetoric.

Zephaniah's descriptions are unrelenting. He is the "literary father of Hebrew eschatology."[3] The prophet sees the end of days. Early on in his prophecy, Zephaniah warns, "Be silent before the Lord GOD! For the day of the LORD is at hand" (1:7). Further, he warns, "The great day of the LORD is near, near and hastening fast; the sound of the day of the LORD is bitter" (1:14) (see the Text Study section at the conclusion of this chapter, "The Day of the LORD.")

---

3. Sandmel, *Hebrew Scriptures*, 110.

This term "Day of the LORD" does not originate with Zephaniah. Amos, some one hundred years earlier, had used it (Amos 5:18-20). For Zephaniah, however, it takes on a more violent and destructive force. The closing lines of chapter 1 clearly are the basis for the *Dies Irae*, a medieval poem that was incorporated into the Roman Catholic Mass of the Dead.[4]

Zephaniah knows the city of Jerusalem. There are references to sections within the city, and to priests, merchants, traders, judges, and prophets (1:4, 10-11; 3:3-4).

Zephaniah 2:4-15; The Nations All About Will Know God's Wrath; Philistia, Moab, Ammon, Ethiopia, and Assyria Are Specifically Named

Zephaniah's major concerns are Judah and Jerusalem. Yet, he likewise addresses Judah's neighbors, both near and far. The Philistine city-states of Gaza, Ashkelon, Ashdod, and Ekron shall be a wasteland. Moab and Ammon will be places of nettles and salt pits not different from Sodom and Gomorrah. Reaching out further, Ethiopia shall fall (2:4; 8-9; 12). Assyria shall be attacked. Nineveh shall be deserted, for "the owl shall hoot at the window, the raven croak on the threshold; . . . [Nineveh will be] a lair for wild animals!" (2:14-15).

Zephaniah 3:1-8; Judgment on Jerusalem and the Nations

Chapter 3 begins with five verses dedicated to condemning Jerusalem. He does not identify Jerusalem by name, but this is clearly his intent. "It has not trusted in the LORD; it has not drawn near to its God" (v. 2). Officials are called "roaring lions" and its judges "evening wolves." "Its prophets are reckless . . . its priests have profaned what is sacred" (vv. 3-4). Nonetheless, God is righteous, and further, God will render judgment.

Verses 6-8 are aimed at the nations. Those nations will be "cut off" and their cities "made desolate, without people, without inhabitants" (v. 6). God will "pour out upon them [divine] indignation . . . [and] all the earth shall be consumed" (v. 8).

---

4. Han, "Nahum, Habakkuk, and Zephaniah," 96-100.

*Zephaniah 3:9-20; A Message of Hope and Salvation
for the Nations and Jerusalem*

The remainder of chapter 3 strikes a new tone. It is a message of hope for the future. In contrast to the previous prophecies, filled with death and destruction, Zephaniah proclaims that a remnant shall remain. "I will leave in the midst of you a people humble and lowly. They shall seek refuge in the name of the LORD—the remnant of Israel; they shall do no wrong, and utter no lies" (3:12–13). Jerusalem's citizens will know fame and renown. Their fortunes shall be restored (3:19–20). It is possible, but not certain, that these words are the additions of a later editor. They offer a balance against the darkness of Zephaniah's earlier statements. Alternatively, Zephaniah holds out high expectations for a saving remnant. (See the Text Study section at the conclusion of this chapter, "Hope for the Future.")

Zephaniah in the Christian Scriptures

Zephaniah is not quoted directly in the Christian Scriptures. There are, however, echoes of Zephaniah's prophecies. In the parable of the weeds of the field, Jesus explains that the "Son of Man will send his angels, and they will collect out of his kingdom all causes of sin and evildoers, and they will throw them into the furnace of fire" (Matt 13:41–42). Zephaniah explains that God will "sweep away humans and animals. . . . I will make the wicked stumble. I will cut off humanity from the face of the earth, says the LORD" (Zeph 1:3).

Paul often addresses the eschatological notion of the coming Day of the Lord. He associates it with the "Parousia," the imminent return of Jesus as the Christ (1 Thess 5:2; 2 Thess 2:2; 1 Cor 1:8; 5:5 et al.; cf. Zeph 1:7, et al.)[5]

Revelation echoes Zephaniah's thoughts (Rev 6:17; Zeph 1:14). This will be a day when the "wrath of God" will be poured "out on the earth" (Rev 16:1 see Zeph 3:8).[6]

In John's Gospel, Jesus is termed "the Son of God! You are the King of Israel!" This appellation resonates with Zephaniah's statement, "The king of Israel, the LORD, is in your midst" (John 1:49; Zeph 3:15).

---

5. See Jenni, "Day of the Lord," 784–85.

6. The Christian Scripture's use of Joel is a more direct connection for the "Day of the LORD" (Acts 2:17–21; Joel 2:28–32 [3:1–5 H]).

Zephaniah in Rabbinic Literature

God will bring the nations to the divine presence. Zephaniah expresses the hope that God will change the speech of the non-Jewish nations so that "all of them may call on the name of the LORD and serve him with one accord" (3:9). This will be in the World to Come. The midrash then quotes the line, "FOR THEN I WILL TURN OVER TO THE PEOPLES A PURE LANGUAGE [FOR ALL OF THEM TO INVOKE THE NAME OF THE LORD, TO SERVE HIM WITH A SINGLE SHOULDER (i.e., with one accord)]" (3:9) (*Midrash Tanhuma, Genesis, Noah*, 2.28, Gen 11:1ff., part VII end).

God knows the secret places. Even if people transgress secretly, and in dark and hidden places, God will find them out. As Zephaniah states, "I will search . . . with lamps" (1:12) (*Tanna Debe Eliyyahu*, ch. 18, p. 108 [236–37]).

God creates everything in the world, but not falsehood or iniquity. Not only does Scripture say that God "is perfect, and all his ways are just. A faithful God, without deceit" (Deut 32:4), but also "The LORD . . . does no wrong" (Zeph 3:5) (*Tanna Debe Eliyyahu*, ch. 3 [*Eliyyahu Zuta*], p. 175 [374]).

When will God's judgment take place? Israel asks God, when will you judge the nations? God replies, "In this matter you have no choice but to wait for Me, as it is said, 'Therefore wait for me, says the LORD, for the day when I arise as a witness. For my decision is to gather nations, to assemble kingdoms, to pour out upon them my indignation, all the heat of my anger'" (3:8) (*Pesikta de-Rab Kahana, Piska* S.2.2).

Text Study

Zephaniah 1:7, 12–17; 2:3; The Day of the LORD

The "Day of the LORD" (*Yom YHWH*) section begins and ends on the same note: specific mention of that day. At the same time, caution in the beginning is replaced by a muted hope at the conclusion.

At the center of this section is verse 15, the Day of Wrath and Trouble: *Dies irae, dies illa*. Like his predecessor Amos, who first spoke of this terror-filled day, Zephaniah pictures an agonizingly distressful time (cf. Amos 5:18–20).

> Zephaniah is as harsh as Amos in preaching the immanent return coming of the Day of Yahweh, and he leaves the people with no illusions concerning its serious character. His preaching is intended to shock, in order to make the people, especially its

leaders, mend their ways and turn to Yahweh in humility and with eagerness to do his will. But like Amos he surely did not expect any repentance from the people, and when he depicted the Day of Yahweh in strong colours he seems to have had no doubt it would come—and come soon.[7]

Verse 1:7. "Be silent before the Lord GOD! For the day of the LORD is at hand." This line echoes Isaiah. That prophet likewise suggests due concern (Isa 13:6). Each prophet uses the exact same phrase in Hebrew, "for the day of the LORD is at hand [is near]." Isaiah counsels, "Wail." Zephaniah suggests, "Be silent." Their effect is similar (cf. Ezek 7:7; 30:2–3; Joel 1:15; Obad 1:15).

Verses 1:14–16. Again Zephaniah states that "the day of the LORD is near" (v. 14). In these three verses, he repeatedly uses the word "day." It is featured nine times, a half dozen occasions in verse 15 alone (1:14–16). Zephaniah's description of this terrible and terrifying day is dramatic, but not because he offers a new and unheard of vision. Others speak of the coming of this terrible time. Zephaniah calls the day "gloom/darkness" (*afelah*). That same word periodically is used in the Torah, Prophets, and Writings (Exod 10:22; Deut 28:29; Isa 8:22; 58:10, 59:9; Jer 23:12; Joel 2:2, and Prov 4:19; 7:9). The day also is called "cloudy" and of "thick darkness" (*anan v'arafel*). These descriptions echo the narrative of the Sinai revelation. In Exodus, God's presence is described as surrounded by clouds and thick darkness (Exod 16:10; 19:16; cf. Num 9:15–22; Deut 4:11).

Zephaniah's portrayal is horrific and horrendous. It draws its strength because it is short, pungent, and dramatic. It is enhanced by its repetition of the word "day." Zephaniah's depiction as a day of "trumpet blast and battle cry" echoes not only the Sinaitic revelation, but also the horn blast/*shofar*'s call for war (Zeph 1:16; Josh 6:5ff.; Judges 7:18).

Verse 2:3. ". . . you humble of the land." These humble, good, righteous people fulfill God's law. They may be able to survive the awesome day. They stand in contrast to the officials, nobility, and others of the power elite (1:8–9).

Zephaniah 3:14–17a; 17b–20; Hope for the Future

Zephaniah begins with a message of devastation and destruction. He concludes with a message of hope. These may be later additions, written in the post-exilic world and appended to Zephaniah. Alternatively, these words of expectation and optimism may be Zephaniah's own words. Earlier in this

---

7. Kapelrud, *Message of the Prophet Zephaniah*, 67.

chapter, comparisons were noted between Micah and Zephaniah. Further, "the threefold title of Jerusalem in 3:14 (daughter of Zion, Israel, daughter of Jerusalem) reverses the three-fold condemnation in 3:1 (the rebellious, the defiled, the oppressing city). Many expressions, too, can be traced more to Isaiah and Jeremiah than to post-exilic writings."[8]

Verse 14. Zephaniah's joyous call to "Sing aloud, O daughter Zion; shout, O Israel! Rejoice and exult with all your heart, O daughter Jerusalem," stands in such contrast to the words found in Lamentations. In that book, the "elders of daughter Zion sit on the ground in silence . . . and put on sackcloth; the young girls of Jerusalem have bowed their heads to the ground" (Lam 2:10).

Zephaniah's invitation to joy is reminiscent of the opening verse of Psalm 47.

Verse 15. These words that God takes away judgments that were set against Jerusalem, and that God is in the people's midst, are similar to thoughts expressed in Second Isaiah—"Speak tenderly to Jerusalem . . . her penalty is paid" (Isa 40:2) and "I am with you . . . I am your God . . . I will uphold you with my victorious right hand" (Isa 41:10).

Verses 19–20. The notion that God will gather the outcasts and change their shame to praise, will bring the people home and restore their fortunes, is part of the theology of the post-exilic prophets. "The major elements of post-exilic eschatology are found here: destruction of the enemy (Ob 15,16; Mic 5.9; Zech 12.9), ingathering of the exiles (Mic 4.6–7; Zech 10.8–12), and return to the Holy Land (Isa 62.1–5; Zech 8.7–8)."[9]

---

8. Boadt, *Jeremiah 26–52*, 227–28. See Boadt for specific verse connections. See Kodell p. 147.

9. *NOAB*, 1216, comment on vv. 19–20.

18

Haggai

Introduction

HAGGAI PROPHESIES IN THE sixth century, about the year 520 BCE. His contemporary is (First) Zechariah. According to the biblical book of Ezra (which is written more than a century later), the two men work together in common purpose (Ezra 5:1; 6:14). Haggai and Zechariah support and encourage Zerubbabel and Joshua in rebuilding the temple in Jerusalem. Haggai does not mention Zechariah, nor does Zechariah mention Haggai. Perhaps their concern is God's word, not that of their peers. Another explanation is that it is obvious in their day that they are working together. To mention it would be superfluous. Personal tensions or differences in approach between the two men and/or their disciples may provide another answer.

Haggai is nineteenth book of the second section of the Hebrew Bible, the Prophets/*Neviim* (see Introduction: "The Order of the Books of the Bible").

Geo-Political Background

Cyrus the Persian (Cyrus II, 558[?]–529 BCE) defeats the Neo-Babylonians in 539. This changes the political landscape of the entire Near East. Cyrus now controls the vast holdings of the Neo-Babylonian Empire, including Syria and Judah. Egypt alone is outside of his direct power. Cyrus' policy is unique. He is benevolent and generous with the nations that he vanquishes. Assyria and Neo-Babylon had displaced conquered peoples. They relocated them within the empire. Cyrus encourages the repatriation of these forced refugees. To instill allegiance to him, Cyrus returns captive peoples to their homes. He financially aids them in rebuilding and in reconstructing their communities, and to reconstruct their sanctuaries. As long as they retain loyalty to him, they can rule themselves. In Cyrus' own words, "I returned to (these) sacred cities . . . the sanctuaries of which have been ruins for a long time . . . and established for them permanent sanctuaries. I (also) gathered all their (former) inhabitants and returned (to them) their habitations."[1]

Among these "(former) inhabitants . . . returned [to] . . . their habitations" are those people from the kingdom of Judah, who were forced into exile by the Babylonians fifty and more years earlier. These particular captive peoples who return to Judah become known as the Jews. "During the Babylonian exile, the Judean exiles retained their communal identity. After their return to Jerusalem, . . . they came to be called by the name *Yehudi* [Jew, plural: *Yehudim*, Jews]. The word became synonymous with the 'descendants of Abraham' . . . Hence, *Jew* developed into a common appellation . . . from which the word *Judaism* was derived to designate the faith of the Jew."[2]

The returning refugees face a land territorially much smaller than the one that they or their family had left. A neighboring tribe, the Edomites, have moved into southern Judah. There are disputes over territory. There are ongoing conflicts with this group and others as well. Likewise, there are internal tensions among those who choose repatriation. Work to rebuild the temple and to resettle the land begins under the leadership of Sheshbazzar in 538 (Ezra 1:8). They face great difficulties. The prophecies and promises of Second Isaiah and Ezekiel are inspiring. Isaiah had said, "Violence shall no longer be heard in your land, devastation or destruction within your borders." "They shall build up the ancient ruins, and shall raise up the former devastations; they shall repair the ruined cities, the devastation of many generations. Strangers shall stand and feed your flocks, foreigners shall till your land and dress your vines" (Isa 60:18; 61:4–5). Ezekiel had prophesied that the mountains of Israel would yield produce and bear fruit, the towns resettled and the ruined sites rebuilt (Ezek 36:8, 10). Reality is considerably grimmer.

Fifteen to twenty years pass by. Their initial enthusiasm dissipates. Then, under the leadership of Zerubbabel, a grandson of exiled King Jehoiachin, a second effort begins. Joshua son of Jehozadak (cf. Jeshua son of Jozadak in Ezra 3:2), a priest of the Zadokite lineage, joins Zerubbabel. They serve respectively as the official governor and the high priest, holding

---

1. Pritchard, *Ancient Near Eastern Texts*, 1:208; see also Meyers and Meyers, *Haggai, Zechariah 1–8*, xxix–xl; Meadowcroft, *Haggai*, 42–45; Matthews and Benjamin, *Old Testament Parallels*, 207–9.

2. "Jew" in Werblowsky and Wigoder, *Oxford Dictionary of the Jewish Religion*, 369; Cohen, *Beginnings*.

commissions under Cyrus's successors Cambyses (530/529-22) and Darius (522-486) (cf. Ezra 3:2ff.; Hag 1:12).

It is not an easy task to accomplish. Local inhabitants oppose the efforts to rebuild the sanctuary (Ezra 4:1-6; 5:2—6:15). The work takes several years. They finally complete a small structure about 515.

At the same time, *not all who may return to Judah actually choose to do so.* Many people decide to remain in Babylon. There are several reasons. A full generation has grown up in Babylon. They are unwilling to return to what is probably a less sophisticated, and certainly more difficult, life in Judah. They have made a new life. The return is fraught with danger. Further, the success of the venture is unknown.[3]

The Book of Haggai

Haggai contains but two chapters. They occur over a mere four months, late in the year of 520 BCE.

Divisions in the Book of Haggai

Haggai 1:1-15a	God commands Haggai to rebuild the temple. This is late summer, c. August–September, 520.
Haggai 1:15b—2:9	Statements about the future glory of the temple. This is a month or so later, early autumn, September–October 520.
Haggai 2:10-19	Ten verses about holiness and cleanliness. This section and the verses following are delivered on the same day in late autumn, November–December 520.
Haggai 2:20-23	God's words to Haggai

Haggai 1:1-15a; God Commands Haggai to Rebuild the Temple

> The temple still lay in ruins when Haggai began to prophesy on 29 August 520 B.C.E. (Hag 1:1); but enormous progress had been made by the time he concluded his brief ministry, some

---

3. Meyers and Meyers, *Haggai, Zechariah 1-8*, xxxvii; Josephus, *Antiquities* 11.1, in *Complete Works of Josephus*.

three and a half months later, on 18 December 520 (Hag 2:10, 20). The book of Haggai itself provides vivid testimony to the effect of the prophet's words on the people as they began the task of rebuilding the temple (Hag 1:12–13), supplementing the cursory notes provided by Ezra (5:1; 6:14).

. . . Haggai was greatly concerned with the reluctance of the Judeans to respond to the Persian mandate to rebuild the temple. In urging them to begin reconstruction, he also supported the pattern of high priestly and gubernatorial joint rule as permitted by the authorities in Ecbatana (Hag 1:1). Zechariah's subsequent focus on the meaning and symbolism of the temple as a legitimate expression of the new dyarchy [the structure of governor and high priest] approved by the Persian authorities that accompanied it complements Haggai's program.[4]

Haggai seeks to rebuild the temple. "Although the book is steeped in temple tradition, it is unlikely that he was a priest, since he seeks priestly guidance concerning a matter of ritual cleanliness (2:10–13)."[5] Haggai is a political activist. Like his prophetical predecessors, Haggai sees God's involvement in history. Initially he blames the people for their lack of commitment to rebuild God's house. He labels the drought they are experiencing as a punishment for their refusal to act. He tells them that they are concerned only with their creature comforts. "Is it a time for you yourselves to live in your paneled houses, while this [i.e. God's] house lies in ruins?" (1:4). (See the Text Study section at the conclusion of this chapter, "A Time to Build.")

Haggai 1:15b—2:9; Statements about the Future Glory of the Temple

Haggai works among the people. He encourages them. Do not be upset, he counsels. The temple may not have its former physical glory, but God is with us, and in time "the latter splendor of this house shall be greater than the former" (2:9) (see the Text Study at the conclusion of this chapter, "A Propitious Time.")

Haggai 2:10–19; Ten Verses about Holiness and Cleanliness

God instructs Haggai to ask the priests certain questions dealing with ritual matters concerning proper ritual cleanliness. Haggai then draws an analogy

---

4. Meyers and Meyers, "Book of Haggai," 3:20.
5. Glazier-McDonald, "Haggai," 228.

with humans. When the foundation of God's house is laid, God will bless the people.

Haggai 2:20–23; God's Words to Haggai

Finally, Haggai presents God's optimistic and apocalyptic message to the governor Zerubbabel. (See the Text Study at the conclusion of this chapter, "God's Choice.")

Unlike most of his prophetic predecessors, Haggai's major concerns are not justice, righteousness, or good deeds. These moral considerations raised by many of the other prophets do not occur here. Haggai's contemporary (and co-worker) Zechariah does address those issues (Zech 7:8–10; 8:16–17), but Haggai is single-minded. His pressing concern is rebuilding God's house. After the ritual aspect is in place and the people have a focal point, then one can speak of the parallel teachings of morality. The building of the temple is not an end in itself. It is a means to bring God's glory and God's teachings to the world.

Haggai in the Christian Scriptures

God sends a message to the people through Haggai. "I am with you, says the LORD." Similar words close out Matthew's Gospel, "I am with you always, to the end of the age" (Hag 1:13; Matt 28:20).

In verse 2:6 Haggai sounds an apocalyptic note. He prophesies that God "will shake the heavens and the earth and the sea and the dry land." This image is repeated in part in Hebrews, and echoed in Matthew and Luke (Hag 2:6, cf. 21–22; Heb 12:26–27; Matt 24:29; Luke 21:26).

Haggai in Rabbinic Literature

Haggai, Zechariah, and Malachi. Haggai, Zechariah, and Malachi are often linked together as contemporaries (*Babylonian Talmud Yoma* 9b; *Babylonian Talmud Sotah* 48b).

The final prophets. Haggai, Zechariah, and Malachi are the last representatives of the prophets. When they died, prophecy ended (*Babylonian Talmud Yoma* 9b; *Babylonian Talmud Sotah* 48b).

Passing the torch of tradition. Haggai, Zechariah, and Malachi passed on the torch and teachings of the tradition to the leaders of the Great Assembly (Great Synagogue), the early Pharisaic leaders (*Avot de Rabbi Natan*, ch. 1).

Psalms attributed to Haggai. "A number of psalms are attributed to Haggai and Zechariah in the [Septuagint, the Vulgate, and the] Peshitta (e.g., Pss. 138; 146–49); this may account for the Christian, as opposed to the Jewish, tradition that the prophet was of priestly descent."[6]

Teach a child a trade, but wealth comes from God. Teach your child a clean and easy craft, but realize that wealth comes not from one's endeavors, but from God, to whom all wealth and property belong. As Haggai explains, "The silver is mine, and the gold is mine, says the LORD of hosts" (2:8) (*Babylonian Talmud Kiddushin* 82b).

Prophets are called angels. The word for "angel" and the word for "messenger" is the same in Hebrew. In Haggai a line reads, "Then Haggai, the messenger [*mal'akh*] of the LORD, spoke to the people with the LORD's message" (1:13), which this midrash understands as the LORD's messenger/angel/prophet (*Midrash Leviticus Rabbah* 1.1; *Midrash on Psalms*, Ps 103:17).

Guardian angels. In a future time, God will cast to earth (i.e., destroy the power of) the nations' guardian angels. Haggai explains, God says "I am about to shake the heavens and the earth, and to overthrow the throne of kingdoms" (2:21–22) (*Midrash on Psalms*, Ps 150:1).

Text Study

Haggai 1:4–6; A Time to Build

Verse 4. "Is it a time for you yourselves to live in your paneled houses, while this [i.e. God's] house lies in ruins?" Haggai asks this rhetorically. He consciously echoes King David's query, nearly five hundred years earlier, when that ruler voices concern that he is sitting in a house of cedar wood while God's house has yet to constructed (2 Sam 7:2). Not too subtly, Haggai suggests to his contemporaries that just as King David sought advice from the prophet Nathan, so should they follow his (Haggai's) advice.

Since the governor Zerubbabel is a descendent of the Davidic line, Haggai also hints that as his forebear listened to Nathan, so should Zerubbabel now listen to Haggai.

---

6. Neil, "Haggai," 509.

Verses 5–6. Failure to follow God's commands brings punishments. Haggai reflects Deuteronomic tradition. Deuteronomy explains that "in the place that [God] will choose as a dwelling for his name, you shall eat the tithe of your grain, your wine, and your oil, as well as the firstlings of your herd and flock . . . you shall eat there in the presence of the LORD your God, you and your household rejoicing together" (Deut 14:23, 26). They will rejoice because they honor God. Leviticus 26:3ff. speaks of God favoring the people in all aspects of their lives as long as they follow God's laws and commandments. Haggai's message is clear. Build God's house and you will prosper too!

Haggai 2:1; A Propitious Time

Chapter 2 begins "in the seventh month, on the twenty-first day of the month." Presumably, this is in the midst of the biblically ordained seven-day festival of *Succot*/Booths/Tabernacles, which begins on the fifteenth day of the seventh month (cf. Lev 23:33ff.; 39ff.) The booth/tabernacle, a temporary dwelling/house, is part of the celebration of the autumn harvest, giving thanks to God for a bountiful crop. In like manner, Haggai is calling for the restoration of God's house here on earth. Centuries earlier, King Solomon had dedicated the temple he built during the seventh month (1 Kgs 8:1ff.). That Haggai's prophecy coincides with these dates is purposeful.

Haggai 2:20–23; God's Choice

Haggai's final oracle begins with a specific date. His message borders on the apocalyptic.

Verse 22. Haggai's images of God overthrowing chariots and drivers, and the fall of these horses and riders, echo God's earlier miracle at the Sea of Reeds (Exod 15). There likewise, God overthrew horses, chariots, and riders. As the hard times in Egypt led to the epiphany at Sinai, so does Haggai suggest that a brilliant future awaits his audience, and specifically Zerubbabel.

Verse 23. Haggai tells Zerubbabel that he will become a "signet ring" for God. Two generations earlier God had told Zerubbabel's grandfather Jehoiachin that were he a signet ring on God's hand, he would be torn off and rejected (Jer 22:24ff.) Now the time has come to rebalance the past. The exact same phrase ("signet ring") is featured in both cases.

Haggai 1:1; 2:1; Unique Dating in Haggai

"The date formulas in Haggai, unlike comparable material in Kings, Chronicles, or other prophets, are tied to the realm of a foreign power. As such, they indicate the extent to which Judean policies and thinking are geared towards Persia. They also suggest prophetic awareness of the imminent conclusion of the seventy-year period of desolation referred to in Jeremiah (Jer 25:11–12; 29:10). Reckoned from the destruction of the first temple in 587–86, the approaching year 517–16 apparently signaled a new era for Judah. This careful reckoning of dates is unique in prophecy and accentuates Haggai's views regarding Yahweh's purposeful control over history."[7]

In Haggai the dating is year-month-day ("In the second year of King Darius, in the sixth month, on the first day of the month," Hag 1:1; "In the second year of King Darius, in the seventh month, on the twenty-first day of the month," Hag 2:1). The exact opposite formula is used in Haggai's contemporary, Zechariah ("On the twenty-fourth day of the eleventh month, the month of Shebat, in the second year of Darius," Zech 1:7).

---

7. Meyers and Meyers, "Book of Haggai," 3:21.

19

Zechariah

Introduction

THE BOOK OF ZECHARIAH, like that of Isaiah, contains the writings of two or possibly three separate authors. Chapters 1–8 form the work of one person (First Zechariah). The last six chapters belong to different voices than the earlier eight chapters. These are termed Second Zechariah (Deutero-Zechariah, chs. 9–11) and Third Zechariah (Trito-Zechariah, chs. 12–14). These separate Zechariahs are based on literary, linguistic, and stylistic grounds. These latter chapters differ in theological outlook and historical reference. The final six chapters present a variety of problems because no one knows the real meaning of the references. A number of the allegories defy clear interpretation.

Zechariah is the twentieth book of the second section of the Hebrew Bible, the Prophets/*Neviim* (see Introduction: "The Order of the Books of the Bible"). The author of the first eight chapters flourished around 520 BCE.

Geo-Political Background

The historical/geo-political background for First Zechariah (Zech 1–8) is the same as that for Haggai (see the Introduction in the chapter on Haggai). The book of Zechariah does not mention Haggai, nor does the book of Haggai mention Zechariah. In Ezra, however, they are described as contemporaries (Ezra 5:1; 6:14).

The date of composition of the latter six chapters (9–14) is problematic. Speculation ranges from the seventh century to the late sixth BCE, although most scholars suggest it is still later. Some posit the period of Alexander the Great, c. 333 and after, to the time of the Maccabees, c. 165 and after. This is quite a range of views. Many feel that these chapters provide some valuable insights into the mind of Jewish thinkers of the Persian or possibly Hellenistic period in the land of Judah.[1] A later date is based on the reference made to Greece (*Yavan* in Hebrew, Zech 9:13).

It is unknown how these latter chapters were appended onto the first eight chapters. Nor is it known who did this editing. When taken together, however, although their vocabulary differs, they share some commonalities. In each line below, the initial verses are from First Zechariah; the second, set within parentheses, come from Second and/or Third Zechariah.

Zechariah 2:5ff. (9:8 and 14:11): Jerusalem with divine protection

Zechariah 8:12 (14:6ff.): An image of paradise

Zechariah 1:18ff. [2:1ff. H] (14:17): A curse on the nations

Zechariah 2:11 [2:15 H], 8:20ff. (14:16): Ultimate conversion of nations/worship of God

Zechariah 8:18ff. (14:20): Cultic rites

Zechariah 3:8; 4:6, [14], (9:9ff.): The idealized figure who triumphs[2]

Although these parallels do exist, there still are significant differences between the first eight chapters (First Zechariah) and the next six (Second/Third Zechariah).

First Zechariah	Second and Third Zechariah
Prose	Poetry
Concern to rebuild the Temple	No concern about building the Temple
Specific dates mentioned (520–18 BCE)	No dates mentioned
Primarily visions oracles	No visions
Hope for the Davidic ruler	Little concern with David
Zerubbabel hinted as idealized figure	No mention of Zerubbabel
Jerusalem as the new center	Judah as a whole as center
Didactic purpose of oracles	Traditional prophetic style[3]

1. Meyers and Meyers, *Zechariah 9–14*, 15–29; see also Neil, "Book of Zechariah," 947; Ollenburger, "Zechariah," 742. "Zechariah 9–14 . . . takes on a darker tone . . . harsh judgment is passed on the nations around Judah and on leaders within the community itself. . . . The final chapters foretell a pending time of conflict and widespread violence." O'Brien, "Zechariah," 346.

2. Childs, *Introduction*, 482–83 (v. 14 not cited in Childs).

3. Adapted from Boadt, *Reading the Old Testament*, 388.

First Zechariah and Haggai are contemporaries, and may be active colleagues. Their messages overlap. They are vitally concerned with the rebuilding of the temple. Zechariah and Haggai address the well-being of their "congregation." Yet these men exhibit different temperaments. Each has his own unique interests and style. Zechariah is primarily a visionary. Haggai is a pragmatic prophet, someone who favors direct action.

Different temperaments notwithstanding,

> Haggai and the first eight chaps. of the canonical book of Zechariah belong together as a composite work. This statement can be justified on thematic grounds alone. Both prophets deal with the reorganization of national life and institutions in the restoration period. The dated prophecies of both Haggai and Zechariah 1–8 take place within a very close time frame (29 August 520 to 7 December 518 B.C.E.). The cast of characters in the two works is virtually the same: the high priest Joshua, the governor Zerubbabel, priests, and the citizenry or representatives of Yehud (Judah). While they diverge to a certain extent in the specifics of their words, the two prophets complement each other, as one might indeed expect of two men of God who are responding to virtually the same questions and quandaries. Together they provide a pragmatic program as well as a world view that looks to the future in the process of dealing with the challenges and opportunities their people confronted at the outset of the reign of Darius I.[4]

Just as Haggai and the first eight chapters of the book of Zechariah "belong together as a composite work," so this will be true of the biblical books of Ezra and Nehemiah.

The Book of Zechariah

Divisions in the Book of Zechariah

Zechariah 1–8; First Zechariah

Zechariah 1:1–6	The prophet's call; God's invitation to repent, October–November 520
Zechariah 1:7—6:15	Eight visions, January–February 519

---

4. Meyers and Meyers, "Book of Zechariah," 6:1061. For a discussion of corresponding literary features between Haggai and Zechariah 7–8, see this citation and Meyers and Meyers, *Haggai, Zechariah 1–8*, xl–xliv, xlix.

Zechariah 7:1—8:23   Oracles on fasting and God's return to Zion, November–December 518

Zechariah 1:1–6; The Prophet's Call; God's Invitation to Repent, October–November 520

This comes some two months after Zerubbabel began work on the temple. It is a month prior to Haggai's final prophecy. Zechariah calls for repentance. He hearkens back to his prophetic predecessors. Yet he does not mention any specifically by name. Zechariah reminds his audience that the prophets' warnings overtook their ancestors, and they had to admit that God "dealt with us according to our ways and deeds" (1:6).

Zechariah 1:7—6:15; Eight Visions, January–February 519

In these visions, there is a threefold pattern. There is a vision, a question is asked about the vision, and then an answer is provided. Verse 7 gives the date of the vision.

- Vision I: 1:8–17. Four horses of different colors. Riders roam or patrol the earth.
- Vision II: 1:18–21 (2:1–4 H). Four horns represent unnamed nations that oppressed Judah, Israel, and Jerusalem.
- Vision III: 2:1–5 (2:5–9 H). A man with a measuring line. He measures Jerusalem. Zechariah is told that Jerusalem shall be so large that it will be measureless. This is followed by an appeal to the exiles that are still living in Babylon to come to Zion (2:6–13 [10–17 H]).
- Vision IV: 3:1–10. Joshua, the high priest, is accompanied by a figure. The figure accuses him before "the angel of the LORD." Different terms are used for this figure: Satan (alternatively Accuser, Adversary), NRSV; the Accuser (alternately Satan) NJPS/*TANAKH*; the Adversary (alternately the Satan), NEB; Satan (with a note that Satan "means *accuser*") NIV; Satan, NAB (see the Text Study at the end of this chapter, "Satan; Filthy Clothes; God's Spirit.")
- Vision V: 4:1–14. A lampstand of gold with a bowl, and two olive trees. The olive trees signify two consecrated figures—presumably, but not explicitly stated, Zerubbabel and Joshua, the high priest. A subdivision of this may feature God's message for Zerubbabel (4:6–10a).

(See the Text Study at the conclusion of this chapter, "Strange Figures; Anointed Figures.")

Vision VI: 5:1–4. A very large flying scroll, wherein names of wrongdoers are inscribed. It is about thirty feet by fifteen feet (twenty cubits by ten cubits; one cubit = eighteen inches).

Vision VII: 5:5–11. A floating basket. Within it is a woman representing wickedness.[5] This "woman 'Wickedness' (=idolatry) may represent a goddess in her shrine and so symbolize non-Yahwistic worship. Another option is to view the woman as human, representing foreign women (in this case Babylonian wives brought back from exile by returning Judeans)."[6] Two other winged women will take the basket to Babylonia (lit. Shinar, cf. Gen 10:10; 11:2, 9).

Vision VIII: 6:1–8. Four chariots. Different colored horses are going out to the four directions of the compass. This is followed by making a crown or crowns of silver and gold. A crown is placed on the high priest, Joshua son of Jehozadak. Mention is made of a man named Branch. He shall branch out from where he is and build the temple. The crown (crowns) shall remain at the temple (6:9–15).

Zechariah 7:1—8:23; Oracles on Fasting and God's Return to Zion, November–December 518

In this section Zechariah raises issues similar to his prophetic predecessors. In chapters 7–8 he suggests familiar standards of morality (7:8–10; 8:16–17). These include: render true judgment; show kindness and mercy; do not oppress the widow, orphan, stranger, or the poor; do not plan evil in secret; do not utter false oaths. Earlier, in chapter 3, he speaks of walking in God's paths and keeping God's charge (3:6f). In chapter 5, Zechariah addresses the evils of theft and false oaths (5:4)

Zechariah 9-11; Second Zechariah (Deutero-Zechariah)

Chapter 9. A condemnation of Israel's neighbors, Syria, Phoenicia and Philistia (9:1–8). This is followed by a prophecy of redemption for Israel (9:9–17)

---

5. Harrington, "Zechariah," 495–96.
6. Glazier-McDonald, "Zechariah," 231.

Chapter 10. A praise of God who brings the natural blessing of rain. Then come statements about false diviners, and God's anger at these leaders (10:1–3a). God's victories for Judah and Ephraim, and how the people will be gathered from distant lands complete this chapter (10:3b–12). (See the Text Study at the conclusion of this chapter, "Words of Hope.")

Chapter 11. An angry God. This chapter is filled with allegory and unknown allusions. The dominant images are shepherds, flocks, and two staves that will be broken (11:1–17). The staves are termed respectively "Favor" and "Unity" (11:7).

In addition to foreign treachery, the local leadership likewise is failing the people. The allegory of dealing with the worthless shepherds (or shepherd) and likewise worthless sheep allows for many interpretations (11:4–14). The image of uncaring shepherds is found elsewhere (in Isa 56:11; Jer 50:6–7; Ezek 34). The staffs labeled "Favor" and "Unity" (11:7), which are broken, serve as an ironic echo of the two pieces of wood in Ezekiel's hand, where they are a positive image (Ezek 37:15ff.) God brutally and powerfully dismisses them with contempt. "So I said, 'I will not be your shepherd. What is to die, let it die; what is to be destroyed, let it be destroyed; and let those that are left devour the flesh of one another!'" (Zech 11:9).

Zechariah 12–14; Third Zechariah (Trito-Zechariah)

Chapter 12. The nations of the world attack Jerusalem, but they shall fail. The clans of Judah shall say, "The inhabitants of Jerusalem have strength through the LORD of hosts, their God" (12:5). All the nations that attack Jerusalem will fail. The people will mourn, regretting that they caused suffering to someone (a king? a prophet?) (Zech 12:10ff.) The NRSV translates this section of verse 10, "when they look on the one whom they have pierced." The NJPS/*TANAKH* translates it, "and they shall lament to Me about those who are slain." It then adds a note that the meaning of these Hebrew words is uncertain.

Chapter 13. This chapter begins with purification and denunciation. Prophecy (or perhaps false prophecy) will end (13:1–2). Parents of prophets reject the false prophecy of their children (v. 3). The wicked will be punished and the virtuous will be purged of any past wrongdoing (13:4–9). The passage ends on a positive note. "They will call on my name, and I will answer them. I will say, 'They are my people'; and they will say, 'The LORD is our God'" (13:9).

Chapter 14. This is the longest and most enigmatic of the latter six chapters. It begins with an announcement of the siege and defeat of Jerusalem, including plunder, rape, and an exile for a part of its population. Immediately thereafter, God will make war on the nations. The Mount of Olives shall be split in two. Other similar earthquake-like events will take place. Miraculously, Jerusalem will be rebuilt. God's rule will be universal. All the surviving nations shall either recognize God and know reward or reject God and in turn be rejected (14:1–21) (see the Text Study at the conclusion of this chapter, "Eschatological Verses").

Third Zechariah commences with the term "oracle." The Hebrew is a formulaic word, *massa* (m-s-'a, mem-sin-alef), meaning "an oracle," "a pronouncement," or possibly "a burden." This is exactly the same term that opens the second section of Zechariah (chs. 9–11, Second Zechariah).

These final three chapters feature a lot of violence surrounding Judah and Jerusalem. Chapter 14 mentions the wondrous day when God will come. The chapter closes on a pleasant note. The eventual disposition of Jerusalem is a time and place of delight. The weather will be temperate. There will be plenty of warm sunshine. Fresh water will be abundant, summer and winter. Best of all, on that day God alone shall be worshipped. For "on that day the LORD will be one and his name one" (14:9).

Zechariah in the Christian Scriptures

First Zechariah

The first eight chapters of Zechariah (First Zechariah) provide abundant material for the author of the book of Revelation. In chapter 1, Zechariah has a vision that features four horses, each of a different color; in chapter six he refers to additional horses. In Revelation, when the Lamb opens a number of the seven seals, horses of various colors appear (Rev 6:2ff.; 19:11; Zech 1:8ff.; cf. Zech 6:2ff.).

Measuring Jerusalem is another shared image between Revelation and First Zechariah (Rev 11:1; 21:15; Zech 2:1f. [2:5f. H]).

Two olive trees are featured as images in both books (Rev 11:4; Zech 4:3, 11–14).

While Zechariah refers to one lampstand and the author of Revelation to two lampstands, this particular item appears next to the olive trees in both books (Zech 4:2; Rev 11:4).

The Accuser/Adversary/Satan provides another link between the books (Rev 12:9–10; 20:2; Zech 3:1–2).

Jude 9 and 23 may echo images in Zechariah 3:2f.

Matthew suggests that the Son of Man will "send out his angels with a loud trumpet call, and they will gather his elect from the four winds, from one end of heaven to the other." This is based on Zechariah's statement to the exiles still in Babylon, for God says to them, "Flee . . . for I have spread you abroad like the four winds of heaven" (Matt 24:31; Zech 2:6 [2:10 H]; cf. Mark 13:27).

In Ephesians, the author speaks of "putting away falsehood, let all of us speak the truth to our neighbors." This thought reflects knowledge of Zechariah's comment to "Speak the truth to one another" (Eph 4:25; Zech 8:16).

Second and Third Zechariah

The later six chapters of Zechariah provide a number of examples of "messianic" predictions for the authors of the Christian Scriptures.

The dominant image is Zechariah's depiction of the king riding into Jerusalem on a donkey, victorious, glorious, and humble. Matthew highlights this figure as Jesus enters the city by the Mount of Olives. Crowds greet him (Matt 21:4ff.; Zech 9:9; cf. 14:4). John presents a similar image. Mark and Luke echo the episode, but with less detail (John 12:12ff.; Mark 11:1ff.; Luke 19:28ff.)

Second Zechariah features the phrase "the blood of my covenant." Jesus uses this image at the Last Supper (Zech 9:11; Matt 26:28; Mark 14:24; Luke 22:20; 1 Cor 11:25; Heb 13:20).

The "thirty shekels [pieces] of silver," paid out to the shepherd in Zechariah 11 are echoed in the same sum paid to Judas for betraying Jesus (Matt 26:15; 27:9; Zech 11:12-13).[7]

Following Jesus' crucifixion, John's Gospel notes that a "passage of scripture says, 'They will look on the one whom they have pierced.'" This refers to Zechariah's statement that the "inhabitants of Jerusalem . . . [will] look on the one whom they have pierced" (John 19:37; Zech 12:10; cf. Rev 1:7). Earlier in this chapter, it was noted that NJPS/*TANAKH* translates this section of verse 10 as "and they shall lament to Me about those who are slain." It then adds a note that the meaning of these Hebrew words is uncertain.

---

7. It is unclear what the figure of thirty shekels means. According to Exodus, thirty shekels was the price of a Hebrew slave (Exod 21:32). In Zechariah, thirty shekels seem like a paltry sum. The "*Lordly price* [in 11:13] is ironic," explain the editors in *NOAB*. Dentan suggests that this is a "not inconsiderable" amount. Dentan, "Book of Zechariah," 1104. Matthew appears to refer to this incident in Zechariah, but he mentions Jeremiah as the author. He then garbles the text in any case, so that Matthew's meaning is not only obscure, but also is a blend between Exodus and Zechariah.

Zechariah's "worthless shepherd" who deserted the flock can be contrasted with John's "good shepherd" (Zech 11:17; John 10:11ff.). Jesus speaks of striking the shepherd and the sheep being scattered, a reference to a passage in Zechariah (Matt 26:31; Mark 14:27; cf. John 16:32; Zech 13:7).

Living waters flowing from Jerusalem, an image reflecting Ezekiel's prophecy appears in Revelation (Zech 14:8; Ezek 47:1–12; Rev 22:1, 17).

The closing words of Zechariah speak of the fact that there will not be "traders in the house of the LORD of hosts on that day." In the Christian Scriptures, Zechariah's apparent comment that there will not be commerce in the temple area may connect to the description of the cleansing of the temple (Zech 14:21; Matt 21:12–13; Mark 11:15–17; Luke 19:45–46; John 2:16).[8] Those descriptions in the Gospels, however, are also connected to the temple sermon passage in Jeremiah (Jer 7:11).

Zechariah in Rabbinic Literature

First Zechariah

Zechariah, Haggai, and Malachi. Zechariah, Haggai, and Malachi are contemporaries (see comments in the chapter on Haggai). All three accompanied the exiles from Babylon (*Babylonian Talmud Zebaḥim* 62a).

The final prophets. When the prophets Malachi, Haggai, and Zechariah died, prophecy ended in Israel (*Babylonian Talmud Yoma* 9b; *Babylonian Talmud Sotah* 48b).

Translating the Targum. Zechariah, Haggai, and Malachi helped Jonathan son of Uzziel to translate the Targum, the Aramaic translation of the Prophets (*Babylonian Talmud Megillah* 3a).

Zechariah is a voice of hope. Some generations following Rome's destruction of the temple, a group of rabbis lamented the fall of Jerusalem. One reminded his colleagues that even as Zion's downfall was prophesied, so was its being rebuilt. As the one prophecy was realized, so will the other. Once again, "Old men and old women shall again sit in the streets of Jerusalem . . . the city shall be full of boys and girls playing" (8:4–5) (*Midrash Lamentations Rabbah* to Lam 5:18; see also *Babylonian Talmud Makkot* 24b end—although there seems to be some confusion between Uriah son of Shamaiah of Kiriath-jearim and Micah the prophet; see Jer 26:20–23 and 26:17ff.).

---

8. Kodell, *Lamentations . . .* , 159.

Measure for measure. If Israel turns from God, God will turn from Israel. "Just as, when I called, they would not hear, so, when they called, I would not hear, says the LORD of hosts" (7:13) (*Midrash on Psalms*, Ps 10:2).

Speak the truth . . . . Rabbi Simeon ben Gamliel had a favorite saying: The world is established on three things: justice, truth, and peace. Zechariah includes all three: "Speak the truth to one another, render in your gates judgments that are true and make for peace" (8:16). Rabbi Simeon explained, "The three are, in fact, one. For when justice is exercised, truth is attained, and peace is achieved" (*Pesikta de-Rab Kahana, Piska* 19.6; cf. *Mishnah Avot* 1.18).

Settle out of court. Zechariah's "Speak the truth to one another, render in your gates judgments that are true and make for peace" (8:16) inspired another idea. Whenever possible, settle litigation out of court. When there is a judgment in court, if there is strict truth then there will *not* be a peaceful judgment. "Wherever there is strict truth there cannot be peaceful judgment; whenever there is peaceful judgment, there cannot be strict truth. How can one combine both? Only by an equitable [compromise] settlement, satisfying both parties" (*Talmud Jerusalem Sanhedrin* 1.1f. 18b, line 19).[9]

Abundant harvests brings contentment among people. When crops are plentiful in the world, people look kindly on each other, and there is peace in the world, as it is said, "On that day, says the LORD of hosts, you shall invite each other to come under your vine and fig tree" (3:10) (*Midrash on Psalms*, Ps 72:3).

If you sin, God will not answer. If you make idols and worship them, God will turn from you. "So if you sin and pray to me, I will not answer you, as stated (in Zech. 7:13) AND IT CAME TO PASS THAT, AS {I} [HE] CALLED, AND THEY DID NOT HEED; SO LET THEM CALL, AND I WILL NOT HEED, SAYS THE LORD OF HOSTS" (*Midrash Tanhuma, Leviticus, Behuqqotay* 10.3, Lev 26:3ff., part III).

Since the people did not bring proper offerings, they were punished. It will be different in the Age to Come. "(Zech. 8:10:) A PERSON HAD NO EARNINGS, after pilgrims [going up to Jerusalem] ceased. [ibid., cont.:] AND THE CATTLE EARNED NOTHING, after the offerings ceased. But in the age to come, the Holy One will not act so. Thus it is stated [in Zech. 8:11–12]: BUT NOW I WILL NOT TREAT THE REMNANT OF THIS PEOPLE AS IN THE FORMER DAYS, SAYS THE LORD OF HOSTS; FOR AS THE SEED OF PEACE, THE VINE SHALL YIELD ITS FRUIT . . . THE

---

9. Quoted in Montefiore and Loewe, *Rabbinic Anthology*, 392.

HEAVENS SHALL YIELD THEIR DEW, AND I WILL BEQUEATH ALL THESE THINGS TO THE REMNANT OF THIS PEOPLE" (*Midrash Tanhuma, Leviticus, Qedoshim* 7.7, Lev 19:23ff., part I).

Liturgical selection. A quote from Zechariah is the prophetical portion for one of the synagogue's weekly reading, in Numbers, *Beha-alotekha*. Zechariah 2:10—4:7 [2:14—4:7 H] complements Numbers 8:1—12:16. That same section in Zechariah is read on the first Sabbath in Hanukah.

Second and Third Zechariah

A messianic reference. Zechariah's statement that "your king comes to you; triumphant and victorious is he, humble and riding on a donkey" (9:9) refers to the future messianic ruler. In this interpretation, the rabbis and the Gospel writers are of the same opinion (*Pesikta Rabbati, Piska* 34.2).

A second messianic reference. The words "triumphant and victorious . . . humble" are translated as "Submissive, and yet He promises salvation" (9:9). This "describes the Messiah, for when they laughed at him while he sat in prison, he submitted for the sake of Israel to the judgment imposed on him, and is therefore properly called submissive . . . *yet he promises salvation* . . . he said . . . you will be saved, every one of you, by the mercy of the Holy One" (*Pesikta Rabbati, Piska* 34.2).

Thirty pieces of silver. In the time of the Messiah, Israel will not require the teaching of the Messiah (with a support text from Isa 11:10). The Messiah, however, will give the nations thirty precepts (Zech 11:12), which the nations will undertake to follow in the new Kingdom (*Midrash Genesis Rabbah* 98.9).[10]

Sufferings of the Messiah. The triumphant appearance of the king, glorious and triumphant, follows years of suffering. A midrashic source describes the difficult days endured by the Messiah in language similar to traditional Christian notions of the suffering of the Messiah (*Pesikta Rabbati, Piska* 34.1–2).[11]

A ram's horn brings salvation. Just as a ram was present when Isaac's life was saved, so will future Israel know its salvation in the same way for God will sound a ram's horn (cf. Gen 22:13; Zech 9:14) (*Midrash Genesis Rabbah* 56.9; *Midrash Leviticus Rabbah* 29.10).

---

10. Ibid., 669 n. 28.
11. See ibid., 583–86 and accompanying notes.

God will save Israel, even though Israel does wrong. In a future time God will save Israel, even though they wander from the path of righteousness, as it is said, "The LORD will give victory to the tents of Judah" (12:7) (*Midrash on Psalms*, Ps 107:2).

A warning against theistic dualism. Zechariah receives credit for warning about Persian religious teachings about theistic dualism. "Do not associate with those who teach that there are two deities in the world." Zechariah explains that those "two" shall perish and die (based on 13:8) (*Midrash Numbers Rabbah* 15.14).

Gog and Magog. Persian dualism and apocalypticism also are seen in the Christian Scriptures. Gog and Magog were merely a person and place in Ezekiel 38–39, but in Christian Scripture, they take on a much larger role (Rev 20:8, the battle of Armageddon). The rabbis also taught of the Gog/Magog terror. They explained that nonetheless God would triumph gloriously. The rabbis' prooftexts included Zechariah's words: "the Lord will go forth and fight against those nations" and then "the Lord will become king over all the earth" (14:3, 9) (*Midrash Leviticus Rabbah* 27.11 and *Midrash Esther Rabbah* 7.23).

God will once again rule the earth—1. Zechariah's concluding chapter provides answers for a number of questions that concern the Talmudic rabbis. In 1 Samuel 8 the people seek an earthly ruler. They are rejecting God's rule. Following the debacle of King Zedekiah of Judah and the fall of the first temple, the people see the error of their ways. They say, now we desire our first ruler. The rabbis explain, God then consents and says, once again I will rule over the earth. "And the LORD will become king over all the earth; on that day the LORD will be one and his name one" (14:9) (*Midrash Deuteronomy Rabbah* 5:11, quoting Zech 14:9).

God will once again rule the earth—2. The Psalms proclaim, "Say among the nations, 'The LORD is king!'" (Ps 96:10). How do we know this? "And the LORD will become king over all the earth; on that day the LORD will be one and his name one" (Zech 14:9) (*Midrash on Psalms*, Ps 96:2).

Liturgical selection. A quote from Zechariah 14:1–21 is the prophetical portion for the synagogue's reading for the first day of the harvest festival *Succot*/Booths/Tabernacles.

Text Study

Zechariah 3:1–5; 4:1–6; Satan; Filthy Clothes; God's Spirit

Verse 3:1. The Hebrew in this passage is *Satan*. The role of this figure is merely to serve as an "Accuser" or "Adversary" against Joshua, the high priest. Satan does not speak. The Accuser does not actually accuse, but rather God accuses the Accuser. Alternatively, an "angel of the LORD" does the accusing of the Accuser because the angel dominates the rest of this and the following chapters.

The figure of Satan has none of the demonic power found in the Christian Scriptures. He also lacks the power and presence depicted in the early chapters of Job. "In the Old Testament *Satan* (literally, "the Adversary") is not the incarnation of evil but a functionary of the heavenly court who accuses mortals of wrong."[12]

Verse 3:4. The priest Joshua's filthy clothes seem to be associated with some sort of guilt. Ritually pure garments replace his older clothes.

Verse 4:6. The angel explains that God said to Zerubbabel, "Not by might, nor by power, but by my spirit, says the LORD of hosts." This means "Zerubbabel will succeed by means of spiritual gifts conferred upon him by the LORD, cf. Isa. 11.2ff."[13]

Zechariah 4:11–14; Strange Figures; Anointed Figures

Verse 13. The angel provides an explanation for Zechariah when the prophet says he does not know the meaning of the symbol. This is similar to Ezekiel's experience at the valley of dry bones. There God asks Ezekiel, "Can these bones live?" Ezekiel admits only God knows (Ezek 37:3).

Verse 14. The "anointed" figures are not designated specifically as Zerubbabel and Joshua. Yet, as the representatives of government and religion, this is the thrust of the passage. Alongside the statement in 3:8, these are "future-oriented" longings expressed by the prophet.

---

12. *NOAB* note to Zech 3:1–10. In the (Roman Catholic) *Jerusalem Bible* a note on Zech 3:1 defines the Accuser as "a malevolent angel, Satan (lit. 'the *satan*,' i.e., 'the accuser')."

13. NJPS/*TANAKH* note on 4:6, note d.

Zechariah 10:1–12; Words of Hope

Verse 1. With the reference to rain and vegetation, it is possible that this line should be linked back to chapter 9 and serve as its closing verse.

Verses 2–3a. God is angry with the shepherds, the leaders of the people. They give false visions. They will be punished.

Verses 3b–5. Judah will flourish. They will produce leaders; working together like warriors in battle, they will fight against their enemies.

Verses 6–7. Not only Judah, but the citizens from the northern kingdom will be empowered. The references to Joseph (v. 6) and Ephraim (v. 7) are synonyms for the northern kingdom (cf. Ezek 37:19).

Verses 8–10. No matter where they are scattered, God shall bring them home.

Verses 11–12. In verse 10 Second Zechariah specifically mentions Egypt and Assyria, and both countries are mentioned again in verse 11. The "sea of distress" and the "waves of the sea" could well be metaphors for times of difficulty, and not refer to specific bodies of water.

Zechariah 14:6–21; Eschatological Verses

These eschatological verses deal with the last days. They announce God's ultimate triumph as world ruler, centered in Jerusalem. The later verses (16ff.) relate an international recognition of God's power. It is a time of universal blessing; God's goodness is open to all who would choose to receive it.

20

Malachi

Introduction

LITTLE IS KNOWN ABOUT the prophet Malachi. As with the prophets Obadiah and Habakkuk, the superscription to his oracles lacks a genealogical heritage. Since the word *Malachi* translates literally as "my messenger," it is unclear if the term is the prophet's actual name or a description of his function (cf. 3:1). Unlike Isaiah's initial words, which mention a time and place for his prophecy, or Haggai's reference to the reign of King Darius, Malachi does not indicate when he speaks. From his message, it is likely that he flourishes c. 500–450 BCE.

Malachi is the twenty-first book of the second section of the Hebrew Bible, the Prophets/*Neviim* (see Introduction: "The Order of the Books of the Bible").

Geo-Political Background

Malachi lives during the period of Persian influence. As noted with previous prophets of this era, life is difficult (see the chapters on Haggai and Zechariah). When the Babylonians exile the inhabitants of Judah in 586, the Edomites, a nearby tribe, confiscate part of their land. When the Judean exiles return, they have less territory. Life in Jerusalem and the surrounding area does not match the hopes expressed by Ezekiel and the Second Isaiah. It takes a great deal of effort to eke out a living. There are tensions with their neighbors. Still, the temple is rebuilt, and the priests are functioning there.

This takes place before Malachi prophesies. People are bringing sacrifices, yet they do not appear to be eager to do so (1:10; 3:10). A secular governor rules the land (1:8).

Malachi's prophecies

> betray a strong interest in the temple, priesthood, and the sacrificial system (cf. 1:6–13; 2:1–4, 8–9; 3:3–4, 6–11). Yet he speaks as one observing that system from the outside (cf. 1:6; 2:2). He possessed a knowledge of both the Deuteronomic (1:8; cf. Deut 15:21) and Priestly (3:10; cf. Num 18:21) legal traditions. Malachi was clearly a man of considerable personal piety, grasping the import of God's holiness and the seriousness of personal sin before God (cf. 2:17—13:4; 3:6–7; 3:13—14:1). His staunch convictions against idolatry (2:10–12), easy divorce (2:13–16), and social injustice (3:5) bespeak a man of commitment and integrity, a throwback to the days of the preexilic prophets. Malachi was also a man of some courage, as seen in his bold upbraiding of the influential priestly class and the social elite (cf. 1:1–14; 2:1–4; 3:2–4).
>
> Finally, Malachi demonstrates an important continuity with the covenantal message of earlier Hebrew prophets. He understood the priority of the internal attitude and motive over the external form (1:9–13; 2:2–3; 3:16–18; cf. Amos 5:12–15, 21–24; Mic 6:6–8). He also understood the blessing and curse of God to be rooted in personal and corporate obedience or disobedience to the stipulations of the divine covenant (3:16—14:3). He recognized that the demands of covenant included a righteous ethic, a code of behavior consistent with the nature of God, the covenant maker (3:5–7; cf. Isa 1:15–20).[1]

The Book of Malachi

Divisions in the Book of Malachi

Malachi 1:1	Superscription
Malachi 1:2–5	God's love for Israel/disdain for Edom (Esau = Edom; cf. Gen 36:1)
Malachi 1:6—2:9	Denunciation of improper priestly behavior

---

1. Hill, "Book of Malachi," 4:479; see also Glazier-McDonald, *Malachi*, 19–23. In "the Jewish Tanakh, Malachi serves as the 'seal' of the prophets. For Christian Bibles, Malachi is the transition to the New Testament." Lilly, "Malachi," 350.

Malachi 2:10–16	Denunciation of mixed marriages and callous divorce
Malachi 2:17—3:5	God will bring justice
Malachi 3:6–12	A call for proper tithes
Malachi 3:13—4:3 (3:13–21 H)	Vindication for righteous, punishment for wicked
Malachi 4:4–6 (3:22–24 H)	Elijah's new message to the people

Protestant versions of Malachi feature four chapters. In the Masoretic, or traditional Hebrew text, there are three chapters. The Masoretic Text's Malachi 3:19–24 are the same verses as the Protestant Malachi 4:1–6. The Vulgate and Roman Catholic Bible feature three chapters.

"Malachi's prophecy is simple, direct, and forceful. Indeed, 47 of the 55 verses in the book are first-person addresses to Israel, presenting a vivid encounter between God and his people."[2]

Malachi 1:1; Superscription

Malachi's lack of genealogical information was mentioned earlier. The literal opening word of his prophecy is "oracle." This is a formulaic word, *massa* (*m-s-'a, mem-sin-alef*), meaning "an oracle," "a pronouncement," or possibly "a burden." It is the same term found in Zechariah 9:1 and 12:1, the opening word of the prophecies of Second and Third Zechariah. Nahum and Habakkuk also begin with the word Oracle. There likewise is some affinity to the opening lines of Hosea, Joel, Micah, Zephaniah, Haggai, and Zechariah, where the prophecy begins with a statement that the "word of the LORD" came to the prophet.

Malachi 1:2–5; God's Love for Israel/Disdain for Edom (Esau = Edom; cf. Gen 36:1)

God affirms love for Israel, even if Israel is skeptical about this preference. At the same time, God makes clear the divine anger toward Esau/Edom. Esau is a different way to refer to the Edomites, the descendants of biblical Esau, Jacob's older brother. Malachi uses the terms Esau and Edom

---

2. Hill, "Book of Malachi," 4:480.

interchangeably (1:2-4). God explains that even if Esau/Edom plans to rebuild broken buildings, God will destroy them again.

Malachi 1:6—2:9; Denunciation of Improper Priestly Behavior

Malachi voices a number of concerns. The priesthood has degenerated. They do not show respect for God. They bring animals to the altar that are blind, lame, or sick, in clear violation of the norms of the Torah (cf. Lev 22:17-25; Deut 15:21) (see the section below, "Malachi and the Deuteronomic Code"). God addresses biting words to the priests. "A son honors his father, and servants their master. If then I am a father, where is the honor due me? And if I am a master, where is the respect due me? says the LORD of hosts to you, O priests, who despise my name" (1:6). God is unrelenting in criticizing the priest's misbehaviors, and is clear about the consequences to follow. "I will rebuke your offering, and spread dung on your faces, the dung of your offerings, and I will put you out of my presence" (2:3).

Malachi 2:10-16; Denunciation of Mixed Marriages and Callous Divorce

"Here Malachi confronts the people with a double abuse that has social and religious consequences: marriage to foreign women and divorce of legitimate wives. These issues are inextricably linked."[3] Ezra and Nehemiah will raise similar anxieties about out-marriage (see the chapters on Ezra and Nehemiah in the companion volume *The Bible's WRITINGS*). "Judah has been faithless . . . and has married the daughter of a foreign god," i.e., foreign, non-Jewish women (2:11). In his denunciation of Jews marrying non-Jews, Malachi states, "Have we not all one father? Has not one God created us?" (2:10). In this context, Malachi promotes the common ancestry of Israel. Taken out of context, Malachi's words read like an endorsement of universalism. It is in fact the opposite; he is arguing for endogamy, for the preservation of Judaism as a particular group. Marriage with non-Jews remains a persistent problem (cf. Ezra 9:1f.; 10:2f., 16-44; Neh 10:30 [31 H]; 13:23-29).

---

3. Glazier-McDonald, "Malachi," 233.

Malachi 2:17—3:5; God Will Bring Justice

At the close of chapter 2 and the beginning of chapter 3, Malachi returns momentarily to a theme he expresses in chapter 1. There he addresses the priests' improper behavior. The priests ask, "How have we despised [God's] name?" (1:6). Here the priests ask, "How have we wearied [God]?" Malachi explains that they have fatigued and disenchanted God by saying, "All who do evil are good in the sight of the LORD." Further, hypocritically they ask, "Where is the God of justice?" (2:17).

God explains that a divine messenger is on the way, but that the people will be sorely tried when the messenger comes. "For he is like a refiner's fire and like fullers' soap" (a fuller is a person who shrinks and thickens cloth with moisture, heat, and pressure). Malachi continues, explaining that the divine messenger "will purify the descendants of Levi and refine them like gold and silver " (3:2–3). Difficult and stressful days await the people. God will draw near in judgment; God "will be swift to bear witness . . . against those who swear falsely, against those who oppress . . . the widow and the orphan, against those who thrust aside the alien, and do not fear [God], says the LORD of hosts" (3:5).

Malachi 3:6–12; A Call for Proper Tithes

Once again, the people feign ignorance of their wrongdoing. God offers to return to them if they repent. Yet, the people say, "How shall we return?" (3:7). God explains, stop your false tithing. If and when Israel changes, then God will reward them, and then nations will count them happy, and the land will be a delight (vv. 10–12). Coincidentally, the people's indifference to proper payments remains a persistent problem (cf. Neh 10:32–39 [33–40 H]; 13:10–14).

Malachi 3:13—4:3 (3:13–21 H); Vindication for Righteous, Punishment for Wicked

The people continue to deny that they are in breach of God's covenant (3:13–15). Yet, there are some who do repent. God takes notice of their change of heart. A "book of remembrance was written before [God] of those who revered the LORD and thought on his name" (3:16). God explains that the righteous will prosper, and the wicked shall be trodden down (Mal 4:1–3 [3:19–21 H]).

Malachi 4:4–6 (3:22–24 H); Elijah's New Message to the People

The book concludes with an admonition to remember the teaching of Moses, and then the final lines are about God sending "the prophet Elijah before the great and terrible day of the LORD" (4:5 [3:23 H]).

Malachi and the Deuteronomic Code

As mentioned above, Malachi addresses matters about proper worship. Which set of laws are the people following? Some years later Ezra reads from the "book of the law of Moses." The Levites assisting Ezra explain these teachings to the people (Neh 8:1–2, 7–8). The assembled appear unfamiliar with these Levitical teachings. One theory is that Ezra brings the Priestly Code from Babylon, and that consequently Malachi is working with an earlier code, that of Deuteronomy.[4] (See the Text Study section at the conclusion of this chapter, "Purifying the Priesthood; Reflecting Deuteronomy; An Added Verse.")

Support for Malachi drawing upon the Deuteronomic tradition comes from several sources within the book. Malachi's "contempt for the offering of blemished [animals] (1:8) rests on Deut. 15:21 ('lame or blind'); 17:1; his demand for the full payment of 'tithe and heave offering [*terumah*]' (3:8–10) corresponds to the law of Deut. 14:22–29 (tithe and *terumah* are mentioned together elsewhere only in Deut. 12:6, 11, 17); the priests are called 'sons of Levi' (3:3; cf. 2:4, 8), as in Deuteronomy (21:5), where Levite and priest are synonymous terms, and not . . . 'sons of Aaron' (as in the Priestly Code)."[5]

There is a further connection between Malachi and the book of Deuteronomy. In Malachi 4:4 (3:22 H) the prophet specifically associates Moses with (Mt.) Horeb. In the book of Deuteronomy, Mt. Sinai consistently is referred to as Horeb (cf. Deut 1:6, 19; 4:10; 5:2; etc.). In fact the word *Sinai* appears but once in Deuteronomy (Deut 33:2).

Like Haggai and Zechariah, Malachi deals with a community that is despondent and depressed. They are apathetic. Those who have returned from Babylon expected to see and experience Israel's former glory. They hoped for, if not actually expected to see the idealized kingdom promised/prophesied by Zechariah. Instead, life is difficult. There is a strong temptation to assimilate into the wider community.

---

4. Pfeiffer, *Introduction*, 614; Dentan, 1117–18.
5. Pfeiffer, *Introduction*, 614.

Malachi in the Christian Scriptures

Malachi concludes with a statement that God will send "the prophet Elijah before the great and terrible day of the LORD." The Synoptic Gospel writers, Matthew, Mark, and Luke, interpret this as a reference to John who baptizes Jesus. Luke directly echoes this passage in Malachi (Luke 1:17). In Matthew Jesus states, "Elijah has already come" but was not recognized by the people (Matt 17:10–13). Mark reflects the idea that John the Baptizer is Elijah (Mark 6:14–17).

There are parallels between Malachi and Elijah (see the Text Study at the conclusion of this chapter, "Malachi and Elijah; Malachi and Moses.") Parallels between Elijah and Moses are discussed in the chapter on the book of Kings. The early church sees Malachi's Elijah (or Malachi-as-Elijah) as a pivotal figure linking Moses and Jesus.

Malachi explains that Elijah will reconcile the parents with their children (4:5–6 [3:23–24 H]). Church leaders suggest Elijah mediates between Moses and Jesus. Alternatively, Elijah mediates between the older and newer generations, or the older and newer teaching.

The transfiguration episode certainly places all three—Moses, Elijah, and Jesus—visibly and unambiguously together in open communication (Matt 17:1–8; Mark 9:2–8; Luke 9:28–36).

Malachi speaks of sending a "messenger to prepare the way" before God. For the church, this has christological overtones (Mal 3:1; Matt 11:10).

Mark's opening words blend statements from Malachi and Isaiah. "See, I am sending my messenger ahead of you, who will prepare your way; the voice of one crying out in the wilderness: 'Prepare the way of the Lord, make his paths straight.'" (Mark 1:2–3; Mal 3:1; Isa 40:3).

Paul quotes Malachi to demonstrate that God makes choices (Rom 9:13; Mal 1:2–3).

James explains, "Draw near to God, and he will draw near to you." This echoes both Malachi and Zechariah (Jas 4:8; Mal 3:7; Zech 1:3).

"Malachi's vision of the pure universal offering (1:11) which will replace the flawed sacrifices in the messianic age may be alluded to in Jesus' description of worship 'in spirit and truth' (Jn 4:23); it was interpreted by the Council of Trent as being fulfilled in the Eucharist."[6]

In the Protestant Bible Malachi directly precedes the Gospels. As noted earlier, Malachi speaks of sending a "messenger to prepare the way" before God (3:1). Malachi then becomes a natural segue into the Christian Scriptures.

---

6. Kodell, *Lamentations . . .* , 95.

Malachi in Rabbinic Literature

The final prophets. Malachi, Haggai, and Zechariah are contemporaries. When they die prophecy ends (*Babylonian Talmud Yoma* 9b; *Babylonian Talmud Sotah* 48b).

Malachi at Sinai. Along with his other prophetic colleagues, Malachi is there at Sinai receiving God's prophecy. The time had not yet come to declare his message (*Midrash Exodus Rabbah* 28.6).

Aaron's personality. Biblical Aaron is the prototype of the peacemaker. Through the force of his personality, Aaron moderates people's behaviors, influencing them toward peaceful action. The prooftext is that "he turned many from iniquity" (2:6) (*Avot de Rabbi Natan*, ch. 12).

Moses' modesty rewarded. "When Moses came down from Sinai [carrying the teaching], the Adversary [Satan] approached God and inquired, 'Where is the Torah?' God replied, 'I have given it to the earth.' The Adversary then went to the earth and said, 'Where is the Torah?' The earth replied, [quoting Job 28:23] 'God . . . knows its place.' Satan then went to the sea and the deep and asked and each said, [again quoting Job (28:14)], 'it is not with me.' The Adversary returned to God and complained that he had asked all over and had not found it. God said, go to Moses, and ask, which the Adversary did. Moses then replied, 'What am I, that God should have given me the Torah?' God then turned to him and said, 'Moses, are you a liar?' Moses replies to God, 'This lovely and hidden thing in which You, God, took so much pleasure, should I take credit for it?' Then God said, 'Because you have been modest therefore shall it be called by your name, as it says [in Mal 4:4 (3:22 H)], 'Remember the teaching of my servant Moses'" (*Babylonian Talmud Shabbat* 89a).

All your words are recorded. "[E]very word which issues from your mouth, whether good, evil, by mistake, or on purpose, is written in a book. Where is it shown that it is so? Where it is stated (in Mal. 3:16): THEN THOSE WHO FEARED THE LORD SPOKE WITH ONE ANOTHER. [THE LORD HAS HEARKENED AND LISTENED, AND A BOOK OF REMEMBRANCE HAS BEEN WRITTEN BEFORE HIM . . .]" (*Midrash Tanhuma, Leviticus, Metsora'* 5.2, Lev 14:1ff., part II; see Matt 12:36–37).

Do not drink while on duty. "Therefore, the High Priest was commanded not to drink wine during the time of the service, lest it confound his knowledge; for he preserves the Torah (and preserves the service) and the knowledge. Thus it is stated (in Mal. 2:6): THE TRUE TORAH WAS IN HIS MOUTH, AND NO INJUSTICE WAS FOUND ON HIS LIPS." It also says, (in vs. 7):

FOR THE LIPS OF A PRIEST PRESERVE KNOWLEDGE. Therefore the Holy One, commanded Aaron (in Lev. 10:9) DRINK NO WINE OR INTOXICATING LIQUOR" (*Midrash Tanhuma, Leviticus, Shemini* 3.7, Lev 10.8ff., part I).

Text Study

Malachi 3:1–5, 10–12; 4:5–6 (3:23–24 H); Purifying the Priesthood; Reflecting Deuteronomy; An Added Verse

Verses 3:1–5. A messenger[7] is going to sift out the priesthood ("descendants of Levi") to distinguish between the righteous (committed) and the merely perfunctory. Malachi presents a drastic image. The priests, like gold and silver, will be put through a smelting of fire.

Verses 3:10–12. Malachi shows his knowledge of Deuteronomic thought. He links God with a cause-effect relationship to proper ritual and the blessings of nature. Malachi's mention of rain/blessing and banishment of insects/prosperity in the fields is essentially a restatement of Deuteronomy, which explains that if the people are faithful then rain will be granted so that field will prosper (Deut 11:13–15; 28:2–12).

Verses 4:5–6 (3:23–24 H), an added verse. In Jewish tradition a prophet's words do not end on a pessimistic note, so line 4:5 [3:23 H] repeats after the final verse in Jewish editions of the Bible.

Malachi and Elijah; Malachi and Moses

Malachi does not associate Elijah with the anonymous "messenger" of 3:1.

Malachi's name, however, which translates as "my messenger," lends itself to the idea that this is coded language for Elijah. Elijah has not died; he is taken to heaven in a fiery chariot (2 Kgs 2). Now perhaps, he is God's messenger. There are some fascinating parallels between Elijah and Malachi's prophecy.[8]

i. Message for all Israel   1 Kgs 18:20; Mal 1:1
ii. Division within the community   1 Kgs 18:21; Mal 3:15–18
iii. Land suffering/need for water 1 Kgs 18:1; Mal 3:9–11

---

7. Note that "angel" and "messenger" are translated from the same Hebrew word.
8. Developed from Childs, *Introduction*, 495–96.

iv. People challenged to decide	1 Kgs 18:21; Mal 3:18
v. An offering is involved	1 Kgs 18:32ff.; Mal 3:3
vi. Fire from heaven	1 Kgs 18:38; Mal 3:2; 4:1 (3:19 H)
vii. Wicked punished	1 Kgs 18:40; Mal 4:3 (3:21 H)

On another level, not only is Malachi connected to Elijah, he also is a latter-day Moses figure. Moses is specifically mentioned in Malachi 4:4 [3:22 H]. Many of the same rubrics that link Elijah and Malachi also link Moses and Malachi. Most are found in the Korah rebellion, where Korah and his followers are called "Levites," and these same words (in Hebrew, *b'nai Levi*) are used in Malachi (Num 16:8; Mal 3:3).

i. Message for all Israel	Num 16:19; Mal 1:1
ii. Division within the community	Num 16:1ff.; Mal 3:15–18
iii. Land suffering/need for water	Num 16:13; Mal 3:9–11
iv. People challenged to decide	Num 16:4ff.; Mal 3:18.
v. An offering involved	Num 16:18; Mal 3:3
vi. Fire from heaven	Num 16:35; Mal 3:2; 4:1 (3:19 H)
vii. Wicked punished	Num 16:31ff.; Mal 4:3 (3:21 H)

In his final chapter, Malachi refers to Moses, and the statutes and ordinances that God "commanded him at Horeb for all Israel" (Mal 4:4 [3:22 H]). Elijah also is associated with Mt. Horeb. As with Moses, God also addressed the prophet there (1 Kgs 19; see the chapter on Kings in this volume for further information).

Glossary

Aggadah — Sermonic material, see Midrash below.

BCE, CE — Before the Common Era, Common Era. The same periods as the religiously exclusive terms Before Christ (BC) and Anno Domini (AD)

Bible — The Hebrew Scriptures; the Jewish Scriptures; the Hebrew Bible; the Jewish Bible; the *TANAKH*; the holy scriptures of Judaism; are comprised of three sections: *Torah*/Teaching, *Neviim*/Prophets, and *Ketuvim*/Writings. The newest standard Jewish translation is *Tanakh: The Holy Scriptures* (Philadelphia: Jewish Publication Society, 1985) (see NJPS/NJPS *TANAKH* below).

Note: Christians will refer to the Bible as comprised of two sacred documents, the Old Testament and the New Testament. While Jews recognize that the Christian Scriptures are sacred to Christians, only those books Christians term the Old Testament are sacred for Jews.

Christian Scriptures — The holy scriptures of Christianity; those books produced by the early Christian church; the New Testament.

Epistles — Part of the Christian Scriptures; the letters written to the early Christian communities (Romans, Corinthians, Galatians, etc.)

Exilic — Time of the Babylonian Exile (c. 586-538 BCE)

Gospels — The first four books of the Christian Scriptures: Matthew, Mark, Luke, John.

Halakhah	Lit. "the Way"; the normative traditional Jewish law/teaching.
Havdalah	The ceremony on a Saturday evening separating the Shabbat/Sabbath from the weekdays
Hebrew	Ancient (and modern) Semitic language; the language of the Jewish Bible.
Hebrew Bible, Hebrew Scriptures	The holy scriptures of Judaism (see Bible above).
Jewish Bible, Jewish Scriptures	See Hebrew Bible, Hebrew Scriptures above.
Judaism	The religion and culture of the Jewish people.
Ketuvim	The Writings, the third section of the *TANAKH*, the Hebrew Bible; comprising Psalms, Proverbs, Job, Song of Songs, Ruth, Lamentations, Ecclesiastes, Esther, Daniel, Ezra, Nehemiah, and 1 and 2 Chronicles.
Lectionary	The tradition of reading set biblical selections at the regular worship service.
Masoretic Text, MT	The traditional exact wording of the Hebrew Bible in Hebrew.
Midrash	A collection of rabbinic sermons and interpretations that supplements the Bible, compiled c. 400–1550 CE, involving many genres: tales and allegories, ethical reflections, epigrams and legends.
Midrashim	Plural of midrash.
Mishnah	Initial section of the Talmud, six volumes, compiled 200 CE.
NAB	New American Bible (a Roman Catholic Bible).
NEB	New English Bible.
Neviim	The Prophets, the second section of the *TANAKH*, the Hebrew Bible; comprising Joshua, Judges, 1 and 2 Samuel, 1 and 2 Kings, and the fifteen literary prophets: Isaiah, Jeremiah, Ezekiel, Hosea, Joel, Amos, Obadiah, Jonah, Micah, Nahum, Habakkuk, Zephaniah, Haggai, Zechariah, and Malachi.

glossary 241

New Testament	See Christian Scriptures above.
NJPS/NJPS *TANAKH*	The newest translation of the Hebrew Scriptures, *Tanakh: The Holy Scriptures* (Philadelphia: Jewish Publication Society, 1985.)
NIV	New International Version
NRSV	New Revised Standard Version.
NOAB	*The New Oxford Annotated Bible with the Apocryphal/Deuterocanonical Books* (New York: Oxford University Press, 1991); the specific edition used in this volume.
Old Testament	See Bible and Hebrew Scriptures above.
Pentateuch	The first five books of the Bible, the Torah: Genesis, Exodus, Leviticus, Numbers, and Deuteronomy.
Post-exilic	The period following the Babylonian Exile (c. 586–538 BCE.
Pre-exilic	The period prior to the Babylonian Exile (c. 586–538 BCE).
Promised Land	Israel, the land promised to Abraham, Isaac, and Jacob.
Prophets	See Neviim above.
Reed Sea/ Sea of Reeds	The "sea" the Israelites passed through (see Exod 14), mistakenly called the Red Sea.
RSV	Revised Standard Version.
Septuagint	The Greek translation of the Torah, completed c. 250 BCE.
Sheol	The underground place where the dead go for a short period of time before they cease to exist.
Sh'ma	"Hear"; first word of the Bible's statement, "Hear, Israel, the LORD is your God, the LORD alone" (Deut 6:4).
Synoptic Gospels	The Gospels of Matthew, Mark, and Luke.

Talmud	The vast compendium of Jewish thought developed in the post-biblical world c. 200 BCE to 500 CE. There are two Talmuds: the Babylonian Talmud, which is more authoritative, and the Jerusalem Talmud.
TANAKH, TANAK	An acronym for the titles of the three divisions of the Hebrew Scriptures: **T**orah/Teaching, **N**eviim/Prophets, and **K**etuvim/Writings.
Targum	The translation of the Bible into Aramaic.
Torah	Teaching, the first section of the *TANAKH*, the Hebrew Bible; comprising Genesis, Exodus, Leviticus, Numbers, Deuteronomy. Can also mean "a Jewish teaching," or by extension Jewish learning in general.
Vulgate	The Latin translation of the Greek Bible by Jerome in the fourth century CE.
Writings	See Ketuvim above.

Bibliography

Ackerman, Susan. "Isaiah." In *The Women's Bible Commentary*, edited by Carol A. Newsom and Sharon H. Ringe. Louisville, KY: Westminster John Knox, 1992.
Alter, Robert. *The Art of Biblical Narrative*. New York: Basic Books, 1981.
———. *The David Story: A Translation with Commentary of 1 and 2 Samuel*. New York: Norton, 1999.
Angel, Marc. "Messiah-Jewish View." In *A Dictionary of the Jewish-Christian Dialogue*, edited by Leon Klenicki and Geoffrey Wigoder. Expanded ed. Mahwah, NJ: Paulist, 1995.
Avot de Rabbi Natan: The Fathers According to Rabbi Nathan. Translated by Judah Goldin. New York: Schocken, 1974.
Babylonian Talmud. Edited by I. Epstein. 18 vols. London: Soncino, 1938.
Bach, Alice. "The Pleasure of Her Text." In *The Pleasures of Her Text: Feminist Readings of Biblical and Historical Texts*, edited by Alice Bach, 25–44. Philadelphia: Trinity, 1990.
———. *Women, Seduction, and Betrayal in Biblical Narrative*. New York: Cambridge University Press, 1997.
Bailey, Randall C. *David in Love and War: The Pursuit of Power in 2 Samuel 10–12*. JSOT Supplement Series 75. Sheffield: JSOT, 1990.
Bakon, Shimon. "Samson: A Tragedy in Three Acts." *Jewish Bible Quarterly* 35/1 (2007) 34–40.
Barton, John. *Joel and Obadiah*. Old Testament Library. Louisville: Westminster John Knox, 2001.
Biblia Hebraica. Edited by Rudolf Kittel. 7th ed. Stuttgart: Wurttembergische Bibelanstalt, 1937 (1951).
Bird, Phyllis. "To Play the Harlot." In *Gender and Difference in Ancient Israel*, edited by Peggy L. Day. Minneapolis: Augsburg Fortress, 1989.
Bledstein, Adrien Janis. "Is Judges a Woman's Satire on Men Who Play God?" In *A Feminist Companion to Judges*, edited by Athalya Brenner, 34–54. Sheffield: JSOT, 1993.
Block, Daniel I. *The Book of Ezekiel*. Vol. 1, *Chapters 1–24*. Grand Rapids: Eerdmans, 1997.
Boadt, Lawrence. "Book of Ezekiel." In *The Anchor Bible Dictionary*, edited by David Noel Freedman. New York: Doubleday, 1992.
———. *Jeremiah 1–25*. Old Testament Message 9. Wilmington, DE: M. Glazier, 1982.

———. *Jeremiah 26–52, Habakkuk, Zephaniah, Nahum.* Old Testament Message 10. Wilmington, DE: M. Glazier, 1982.

———. *Reading the Old Testament: An Introduction.* 2nd ed. Revised and updated by Richard Clifford and Daniel Harrington. New York: Paulist, 2012.

Boling, Robert G., and G. Ernest Wright. *Joshua.* Anchor Bible 6. Garden City, NY: Doubleday, 1982.

Boxall, Ian K. "Exile, Prophet, Visionary: Ezekiel's Influence on the Book of Revelation." In *The Book of Ezekiel and Its Influences*, edited by Henk Jan de Jonge and Johannes Tromp. Burlington, VT: Ashgate, 2007.

Bratcher, Dennis R. "Elisha." In *Harper's Bible Dictionary*, edited by Paul J. Achtemeier. San Francisco: Harper, 1985.

Brettler, Marc Z. "The Book of Obadiah." In *Harper's Bible Dictionary*, edited by Paul J. Achtemeier. San Francisco: Harper, 1985.

Bright, John. *A History of Israel.* 4th ed. Louisville: Westminster John Knox, 2000.

———. *Jeremiah.* Anchor Bible 21. Garden City, NY: Doubleday, 1965.

Brooks, Simcha Shalom. *Saul and the Monarchy: A New Look.* Burlington, VT: Ashgate, 2005.

Bronner, Leila Leah. "Valorized or Vilified?: The Women of Judges in Midrashic Sources." In *A Feminist Companion to Judges*, edited by Athalya Brenner, 72–95. Sheffield: JSOT, 1993.

Brown, Cheryl Anne, "Jephtha's Daughter," *No Longer Silent: First Century Jewish Portraits of Biblical Women*, Louisville: Westminster John Knox, 1992.

Brueggemann, Walter. *A Commentary on Jeremiah: Exile and Homecoming.* Grand Rapids: Eerdmans, 1998.

———. *Divine Presence amid Violence: Contextualizing the Book of Joshua.* Eugene, OR: Cascade, 2009.

———. *An Introduction to the Old Testament: The Canon and Christian Imagination.* Louisville, KY: Westminster John Knox, 2003.

Buitenwerf, Rieuwerd. "The Gog and Magog Tradition in Revelation 20:8." In *The Book of Ezekiel and Its Influences*, edited by Henk Jan de Jonge and Johannes Tromp. Burlington, VT: Ashgate, 2007.

Camp, Claudia V. "1 and 2 Kings." In *The Women's Bible Commentary*, edited by Carol A. Newsom and Sharon H. Ringe. Louisville, KY: Westminster John Knox, 1992.

Childs, Brevard S. *Introduction to the Old Testament as Scripture.* Philadelphia: Fortress, 1979.

Claassens, L. Juliana M. "Obadiah." In *Women's Bible Commentary*, edited by Carol A. Newsom, Sharon H. Ringe, and Jacqueline E. Lapsley. 3rd ed. Louisville: Westminster John Knox, 2012.

Clifford, Richard J. "Book of Isaiah (Second Isaiah)." In *The Anchor Bible Dictionary*, edited by David Noel Freedman. New York: Doubleday, 1992.

Cohen, A. *Everyman's Talmud.* New York: Dutton, 1949.

Cohen, Shaye J. D. *The Beginnings of Jewishness.* Berkeley: University of California Press, 1999.

Cottrill, Amy C. "Joshua." In *Women's Bible Commentary*, edited by Carol A. Newsom, Sharon H. Ringe, and Jacqueline E. Lapsley. 3rd ed. Louisville: Westminster John Knox, 2012

Davidson, Richard M. "Did King David Rape Bathsheba?: A Case Study in Narrative." *Journal of the Adventist Theological Society* 17/2 (Autumn 2006) 81–95.

Dearman, J. Andrew. *The Book of Hosea*. Grand Rapids: Eerdmans, 2010.
Dentan, Robert C. "Book of Malachi." In *The Interpreter's Bible*, edited by George Arthur Buttrick. 12 vols. Nashville: Abingdon, 1956.
———. "Book of Zechariah." In *The Interpreter's Bible*, edited by George Arthur Buttrick. 12 vols. Nashville: Abingdon, 1956.
Edelman, Diana. "Huldah the Prophet—of Yahweh or Asherah?" In *A Feminist Companion to Samuel and Kings*, edited by Athalya Brenner, 231–50. Sheffield: Sheffield Academic, 1994.
Encyclopedia Judaica. Edited by Cecil Roth. 16 vols. New York: Macmillan; Jerusalem: Keter, 1972.
Encyclopedia Judaica (2nd ed.). Edited by Fred Skolnik and Michael Berenbaum. 22 vols. Detroit: Thompson Gale, 2007.
Exum, J. Cheryl. "Michal, the Whole Story." In *Fragmented Women: Feminist (Sub) Versions of Biblical Narratives*, 42–60. Sheffield: Sheffield Academic, 1993.
———. "Murder They Wrote: Ideology and the Manipulation of Female Presence in Biblical Narrative." In *The Pleasures of Her Text, Feminist Readings of Biblical and Historical Texts*, edited by Alice Bach. Philadelphia: Trinity Press International, 1990.
Falk, Harvey. *Jesus the Pharisee*. Mahwah, NJ: Paulist, 1985.
Fewell, Danna Nolan. "Joshua." In *The Women's Bible Commentary*, edited by Carol A. Newsom and Sharon H. Ringe. Louisville, KY: Westminster John Knox, 1992.
———"Judges." In *The Women's Bible Commentary*, edited by Carol A. Newsom and Sharon H. Ringe. Louisville, KY: Westminster John Knox, 1992.
Finkelstein, Israel, and Neil Asher Silberman. *David and Solomon: In Search of the Bible's Sacred Kings and the Roots of the Western Tradition*. New York: Free Press, 2006.
Flanagan, James W. "Book of 1–2 Samuel." In *The Anchor Bible Dictionary*, edited by David Noel Freedman. New York: Doubleday, 1992.
Fontaine, Carole R. "A Response to 'Hosea.'" In *A Feminist Companion to the Latter Prophets*, edited by Athalya Brenner. Sheffield: Sheffield Academic, 1995.
Fritz, Volkmar. *1 and 2 Kings*. Translated by Anselm Hagedorn. Minneapolis: Fortress, 2003.
Galambush, Julie. "Nahum." In *Women's Bible Commentary*, edited by Carol A. Newsom, Sharon H. Ringe, and Jacqueline E. Lapsley. 3rd ed. Louisville: Westminster John Knox, 2012.
Gaster, Theodor H. *Myth, Legend, and Custom in the Old Testament*. 2 vols. Gloucester: Peter Smith, 1981.
Ginsberg, H. L. "Hosea." In *Encyclopedia Judaica*, edited by Cecil Roth. 16 vols. New York: Macmillan; Jerusalem: Keter, 1972.
Ginzberg, Louis. *The Legends of the Jews*. 7 vols. Philadelphia: Jewish Publication Society, 1967.
Gitay, Yehoshua. "The Book of Isaiah." In *Harper's Bible Dictionary*, edited by Paul J. Achtemeier. San Francisco: Harper, 1985.
Glazier-McDonald, Beth. "Haggai." In *The Women's Bible Commentary*, edited by Carol A. Newsom and Sharon H. Ringe. Louisville, KY: Westminster John Knox, 1992.
———. "Malachi." In *The Women's Bible Commentary*, edited by Carol A. Newsom and Sharon H. Ringe. Louisville, KY: Westminster John Knox, 1992.
———. "Zechariah." In *The Women's Bible Commentary*, edited by Carol A. Newsom and Sharon H. Ringe. Louisville, KY: Westminster John Knox, 1992.

———. *Malachi: The Divine Messenger*. Atlanta: Scholars, 1987.

Goldingay, John, and Pamela Scalise. *Minor Prophets II* (Nahum, Habakkuk, Zephaniah, Haggai, Zechariah, Malachi). Peabody, MA: Hendrickson, 2009.

Greenberg, Moshe. "Ezekiel." In *Encyclopedia Judaica*, edited by Cecil Roth. 16 vols. New York: Macmillan; Jerusalem: Keter, 1972.

———. *Ezekiel 21–37*. Anchor Bible 22A. New York: Doubleday, 1997.

Greenspahn, Frederick E., editor. *Scripture in the Jewish and Christian Traditions: Authority, Interpretation, Relevance*. Nashville: Abingdon, 1982.

Hackett, Jo Ann. "1 and 2 Samuel." In *Women's Bible Commentary*, edited by Carol A. Newsom, Sharon H. Ringe, and Jacqueline E. Lapsley. 3rd ed. Louisville: Westminster John Knox, 2012.

Halpern, Baruch. *David's Secret Demons: Messiah, Murderer, Traitor, King*. Grand Rapids: Eerdmans, 2001.

Han, Jin H. "Nahum, Habakkuk, and Zephaniah." In *Six Minor Prophets Through the Centuries: Nahum, Habakkuk, Zephaniah, Haggai, Zechariah, and Malachi*, Richard Coggins and Jin H. Han. Blackwell Bible Commentaries 29. Malden, MA: Blackwell-Wiley, 2011.

Haran, Menahem. "Amos." In *Encyclopedia Judaica*, edited by Cecil Roth. 16 vols. New York: Macmillan; Jerusalem: Keter, 1972.

Harper, Elizabeth A. "Jonah." In *The IVP Women's Bible Commentary*, edited by Catherine Clark Kroeger and Mary J. Evans. Downer's Grove, IL: InterVarsity, 2002.

———. "Micah." In *The IVP Women's Bible Commentary*, edited by Catherine Clark Kroeger and Mary J. Evans. Downer's Grove, IL: InterVarsity, 2002.

Harrington, Hannah K. "Zechariah." In *The IVP Women's Bible Commentary*, edited by Catherine Clark Kroeger and Mary J. Evans. Downer's Grove, IL: InterVarsity, 2002.

Heffelfinger, Katie M. "Zephaniah." In *Women's Bible Commentary*, edited by Carol A. Newsom, Sharon H. Ringe, and Jacqueline E. Lapsley. 3rd ed. Louisville: Westminster John Knox, 2012

Herbert, A. S. *The Book of the Prophet Isaiah 1–39*. New York: Cambridge University Press, 1973.

Hertzberg, Hans Wilhelm. *I and II Samuel*. Translated by J. S. Bowden. Old Testament Library. Philadelphia: Westminster, 1964.

Heschel, Abraham Joshua. *The Prophets*. New York: Harper, 1962.

Hill, Andrew E. "Book of Malachi." In *The Anchor Bible Dictionary*, edited by David Noel Freedman. New York: Doubleday, 1992.

Holloway, Steven W. "Book of 1–2 Kings." In *The Anchor Bible Dictionary*, edited by David Noel Freedman. New York: Doubleday, 1992.

Horbury, William. *Jewish Messianism and the Cult of Christ*. London: SCM, 1998.

Howard, Cameron B. R. "1 and 2 Kings." In *Women's Bible Commentary*, edited by Carol A. Newsom, Sharon H. Ringe, and Jacqueline E. Lapsley. 3rd ed. Louisville: Westminster John Knox, 2012

Howie, Carl G. "Ezekiel." *The Interpreter's Dictionary of the Bible*. Edited by George Arthur Buttrick. 4 vols. Nashville: Abingdon, 1962.

Huwiler, Elizabeth. *Biblical Women: Mirrors, Models, and Metaphors*. Cleveland, OH: United Church Press, 1993.

Irenaeus. "Joshua as a Type." *Against Heresies*. Translated by John Keble. Oxford and London: James Parker, 1872.

Jenni, Ernst. "Day of the Lord." *The Interpreter's Dictionary of the Bible*. Edited by George Arthur Buttrick. 4 vols. Nashville: Abingdon, 1962.

Jenson, Philip Peter. *Obadiah, Jonah, Micah: A Theological Commentary*. London: T. & T. Clark, 2008.

The Jewish Annotated New Testament—New Revised Standard Version. Edited by Amy-Jill Levine and Marc Zvi Brettler. New York: Oxford University Press, 2011.

The Jerusalem Bible. Garden City: Doubleday, 1966.

The Jewish Encyclopedia. Edited by Cyrus Adler and Isidore Singer. New York: Funk & Wagnall, 1903.

Jobling, David. *1 Samuel*. Berit Olam. Collegeville, MN: Liturgical, 1998.

Jones, Alexander. "Introduction to the Books of Joshua, Judges, Ruth, Samuel and Kings." In *The Jerusalem Bible*, edited by Alexander Jones. Garden City, NY: Doubleday, 1966.

Josephus, Flavius. *The Antiquities*. In *The Complete Works of Josephus*, translated by William Whiston. Boston: Walker, 1823.

Kaiser, Otto. *Isaiah 1–12: A Commentary*. Translated by R. A. Wilson. Old Testament Library. Philadelphia: Westminster, 1976.

Kamionkowski, S. Tamar. "Gender Reversal in Ezekiel 16." In *Prophets and Daniel: A Feminist Companion to the Bible*, edited by Athalya Brenner. 2nd ser. Sheffield: Sheffield Academic, 2001.

Kapelrud, Arvid S. *The Message of the Prophet Zephaniah*. Oslo: Universitetsforlaget, 1975.

Keefe, Alice A. "The Female Body, the Body Politic, and the Land: A Sociopolitical Reading of Hosea 1–2." In *A Feminist Companion to the Latter Prophets*, edited by Athalya Brenner. Sheffield: Sheffield Academic, 1995.

Keener, Craig S. *A Commentary on the Gospel of Matthew*. Grand Rapids: Eerdmans, 1999.

Klein, Lillian R. "Bathsheba Revealed." In *A Feminist Companion to Samuel and Kings*, edited by Athalya Brenner, 47–64. 2nd ser. Sheffield: Sheffield Academic, 2000.

———. *From Deborah to Esther: Sexual Politics in the Hebrew Bible*. Minneapolis: Augsburg Fortress, 2003.

Klitsner, Judy. *Subversive Sequels in the Bible: How Biblical Stories Mine and Undermine Each Other*. Philadelphia: Jewish Publication Society, 2009.

Kodell, Jerome. *Lamentations, Haggai, Zechariah, Malachi, Obadiah, Joel, Second Zechariah, Baruch*. Wilmington, DE: M. Glazier, 1982.

Kselman, John S. "Book of Zephaniah." In *The Anchor Bible Dictionary*, edited by David Noel Freedman. New York: Doubleday, 1992.

Lacocque, André. "Messiah—Christian View." In *A Dictionary of the Jewish-Christian Dialogue*, edited by Leon Klenicki and Geoffrey Wigoder. Expanded ed. Mahwah, NJ: Paulist, 1995.

Lanner, Laurel, *"Who Will Lament Her?": The Feminine and the Fantastic in the Book of Nahum*. London: T. & T. Clark, 2006.

Lapsley, Jacqueline E. "Ezekiel." In *Women's Bible Commentary*, edited by Carol A. Newsom, Sharon H. Ringe, and Jacqueline E. Lapsley. 3rd ed. Louisville: Westminster John Knox, 2012

Leslie, Elmer A. "Habakkuk." *The Interpreter's Dictionary of the Bible*. Edited by George Arthur Buttrick. 4 vols. Nashville: Abingdon, 1962.

Levine, Amy-Jill, "Matthew," Carol A. Newsom, Sharon H. Ringe, and Jacqueline E. Lapsley, Eds., *Women's Bible Commentary: Revised and Updated*, 3rd ed., Louisville, KY: Westminster John Knox, 2012.

Lilly, Ingrid E. "Malachi." In *Women's Bible Commentary*, edited by Carol A. Newsom, Sharon H. Ringe, and Jacqueline E. Lapsley. 3rd ed. Louisville: Westminster John Knox, 2012.

Limburg, James. *Jonah: A Commentary*. Old Testament Library. Louisville: Westminster John Knox, 1993.

Linafelt, Tod. *Surviving Lamentations: Catastrophe, Lament, and Protest in the Afterlife of a Biblical Book*. Chicago: University of Chicago Press, 2000.

Liver, Jacob. "Deborah." In *Encyclopedia Judaica*, edited by Cecil Roth. 16 vols. New York: Macmillan; Jerusalem: Keter, 1972.

Longman III, Tremper. *Jeremiah, Lamentations*. New International Biblical Commentary. Peabody, MA: Hendrickson, 2008.

MacKenzie, Iain M. *Irenaeus' Demonstration of the Apostolic Preaching*. Burlington, VT: Ashgate, 2002.

Magdalene, F. Rachel. "Ancient Near Eastern Treaty-Curses and the Ultimate Texts of Terror: A Study of the Language of Divine Sexual Abuse in the Prophetic Corpus." In *A Feminist Companion to the Latter Prophets*, edited by Athalya Brenner. Sheffield: Sheffield Academic, 1995.

Magonet, Jonathan. "Book of Jonah." In *The Anchor Bible Dictionary*, edited by David Noel Freedman. New York: Doubleday, 1992.

Matthews, Victor H. *Judges and Ruth* New Cambridge Bible Commentary. New York: Cambridge University Press, 2004.

Matthews, Victor H., and Don C. Benjamin. *Old Testament Parallels*. 3rd ed. Mahwah, NJ: Paulist, 2006.

Mays, James Luther. *Hosea: A Commentary*. Old Testament Library. Philadelphia: Westminster, 1969.

McCarter, P. Kyle. *II Samuel*. Anchor Bible 9. Garden City, NY: Doubleday, 1984.

McConville, J. Gordon, and Stephen N. Williams. *Joshua*. Two Horizons Old Testament Commentary. Grand Rapids: Eerdmans, 2010.

McKenzie, John L. *Second Isaiah*. Anchor Bible 20. Garden City, NY: Doubleday, 1968.

McKenzie, Steven L. *The Trouble with Kings: The Composition of the Book of Kings in the Deuteronomistic History*. Leiden: Brill, 1991.

Meadowcroft, Tim. *Haggai*. Readings. Sheffield: Sheffield Phoenix, 2006.

Mekilta de Rabbi Ishmael. Translated by Jacob Z. Lauterbach. Philadelphia: Jewish Publication Society, 1949.

Mendelhall, G. E. "The Census Lists of Numbers 1 and 26." *Journal of Biblical Literature* 77 (1958) 52–66.

Metzger, Bruce, "Narrative Books—Gospels and Acts," in *New Oxford Annotated Bible with the Apocryphal/Deuterocanonical Books*.

Meyers, Carol L., and Eric M. Meyers. "Book of Haggai." In *The Anchor Bible Dictionary*, edited by David Noel Freedman. New York: Doubleday, 1992.

———. "Book of Zechariah." In *The Anchor Bible Dictionary*, edited by David Noel Freedman. New York: Doubleday, 1992.

———. *Haggai, Zechariah 1–8*. Anchor Bible 25b. Garden City, NY: Doubleday, 1987.

———. *Zechariah 9–14*. Anchor Bible 25c. New York: Doubleday, 1993.

The Midrash on Psalms. Translated by William G. Braude. 2 vols. New Haven, CT: Yale University Press, 1959.
Midrash Rabbah (The Midrash). 10 vols. London: Soncino, 1939.
Midrash Tanhuma, Exodus and Leviticus. Vol. 2. Buber recension. Translated by John T. Townsend. Hoboken, NJ: Ktav, 1997.
Midrash Tanhuma, Genesis. Vol. 1. Buber Recension. Translated by John T. Townsend. Hoboken, NJ: Ktav, 1989.
The Mishnah. Edited by Philip Blackman. 6 vols. New York: Judaica, 1965.
Montefiore, Claude G., and Herbert Loewe, editors. *A Rabbinic Anthology*. Philadelphia: Jewish Publication Society, 1960.
Morrell, Keren E., and Catherine Clark Kroeger. "Hosea." In *The IVP Women's Bible Commentary*, edited by Catherine Clark Kroeger and Mary J. Evans. Downer's Grove, IL: InterVarsity, 2002.
Neil, William. "Haggai." In *The Interpreter's Dictionary of the Bible*, edited by George Arthur Buttrick. 4 vols. Nashville: Abingdon, 1962.
———. "Book of Zechariah." In *The Interpreter's Dictionary of the Bible*, edited by George Arthur Buttrick. 4 vols. Nashville: Abingdon, 1962.
New American Bible. Cleveland, OH: Collins World, 1970.
The New English Bible with the Apocrypha. Oxford, Cambridge: Oxford University Press, Cambridge University Press, 1970.
New International Version [The Holy Bible: New International Version]. Grand Rapids: Biblia/Zondervan, 2011.
New Oxford Annotated Bible with the Apocryphal/Deuterocanonical Books. Edited by Bruce M. Metzger and Roland E. Murphy. New York: Oxford University Press, 1991.
Newsom, Carol A., and Sharon H. Ringe, editors. *The Women's Bible Commentary*. Louisville: Westminster John Knox, 1992.
Newsome, James D. *The Hebrew Prophets*. Atlanta: Knox, 1984.
Nicol, George G. "The Alleged Rape of Bathsheba: Some Observations on Ambiguity in Biblical Narrative." *Journal for the Study of the Old Testament* 22/73 (March 1997) 43–54.
Niditch, Susan. "Eroticism and Death in the Tale of Jael." In *Women in the Hebrew Bible: A Reader*, edited by Alice Bach, 305–15, New York: Routledge, 1999.
———. *Judges: A Commentary*. Old Testament Library. Louisville: Westminster John Knox, 2008.
North, Christopher R. "Immanuel." In *The Interpreter's Dictionary of the Bible*, edited by George Arthur Buttrick. 4 vols. Nashville: Abingdon, 1962.
O'Brien, Julia M. *Nahum*. Readings. 2nd ed. Sheffield: Sheffield Phoenix, 2009.
———. "Zechariah." In *Women's Bible Commentary*, edited by Carol A. Newsom, Sharon H. Ringe, and Jacqueline E. Lapsley. 3rd ed. Louisville: Westminster John Knox, 2012
O'Connor, Kathleen M. "Jeremiah." In *Women's Bible Commentary*, edited by Carol A. Newsom, Sharon H. Ringe, and Jacqueline E. Lapsley. 3rd ed. Louisville: Westminster John Knox, 2012.
———. "Lamentations." In *Women's Bible Commentary*, edited by Carol A. Newsom, Sharon H. Ringe, and Jacqueline E. Lapsley. 3rd ed. Louisville: Westminster John Knox, 2012.

Ollenburger, Ben C. "Zechariah." In *The New Interpreter's Bible*, vol. 7. Nashville: Abingdon, 1996.

Origen. "Homily 2." In *Homilies on Joshua*, translated by Barbara J. Bruce, edited by Cynthia White. Washington, DC: Catholic University of America, 2002.

Paul, Shalom M. *Isaiah 40–66: Translation and Commentary*. Eerdmans Critical Commentary. Grand Rapids: Eerdmans, 2012.

Pesikta Rabbati: Discourses for Feasts, Fasts and Special Sabbaths. Translated by William G. Braude. New Haven, CT: Yale University Press, 1968.

Pesikta de-Rab Kahana: Rabbi Kahana's Compilation of Discourses for Sabbaths and Festal Days. Translated by William G. Braude and Israel J. Kapstein. Philadelphia: Jewish Publication Society, 1975.

Pfeiffer, Robert H. *Introduction to the Old Testament*. New York: Harper, 1948.

Pirke de Rabbi Eliezer. Translated by Gerald Friedlander. New York: Sepher-Hermon, 1981.

Porton, Gary G. "Midrash." In *The Anchor Bible Dictionary*, edited by David Noel Freedman. New York: Doubleday, 1996.

Pritchard, James B., editor. *Ancient Near Eastern Texts*. Vol. 1. Princeton, NJ: Princeton University Press, 1958.

Reis, Pamela Tamarkin. "Uncovering Jael and Sisera: A New Reading." *Scandinavian Journal of the Old Testament* 19:/1 (2005) 24–47.

Roberts, J. J. M. *Nahum, Habakkuk, and Zephaniah*. Old Testament Library. Louisville: Westminster John Knox, 1991.

Robertson, Amy H. C. "Rahab and Her Interpreters." In *Women's Bible Commentary*, edited by Carol A. Newsom, Sharon H. Ringe, and Jacqueline E. Lapsley. 3rd ed. Louisville: Westminster John Knox, 2012

Rosenblatt, Naomi Harris. *After the Apple: Women in the Bible*. New York: Miramax/Hyperion, 2005.

Rosenthal, Gilbert S. "Messianism Reconsidered." *Judaism* 40/4 (Fall 1991) 552–69.

Sanderson, Judith E. "Amos." In *The Women's Bible Commentary*, edited by Carol A. Newsom and Sharon H. Ringe. Louisville, KY: Westminster John Knox, 1992.

———. "Habakkuk." In *The Women's Bible Commentary*, edited by Carol A. Newsom and Sharon H. Ringe. Louisville, KY: Westminster John Knox, 1992.

———. "Nahum." In *The Women's Bible Commentary*, edited by Carol A. Newsom and Sharon H. Ringe. Louisville, KY: Westminster John Knox, 1992.

———. "Zephaniah." In *The Women's Bible Commentary*, edited by Carol A. Newsom and Sharon H. Ringe. Louisville, KY: Westminster John Knox, 1992.

Sandmel, Samuel. *The Hebrew Scriptures: An Introduction to Their Literature and Religious Ideas*. New York: Knopf, 1963.

———. *A Jewish Understanding of the New Testament*. Cincinnati: Hebrew Union College Press, 1956.

Scholz, Susanne. "Judges." In *Women's Bible Commentary*, edited by Carol A. Newsom, Sharon H. Ringe, and Jacqueline E. Lapsley. 3rd ed. Louisville: Westminster John Knox, 2012.

Schreiber, Mordecai. *The Man Who Knew God: Decoding Jeremiah*. Lanham, MD: Lexington Books, Rowman and Littlefield, 2010.

Seitz, Christopher R. "Book of Isaiah (First Isaiah)." In *The Anchor Bible Dictionary*, edited by David Noel Freedman. New York: Doubleday, 1992.

Seltzer, Robert M. *Jewish People, Jewish Thought: The Jewish Experience in History.* New York: Macmillan, 1980.
Seow, C. L. "Book of Hosea." In *The Anchor Bible Dictionary*, edited by David Noel Freedman. New York: Doubleday, 1992.
Setel, T. Drorah. "Prophets and Pornography: Female Sexual Imagery in Hosea." In *Feminist Interpretation of the Bible*, edited by Letty M. Russell, 86–95. Louisville: Westminster John Knox, 1985.
Shinan, Avidor, and Yair Zakovitch. *From Gods to God: How the Bible Debunked, Suppressed, or Changed Ancient Myths and Legends.* Translated by Valarie Zakovitch. Philadelphia: Jewish Publication Society; Lincoln: University of Nebraska Press, 2012.
Sifre: A Tannaitic Commentary on the Book of Deuteronomy. Translated by Reuven Hammer. New Haven, CT: Yale University Press, 1986.
Signer, Michael A. "Searching the Scriptures: Jews, Christians, and the Book." In *Christianity in Jewish Terms*, edited by Tikva Frymer-Kensky and David Novak, et al. Boulder, CO: Westview, 2000.
Smart, James D. "Amos." In *The Interpreter's Dictionary of the Bible*, edited by George Arthur Buttrick. 4 vols. Nashville: Abingdon, 1962.
Sternberg, Meir. *The Poetics of Biblical Narrative: Ideological Literature and the Drama of Reading.* Indiana Literary Biblical Series. Bloomington: University of Indiana, 1985.
Stewart, Anne W. "Deborah, Jael, and Their Interpreters." In *Women's Bible Commentary*, edited by Carol A. Newsom, Sharon H. Ringe, and Jacqueline E. Lapsley. 3rd ed. Louisville: Westminster John Knox, 2012
———. "Jephtha's Daughter and Her Interpreters." In *Women's Bible Commentary*, edited by Carol A. Newsom, Sharon H. Ringe, and Jacqueline E. Lapsley. 3rd ed. Louisville: Westminster John Knox, 2012
Stulman, Louis. *Jeremiah.* Abingdon Old Testament Commentaries. Nashville: Abingdon, 2005.
Sweeney, Marvin A. "Book of Habakkuk." In *The Anchor Bible Dictionary*, edited by David Noel Freedman. New York: Doubleday, 1992.
TANAKH: The Holy Scriptures. Philadelphia: Jewish Publication Society, 1985.
Tanna Debe Eliyyahu: The Lore of the School of Elijah. Translated by William G. Braude and Israel J. Kapstein. Philadelphia: Jewish Publication Society, 1981.
Thompson, Joel A. "Joel." In *The Interpreter's Bible*, edited by George Arthur Buttrick. 12 vols. Nashville: Abingdon, 1956.
Trible, Phyllis. *Texts of Terror: Literary-Feminist Readings of Biblical Narratives.* Philadelphia: Fortress, 1984.
Tull, Patricia K. "Isaiah." In *Women's Bible Commentary*, edited by Carol A. Newsom, Sharon H. Ringe, and Jacqueline E. Lapsley. 3rd ed. Louisville: Westminster John Knox, 2012
Waltke, Bruce K. *A Commentary on Micah.* Grand Rapids: Eerdmans, 2007.
Weinfeld, Moshe. *Deuteronomy 1–11.* Anchor Bible 5. New York: Doubleday, 1991.
Werblowsky, R. J., and Geoffrey Wigoder, editors. *The Oxford Dictionary of the Jewish Religion.* New York: Oxford University Press, 1997.
West, James King. *Introduction to the Old Testament.* 2nd ed. New York: Macmillan, 1981.

Westermann, Claus. *Isaiah 40–66*. Translated by David M. G. Stalker. Old Testament Library. Philadelphia: Westminster, 1969.
White, Marsha C. "Jonah." In *The Women's Bible Commentary*, edited by Carol A. Newsom and Sharon H. Ringe. Louisville, KY: Westminster John Knox, 1992.
Willoughby, Bruce E. "Book of Amos." In *The Anchor Bible Dictionary*, edited by David Noel Freedman. New York: Doubleday, 1992.
Wilson, Marvin R. *Our Father Abraham: Jewish Roots of the Christian Faith*. Grand Rapids: Eerdmans: Center for Judaic-Christian Studies, 1989.
Winward, Stephen F. *A Guide to the Prophets*. Richmond: Knox, 1969.
Wolff, Hans Walter. *Micah: A Commentary*. Translated by Gary Stansell. Minneapolis: Augsburg Fortress, 1990.
———. *Micah the Prophet*. Translated by Ralph D. Gehrke. Philadelphia: Fortress, 1981.
Wright, N. T. *Jesus and the Victory of God*. Vol. 2 of *Christian Origins and the Question of God*. Minneapolis: Fortress, 1996.
Yee, Gale A. "Hosea." In *Women's Bible Commentary*, edited by Carol A. Newsom, Sharon H. Ringe, and Jacqueline E. Lapsley. 3rd ed. Louisville: Westminster John Knox, 2012.
Zucker, David J. *The Bible's WRITINGS: An Introduction for Christians and Jews*, Eugene, OR: Wipf & Stock, 2013.
———. "Cold Case: The Micaiah Mysteries." *CCAR Journal/The Reform Jewish Quarterly* 58/4 (Fall 2011) 3–9.
———. *Israel's Prophets: An Introduction for Christians and Jews*. Mahwah, NJ: Paulist, 1994.
———. "Jesus and Jeremiah in the Matthean Tradition." *Journal of Ecumenical Studies* 27/2 (Spring 1990) 288–305.
———. "Jonah's Journey." *Judaism* 44/3 (Summer 1995) 362–68.
———. "The Marvels of Midrash: Jonah as Defender of the Jews." *Midstream* 32/6 (August–September 1996) 5–6.
———. *The Torah: An Introduction for Christians and Jews*. Mahwah, NJ: Paulist, 2005.
———, with Jane Smith. "Jerusalem, the Sacred City: Perspectives From Judaism and Islam." *Journal of Ecumenical Studies* 32/2 (Spring 1995) 227–56.

www.ingramcontent.com/pod-product-compliance
Lightning Source LLC
Chambersburg PA
CBHW051104230426
43667CB00013B/2442